BEYOND COMMUNITY POLICING

BEYOND COMMUNITY POLICING

FROM EARLY AMERICAN BEGINNINGS TO THE 21ST CENTURY

James J. Chriss

Routledge
Taylor & Francis Group

LONDON AND NEW YORK

First published 2011 by Paradigm Publishers

Published 2016 by Routledge
2 Park Square, Milton Park, Abingdon, Oxon OX14 4RN
711 Third Avenue, New York, NY 10017, USA

Routledge is an imprint of the Taylor & Francis Group, an informa business

Library of Congress Cataloging-in-Publication Data

Chriss, James J., 1955-
    Beyond community policing : from early American beginnings to the 21st century / James J. Chriss.
        p. cm.
    Includes bibliographical references and index.
    ISBN 978-1-59451-846-1 (hbk. : alk. paper)
    1. Police--United States—History.   2. Community policing—United States—History.   3. Police-community relations—United States—History.   I. Title.
    HV8138.C535 2011
    363.2'30973--dc22

                                                                                2010025257

ISBN 13 : 978-1-59451-846-1 (hbk)
ISBN 13 : 978-1-59451-847-8 (pbk)

Designed by Straight Creek Bookmakers.

Contents

List of Tables and Figures

Acknowledgments

This book represents my admittedly limited attempt to contribute to the study of police and society. The sociologists I have looked up to over the years—Parsons, Ward, and Gouldner most immediately—worked in the area of grand or cosmological theorizing, and this is the perspective on which I cut my teeth. For me cosmological grand theory is useful because every once in awhile, whenever the spirit moves me, I can climb down from those dizzying heights and try to grapple with any particular substantive topic in real time. Recently my chosen substantive topic has been policing and the criminal justice system, so this book is simply a reflection of how I "make sense" of this field going back and forth between grand sociological theory, pertinent criminological theories, and the rapidly growing scholarly literature on policing.

Each of us has tastes for certain topics, and when considering all the possible topics within criminal justice, my penchant has always been toward policing rather than the other two major subsystems, namely courts and corrections. More than the other two, for me policing is "where the action is." Unlike the drudgery of plowing through the scholarly literature in sociology and criminology writ large, I actually look forward to reading the latest issues of scholarly journals in the policing field. And of course, books and monographs on various aspects of policing are important and worthwhile as well. Although Egon Bittner has been the single most influential police scholar informing my take on policing, there are of course others who deserve mention. Some of the scholars listed here I have been in contact with over the years or during the writing of this book, while others I have only read but certainly appreciate from afar. In addition to Bittner, police scholars who have been important to me include Jerome Skolnick, Wesley Skogan, Michael White, Rod Brunson, Stephen Mastrofski, Peter Manning, Tim Prenzler, Jeremy Wilson, John Crank, David Klinger, Eric Monkkonen, Steve Herbert, Carl Klockars, Donald Black, Sam Walker, and John Van Maanen. There are others of course, dutifully noted in the bibliography, but these are the ones that readily come to mind.

My family deserves a round of applause as well, perhaps even more so than the veritable list of Who's Who in policing offered above. My daughter Ariana asked interesting questions throughout the time of the writing of this book, and she is always a delight. Whenever I was home working on the book my son Johnny would come into the study and ask "Are you finished yet?" Sadly, most of the time I had to tell him no, that is until now. "Yes, Johnny, I am through. Let's go play badminton." And my wife Mandy put up patiently with my many late nights buried in writing, reading, and printing countless versions of drafts of chapters. For these reasons and many more, I dedicate this book to them.

Some of the material that found its way into chapters of the book was presented as talks in various forums over the last seven years. In 2004 I presented the paper "The Concept of Proactivity in Social and Criminal Justice Policy" in Cleveland at the North Central Sociological Association meetings. In 2007 I presented the paper "From Generalist to Specialist Back to Generalist: The Shifting Roles of Police over Time," in Atlanta at the annual meeting of the American Society of Criminology. Two versions of Chapter 8 on police as contact men were presented as papers, the first as an invited lecture in 2008 before the Sociology Department at the University of Connecticut, and the second in 2009 at the annual meeting of the American Society of Criminology held in Philadelphia. In 2008 I presented a paper titled "Institutionalism versus Functionalism: The Case of Post 9-11 Policing" in St. Louis at the annual meeting of the American Society of Criminology. Finally, in 2009 I gave a talk to the Sociology–Criminology Club at Cleveland State University on "Policing in the Wild West." I of course thank all—too numerous to mention individually—who provided comments and feedback on these various talks.

Finally, I should mention that one of my students at Cleveland State University, Jason Scott, mentioned to me a book by Peter Moskos, *Cop in the Hood,* of which I was unaware. I ended up getting a copy of the book and it eventually made its way into the bibliography, thanks to Jason. It is students like Jason who fan the flames of eternal optimism about working in higher education.

James J. Chriss
Cleveland
September 2010

Permissions

Figure 1.1.—Reprinted by permission of the publisher from *The American University* by Talcott Parsons and Gerald M. Platt, with contributions by Neil J. Smelser, p. 12, Cambridge, MA: Harvard University Press, Copyright © 1973 by the President and Fellows of Harvard College.

Picture of Wild Bill Hickok in Chapter 3—Used by permission of the Nebraska State Historical Society, reference number RG2603-6.

The quote on page 186—Reprinted by permission of the publisher from *Off the Books: The Underground Economy of the Urban Poor* by Sudhir Alladi Venkatesh, p. 203, Cambridge, MA: Harvard University Press, Copyright © 2006 by Sudhir Alladi Venkatesh.

1

Explaining the Police

On December 6, 2008, riots broke out in several Greek cities after word spread of the fatal police shooting of Alexandros Grigoropoulos, a fifteen-year-old youth living in Exarchia, a central district of Athens.[1] The rioting started in Athens, then spread north to Thessaloniki, Komotini, Ionnina, and later as far south as Crete. Although as of mid-December, 2008 no deaths had been attributed to the rioting, there was substantial damage to banks and stores in the main shopping districts of these cities. Indeed, Greece's retail association estimated that the losses were at least 100 million Euros (about 135 million dollars).

Two officers involved in the shooting were immediately suspended pending further investigation, and Greek authorities pleaded with the rioters to stop the violence. There had been longstanding tense relations between the police and anarchists who viewed Exarchia as their fortress or home base. Indeed, the last round of serious rioting in Greece occurred twenty years earlier, and it too pitted anarchists against the local police. The rioters eventually moved inside the gates of Athens University, where they took sanctuary thanks to a Greek law which bars police from university campuses. Now ensconced safely out of reach of the police, the rioters were free to pelt them with rocks, bottles, and whatever else was available.

Since the 1820s Greece has experienced persistent levels of instability brought about by conflicts and sometimes open warfare both internally and externally. After gaining its independence from the Ottoman Empire in 1832, a Bavarian monarch was installed to reign over the kingdom as decreed by the Convention of London. Further conflicts continued, including Greece's involvement in the Balkan Wars, World War I, ongoing skirmishes against Turkish nationalists, and the German occupation of Greece leading to a devastating civil war which pitted royalists against communists. As a result of these military exigencies Greece's municipal police force, first established in the 1830s, was oftentimes indistinguishable from national military forces. (Indeed, during some periods the police force was disbanded altogether.) Because of this,

Greek police have historically been actively engaged in the political policing of its citizens. As Rigakos and Papanicolaou (2003, p. 283) note, "This engagement had been a direct consequence of institutional, and even constitutional, arrangements that allowed continuous surveillance and suppression of individuals and organizations (political or other) connected with, or friendly to, the Greek Communist Party."[2]

Much of the actions of the anarchists (far leftists in ideology, many of whom are openly communistic) are driven by general opposition to the current conservative government of Prime Minister Costas Karamanlis and, by extension, the police as the most visible defenders of the status quo. Socialist opposition leader George Papandreou called for early elections, and proclaimed that the current Greek government cannot identify with the anxieties felt by the younger generation.[3]

For years local police in Greece realized they had their hands full attempting to control increasingly restless groups, whether they identified themselves as anarchists—groups overtly and avowedly opposed to the government and its police forces—or in other ways (see, e.g., Di Paola 2007). These "other ways" or reasons often amount to groups claiming oppression on the basis of race, class, nationality, religion, or other aspects of group identity which the broader society is alleged to devalue (Feldman 2002; Taylor 1994; Walby 2001). For example, in the United States, England, and other western nations persons of color (Blacks, Hispanics, and increasingly those of Middle Eastern descent) are apt to view the police less favorably than Whites (see Brunson 2007).

Although this observation holds in a general sense, a more fine-grained analysis reveals some intriguing nuances. One recent study asked survey respondents about the nature of their contact with police under various circumstances (Durose et al. 2007, p. 3). The research focused on the percentage of persons who felt that the police acted properly during contact, and whether or not these opinions varied significantly on the basis of race (the categories being White, Black/African-American, and Hispanic/Latino). There were no significant differences by race when the reason for the contact involved routine police actions such as responding to a traffic accident, providing assistance or service to citizens, or when persons reported a crime or problem to the police. Specifically, under these circumstances the percent who felt police acted properly was 95% for Whites, 93.1% for Blacks, and 93.6% for Hispanics.

However, when persons were asked about situations in which they were the target of police actions, clear differences by race began to emerge. When persons were the driver during a traffic stop, the percent who felt police acted properly during the contact was as follows: Whites 91.7%; Blacks 83.7%; and Hispanics 87.5%. Even more dramatically, when persons were under police investigation for a crime or suspected of wrongdoing, the percent who felt police acted properly was as follows: Whites 79.7%; Blacks 55.3%; and Hispanics 73.4%. The steep decline in favorable attitudes toward the police among Blacks being targeted for police actions is reflective of a pervasive sense, especially among minority residents of poor, inner-city areas, that police are biased against

African-Americans as a group, whether in the form of police violence or neglect, heightened levels of suspicion or circumspection, the problem of Driving while Black, or racial profiling more generally (see, e.g., Anderson 1999; Chriss 2007b; Kowalski and Lundman 2007; Weitzer and Brunson 2009).

The bottom line is that citizen encounters with the police may best be described as "asymmetrical." A clarification of this idea is provided by Wesley Skogan (2006b), who suggests that negative encounters with the police are weighted far more heavily than positive encounters. Indeed, the impact of having a bad encounter with the police is four to fourteen times greater than the impact of a positive encounter (Skogan 2006b, p. 100).

THE ANOMALY OF THE POLICE

These events illustrate the somewhat paradoxical and precarious place the police hold in modern society. We want the police to come to our aid when we call them, and put away the "bad guys" in the name of public order and preserving the peace. But when the police turn their attention to us, when we are under suspicion or arrest, then we are less apt to think of them in positive terms. Indeed, ever since the 1960s, a period marked by increasingly visible clashes between the police and a restless citizenry embroiled in any number of social movements—gay rights, antiwar protest, civil rights, school protest, and experimentation with drugs and lifestyle choices—the police have been searching for ways to present themselves in a more favorable light. For example, where once the police viewed the media as an enemy because of its penchant for portraying the police in a negative and critical way, now most police departments have their own media relations departments which overtly are concerned with citizen satisfaction regarding police operations and services. Indeed, community policing arises as much as anything as a statement that today's police care about citizens, and are eager to present themselves as more "user friendly" and compassionate about the various problems facing citizens (Meliala 2001).

Although this turn toward "soft" policing strategies has been hailed by many as reflective of a more educated, thoughtful, and professional police force positioned to deal effectively with an increasingly diverse citizenry, others are not so confident it is for the better. A cynical perspective on the rise of community policing is that it is simply a ruse whereby police slip a new and softer "velvet glove" over the old "iron fist" of brute force and coercion, the latter of which has always been, and always will be, the true work police do at the behest of the state (Loader and Walker 2006, p. 174).

Community policing is real, in terms of how police talk about it and how everyday citizens understand it. But from a scholarly perspective, there is a need to be more precise about the concepts being discussed. One goal of this book, then, is to provide a systematic overview and understanding of policing in modern society, including various types of policing such as community policing. In order to achieve this goal it must be clear what I am referring to when I talk about the "police." By *police* I mean sworn, uniformed law enforcement officers with arrest powers covering some legal and/or territorial jurisdiction. Although legal jurisdiction can encompass the federal, state, county, or local levels, for the most part in this book I will be interested in the situation of local policing, that is, modern municipal police departments which are concerned with enforcing the laws of their local cities or municipalities. Nevertheless, on occasion I will be discussing state, federal, and cross-national policing issues, especially as these relate to the problem of terrorism which has profoundly affected the organization of law enforcement in America in general and local or municipal policing in particular since September 11, 2001.

SOCIOLOGY AND CRIMINOLOGY

Although police can be understood and studied from a variety of perspectives including common sense, journalism, psychology, or politics, my approach to the topic is influenced by my training in sociology and criminology. *Sociology* is the scientific study of society, although within sociology itself there are a variety of competing perspectives for explaining the social world. *Criminology*, the study of crime and criminals, but also those social organizations dedicated to dealing with crime (police, courts, and corrections), is a specialized social science discipline which began with the rise of the Classical School of Criminology in Europe in the mid-1700s, and which has been most closely aligned with sociology since its founding beginning in the late 1800s.

Like all social sciences, sociology is multiparadigmatic, meaning that there are a variety of theories vying for attention within the field (Ritzer 1975). A *paradigm* represents the shared commitments of a group of theorists, and in this sense is broader than a theory. Another way of thinking about a paradigm is that it represents a worldview, or a specific way of seeing the subject matter to which members of a theory group turn their attention. A paradigm, then, allows theorists sharing the same or similar sets of assumptions to solve the puzzles that are of interest to them, and the theories that are produced are the tools for this puzzle solving (see Eckberg and Hill 1979; Kuhn 1962; Merton 1968). Each paradigm contains or encompasses a family of theories, each one somewhat distinct but nevertheless sharing certain basic assumptions about reality, about society, and about knowledge with other theories that are consistent with the paradigm.

I would argue that both sociology and criminology are dominated by three basic paradigms, which are the positivist, the interpretive, and the evaluative (Wagner 1963). A handy way of distinguishing the three paradigms is to think about the major goal of each, these being:

- **Positivist**—To discover the laws of society;
- **Interpretive**—To learn how persons make the social world meaningful;

- **Evaluative**—To change the social world.

The *positivist* approach is modeled after the natural sciences, and it operates with the assumption that timeless laws of the social universe can be derived through systematic observation and experimentation. The goal of the positivistic approach is to develop causal theories by way of deducing hypotheses from more general covering laws, with the findings in turn being generalizable beyond the specific data that are being analyzed (Roth and Mehta 2002, p. 133). The founder of positivism (and sociology for that matter) was French philosopher Auguste Comte (1798–1857). Comte believed in the unity of knowledge, and also that later social science disciplines (such as economics, political science, psychology, and sociology) build upon the basic findings (or "first principles") of the earlier natural science disciplines such as mathematics, biology, chemistry, astronomy, and geology (Ward 1883).

The primary distinguishing characteristic of the positivist paradigm is that its authors consider, or actually treat, sociology as a natural science. As such, positivist theorists view society as akin to a machine, or an organism, or see human beings as carbon-based life forms subject to the same laws of physics as other natural objects. I am in agreement with Comte about the nature of knowledge and science, and for the most part I will be utilizing a positivistic theory called functionalism to explain modern municipal policing in this book. But I will also be crossing paradigmatic boundaries occasionally as well, as some aspects of policing—especially the "micro" realm of face-to-face behavior—can be fruitfully explored from the interpretive perspective.

The primary distinguishing characteristic of the *interpretive* paradigm is that its authors consider, or actually treat, sociology as a social science rather than as a natural science. Interpretive theorists assume social phenomena are fundamentally different than natural phenomena, and as a result sociology and criminology require distinct methodological and explanatory approaches from those found in the natural sciences. Rather than seeking to discover the timeless laws of the social universe, interpretive theorists emphasize the importance of meaning and the subjective orientations of persons as they do things together. Additionally, "The *interpretivist* approach does not seek an objective truth so much as to unravel patterns of subjective understanding" (Roth and Mehta 2002, p. 132).

For example, behaviorism is a type of positivist theory which suggests that one may develop general explanations about human behavior if one assumes that human beings—like other animals—respond to external stimuli in the same way. That is, human beings will repeat behavior that is pleasurable or rewarding, and desist from or try to avoid behaviors that are painful. This is known as the stimulus–response (S-R) theory, namely, that as sentient life forms human beings are predictable insofar as pleasurable stimuli will produce certain forms of concrete, observable behavior and painful stimuli will produce other types.

Interpretive theorists would respond by suggesting that the behaviorist or S-R approach is leaving one crucial element out of its explanation: human cognition. From the interpretive perspective, the S-R approach is overly deterministic in that it sees human beings as empty vessels being buffeted about by various external stimuli. This, they would contend, is simply not an accurate portrayal of human behavior. Between the external stimulus (S) and the response (R) of the organism to that stimulus is the cognitive process at work within the organism (O), whereby the organism *interprets* what the stimulus *means*. For example, a person who gets kicked in the shin will react very differently to this "painful" stimulus in different social situations. Someone walking down the street minding his or her own business who gets kicked in the shin out of the blue by a passerby would likely interpret the kick as both painful and shocking, while a soccer player who likewise gets kicked might not even notice the pain because of the heat of the battle and because kicks to the shin are a rather routine part of the game of soccer.

Rather than attempting to develop causal explanations of social phenomena à la positivist theory, or seeking to develop deeper understanding about social life from the perspective of the human subjects being studied à la interpretive theory, *evaluative* theories attempt to effect some fundamental change in the world, and thus contain an explicit normative or ideological agenda. Whereas both positivist and interpretive theories report on *what is*, evaluative theories are at least as concerned with *what ought to be*. For example, Marxist or critical theory is a type of evaluative theory concerned with examining the ways in which certain social classes (owners or capitalists) dominate and oppress other social classes (workers) within capitalist society, the purpose of which is to reduce or eliminate such oppression toward the ultimate goal of establishing a classless (i.e., socialist or communist) society. Likewise, feminist theory is evaluative to the extent that it seeks to end the historical advantages men have enjoyed over women and to assure that women as a group are provided access to full participation in society alongside men.

SOME CONCEPTUAL ISSUES

Above I suggested that sociology is the scientific study of society. Even given this general understanding of what sociology is, there are still disagreements over just how a scientific discipline such as sociology could claim to study the totality of the human experience, including the structure, functioning, and culture of the social system as experienced by its members. American sociologist Talcott Parsons had a particular take on this issue that has always struck me as reasonable, and so I have followed many of his recommendations for making sense of human social systems and the various units within the system. In order to reduce the complexity of the social system in its totality, Parsons suggested that sociologists should focus on the basic functions which operate at all levels of the social system. Parsons went on to suggest that any social system must solve four critical functional problems if it is to remain viable as a going concern over time. These will be specified shortly.

Although early in his career Parsons rejected the evolutionism and positivism of Herbert Spencer (see especially Parsons 1937), by the time of the establishment of his functionalist theory of social systems in the 1950s and 1960s, Parsons was firmly located within the positivist paradigm. Parsons followed Spencer's (1864) "first principles" in applying basic laws of physics, matter, motion, and time to the human social world. In a nutshell, human cognition can recognize the cosmic truth that matter moves from the undifferentiated, unorganized, and homogeneous to the differentiated, organized, and heterogeneous (Haines 1992, 2005). Life begins as an undifferentiated mass of protoplasm, arising from a chemical stew which, through the process of elective affinities, in turn gives rise to simple, single-celled organisms seeking to extend and expand the vital life force—through food quests and procreation—while operating in a physical environment. Eventually these simple organisms begin dividing into more complex, multi-cellular organisms, and their physical organizations become more complex as well with increasing population densities. Through evolutionary adaptation and upgrading, human beings appear, and over time they, too, grow in number and their social organization becomes more complex. Life, in any of its forms, strives toward organization and complexity, thereby comprising a system of parts fulfilling specific functions which contribute to the maintenance of the whole. Eventually, of course, as a result of the law of entropy, all forces eventually dissipate and return all matter once again to the primordial chemical stew. In other words, all organisms and systems created by their physical strivings will die.

This is the physical template—the first principles—upon which all life on earth appears, proliferates, becomes organized, and eventually dies off. But with the rise of the human species and the extraordinary properties of the human mind, human beings are freed somewhat from the trappings and the limitations of the physical environment and the destiny of the laws of physics. Yet the continuity of the four functions remains, and ramifies across all physical and human realities. The four functions specified by Parsons are logically derived from the rise of organized systems and their relation to an external environment. The two key axes which generate, analytically, the four functions are internal–external and instrumental–consummatory.

The *internal–external* axis simply refers to those functions which are pertinent to the internal workings of the system, as well as those functions which deal with the external conditions of the system in relation to its environment or environments. Parsons assumes that social systems are *open*, meaning that there is a continual interchange of information and resources between the system (internal) and the environment (external). The two functions that fall on the internal side of the ledger are integration (I) and latent pattern maintenance (L). Another way to say this is that integration and latent pattern maintenance are problems internal to social systems, and specialized structures must be in place to solve these two vital functional problems. Likewise, two key functions fall on the external (or environmental) side, and these are adaptation (A) and goal attainment (G).

The other analytical axis is instrumental–consummatory. This is the time dimension of the system, in that in however it occurs within any particular subsystem, resources must be created, built up, or stored for later utilization by the system. The "building up" or earlier aspect of the timeline represents the instrumental end of the axis, while the later aspect of the timeline, where resources are actually consumed, is the consummatory or expressive side of the axis. The two functions which are grouped on the consummatory side of the axis are integration and goal attainment, while those grouped on the instrumental side are latent pattern maintenance and adaptation. Notice that the four functions— adaptation (A), goal attainment (G), integration (I), and latent pattern maintenance (L), are the key elements for the conceptualization of social systems and their units or parts, hence following Parsons, we refer to this as the AGIL schema (see Figure 1.1).

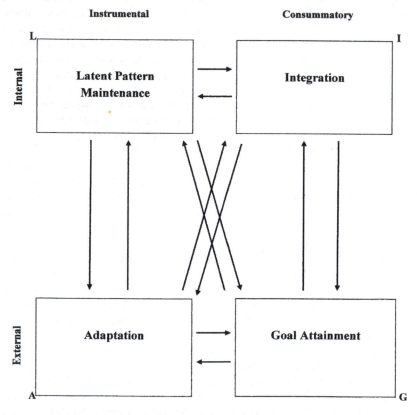

Figure 1.1. Parsons' AGIL Schema
(Adapted from Parsons and Platt 1973, p. 12)

The specifics of how this analytical scheme explains the empirical aspects of the functioning of human social systems and their various subsystems, including of course the criminal justice system and the policing subsystem, will be taken up over the course of the book. But generally, and to provide a glimpse of what is to come, a human society may be described as a relatively self-sufficient social system which gives its members access to economic resources (A), steered in varying degrees by territorially oriented political organizations (G), marked by the recruitment and socialization of members of the population (I), and which possesses cultural legitimation as an independent entity (L; Parsons 1968, p. 321). Much of the action of the criminal justice system and the police occurs within the sphere of the G or goal-attainment function, especially as this applies to jurisdictional issues within geographical territories and the vesting of coercive power among specific agents of formal control (the police) by political organizations.

Parsons' thought is also useful in explaining elements of police organization, and how such organizations are configured within broader institutional contexts. When we speak of municipal police organizations we always take for granted that they exist within specific locations, usually within cities or communities. This means that police departments serve some functions relative to the citizens of a municipality, and that there are general concepts available for understanding how these organizational transactions occur. Although we will be getting into more detail on organizational theory in Chapters 5 and 8, for now it is sufficient to consider Parsons' (1960a, pp. 45–47) extension of the AGIL schema to identify four basic kinds of organizations. *First*, organizations may be oriented primarily to economic production, the paradigmatic case being the business firm. *Second*, organizations may take as their primary orientation a range of political goals. Most organs of government, but primarily the executive branch since it is overtly set up to establish a hierarchy of goals whereby the executive pursues them according to the mandate given to him or her by popular election, are concerned with the production and allocation of power in society (Parsons 1966). Regulatory and administrative agencies are also political in nature to the extent that laws are promulgated and enforced within some political jurisdiction. It might appear that modern law enforcement should be categorized as a political organization, to the extent that in the incipient stages of its formation and institutionalization it served an overtly political function since enforcement functionaries did their work at the behest of some government entity whether local, state, or national. However, although policing has a "leg" in political organization especially in its earliest stages, it is not placed only there since its institutional environment is broader than the polity.

A *third* kind of organization, according to Parsons, is concerned first and foremost with integration, that is, with the "adjustment of conflicts and the direction of motivation to the fulfillment of institutionalized expectations" (Parsons 1960a, p. 46). Parsons suggests that the law profession and the court system should be placed here, but also interest groups, hospitals, and others concerned with ensuring the proper functioning of parts within the system. This means also that social control in the broadest sense should be included here, which opens up the possibility that police organizations should be placed in the integrative camp as well. This will be returned to shortly.

A *fourth* kind of organization is concerned primarily with pattern maintenance, and the examples Parsons provides include schools, churches, kinship groups, as well as creative organizations emphasizing "expressive functions" such as various arts industries. To summarize, organizations can be described as oriented primarily to economic production (A); to the pursuit of political goals and the maximization of power within its sphere (G); to the adjustment of conflicts and motivation of relevant actors (or collective actors such as groups) to operate in line with institutionalized expectations (I); or to maintaining value patterns to ensure continuity over time and across generations (L).

Given these four basic types of organizations, where should the municipal police be placed? For one thing, we know that for most of its history, police adopted a quasi-military organizational structure, complete with a rank system for promotion and demotion, a chain of command, a written set of rules for management and operations, and an explicit system of rewards and punishments marking, respectively, meritorious or detrimental service. Parsons (1960a, p. 48) considers the military to be a type of political or goal-oriented organization, yet views the military as an "emergency" function specializing in defensive actions for the protection of the state, or to engage enemy combatants out in (typically) distant battlefields for the protection of national interests. On the other hand, the social control agencies operate more on the logic of integration, according to Parsons, because of the routine and recurrent nature of the problems they are created to address, such as disease by medical organizations, disputes by civil trial lawyers, and crime by agents of the criminal justice system (police, courts, and corrections). But how do the police assure this work of integration? By what magic or miracle is this accomplished? Do they simply cajole persons to settle their differences on the basis of the great respect and admiration heaped upon them by the general public? Do they influence compliance of potential or real deviants as the stern but steady hand of a father to a wayward son?

No, they do not. Such an approach has really never worked in American society. Since its inception police officers have been armed with service revolvers and other instruments of force, and for a long time they indeed have had all the trappings of a military battalion. In other words, police may indeed extract compliance by mere presence or respect, but the underlying reality which makes policing "work" is police officers' ability to resort to coercive force in the end, and if need be. This coercive force may indeed be applied only sporadically and unpredictably, just as is the general case for military engagements out on the battlefield, but it is always potentially there, reflecting a battle readiness among police much more in line with military preparedness than not. Along these lines, Egon Bittner (1990, pp. 137–138) explains why throughout most of its history a military style of organization was viewed favorably by police planners. First, to reiterate from above, both the military and the police are instruments of force and must apply that force sporadically and often under unpredictable circumstances. Second, during the second era of reform and early professionalization as police organizations were attempting to distance themselves from local political influence, the military model of harsh and punitive internal discipline seemed well suited to keeping officers in line and away from the "sloth and corruption" of the vestiges of political cronyism and quid pro quo arrangements of the first era. Third, the police adopted the military style of organization because there was no other working model available for doing the things police set for themselves, namely, crime control, order maintenance, and service. In addition, the work being done required that officers spend time out in the field away from immediate supervision, so a punitive set of military–bureaucratic directives could at least give the appearance that the line staff was under control.

Although Parsons specifies how various parts of the social system fulfill specific functions which are said to contribute to the maintenance of the system, it is also the case that strains and perturbations exist within the system as well. And if these strains become severe enough, the system may reach entropy or death. Parsons, then, sees sociology as the social science discipline especially concerned with those structures and processes associated with the *integration* of social systems. But integration is only one side of the analytical coin, because there would also be an interest in explaining when, how, and why social systems *fail* to achieve integration or smooth functioning. As Parsons (1968, p. 322) explains,

> By integration in this context I mean the structures and processes by which the relations among the parts of a social system—persons in roles, collectivities, and normative pattern components—either become so ordered as to promote harmonious functioning in their respective involvements with each other in the system, or in specific and understandable ways fail to do so. Integration has both a negative and a positive aspect.

THE TRIALS AND TRIBULATIONS OF POLICE AUTHORITY

This quote from Parsons is instructive, for it serves to illustrate a contentious point in sociology, criminology, and other social sciences. For a long time within sociology especially, there has been an ideological harangue that if one seeks to explain social order, then one is a "conservative" and unable or unwilling to face the very real possibility that not all social orders are created equal. Conservative thinkers like Parsons, so the criticism goes, paint too rosy a picture about how social order is maintained, namely, through a broad consensus of the citizenry about right and wrong, good and bad, moral and immoral, and so forth. These "consensus" theorists do not seem to understand that social order can also be maintained through threats and outright coercive force, and so those in power can use their power advantage to coerce those who do not have power to fall in line or pay the consequences.

This means that those who make such accusations also tend to self-identify as "liberals" who are concerned with the "underdogs" of society, namely, those who hold fewer valued social resources such as wealth, status, and power (Gouldner 1970). This unequal distribution of valued resources is viewed as inherently evil, and the goal is to understand why the system creates this kind of inequality with an eye toward eliminating it. Persons described thusly tend to be proponents of the evaluative paradigm mentioned above. This also means that, at least on a vulgar and simplistic level, evaluative theorists are likely to be critical of the police and the criminal justice system because of the heavily skewed power imbalance which exists between the average citizen on the one hand and representatives of the government on the other.

Jerome Skolnick (1966) has captured the essence of this dilemma perhaps as well as anyone, when he argued that law enforcement in a democratic society is an increasingly unsure and perilous undertaking. The title of his book *Justice without Trial*, refers to the fact that police out on the streets have the ability within face-to-face encounters with citizens to pretty much call the shots as they see fit, primarily because they are the ones that have the power of the police report whereby their version of reality tends to win out after all is said and done. Studies tend to support the notion that in the courtroom, when it comes down to competing accounts of what happened, jurors are more apt to believe government officials and police witnesses than those accused of a crime or their witnesses or defense attorneys (Manning 1997, pp. 94–95). The criminal justice system is set up so that those accused of crimes—especially indigent defendants who do not have the resources to adequately fight criminal charges—do not go to trial, and they do this primarily through the use of plea bargaining. Just so long as some semblance of fidelity to proper police procedure is evident, the police officer's word is typically sufficient to gain a conviction against a defendant.

Herbert Packer (1968) has extended this insight of Skolnick's into a general observation that the criminal justice system attempts to fulfill two major goals which often come into conflict. The *crime control* model of the criminal justice system is concerned with doing something about crime, and police officers are vested with the coercive power of the state to detain and possibly arrest people who are suspected of violating criminal laws. Notice that police can make arrests according to probable cause as specified in the Fourth Amendment, which deals with search and seizure issues. When someone is arrested, booked, and held in jail to await trial, it is obvious that the front end of the criminal justice system, where initial contacts between police and citizens take place, operates by the standard of "guilty until proven innocent." Indeed, if it were not for the reasonableness clause of the Fourth Amendment which informs all formal police actions and which allows them to assume the guilt of suspects, no one could ever be detained, arrested, or held over for trial.

The second model of the criminal justice system is represented by the *due process* model. Although police are vested with the coercive power of the state to carry out their enforcement powers, they must carry out their formal actions in such a way as to meet constitutional requirements of due process (such as the Fourth Amendment probable cause requirement for searches and seizures). However, the motto "innocent until proven guilty" applies at the time of a criminal trial, that is, when the state as plaintiff carries the burden of proof—beyond a reasonable doubt—in seeking to convict a criminal defendant. The police operate with a reasonableness clause (that is, probable cause) which gives them more leeway in their dealings with *prima facia* cases of suspect misconduct. Along the way of course, proper police procedures are supposed to assure that actions taken further along the criminal justice conveyor belt hold up under the more stringent requirements of "innocent until proven guilty" and constitutional due process. The latter stages of the criminal justice process also scrutinize police procedures residing at the front end, thereby contributing to the checks and balances which are presumably in place to ensure those accused are treated fairly.

Law is supposed to be applied dispassionately, blindly, and equally to all, whether at the point of police actions, prosecutorial conduct, judicial deliberations, or corrections administration. This impulse toward equality or egalitarianism as a primary policy directive across western society means that wherever raw inequalities exist in status, power, or opportunity, there will be attempts to examine these with an eye toward eliminating them. The evaluative theorists have established this as the primary problematic to be addressed, and there are good reasons to examine social structural arrangements which have imbedded within them raw inequalities of power.

Contrary to how evaluative theorists would approach this matter, it is not my position that the existence of such inequalities makes them *ipso facto* evil and worthy of dismantling. Some inequalities are necessary for the functioning of the social system. For example, there is still good reason to believe that the imbalance of power, authority, and status between parents and their children is functional for society. After all, children lack knowledge of and experiences with the world, and competent parents intervene on their behalf to keep them safe and to instruct them regarding their daily needs. This is a type of paternalistic power imbalance. Not all imbalances in the name of paternalism are necessarily good, but this one is.

The major imbalance of power that will occupy our time here is that between the citizens of a municipality and the police who are sworn to enforce the laws of a jurisdiction. It is interesting to note that the Greek word for police is αστυνομία ("astinomia"), which means in the literal sense "urban law." It makes sense that the meaning of the police would be connected to both "urban" and "law," as the police as a structural feature of society arise only with the advent of the modern state and its political/governmental apparatus. In rural or folk societies, law tends to be less well defined and specialized, and the people employ means of self-help to settle disputes, solve problems, and provide for local social order.

When a society grows and spreads out across an area, more impersonal systems of control arise to take charge of an increasingly well-defined and -bounded jurisdiction. Because as a society grows the people become less and less familiar with each other—indeed, many do not even know others living in the vicinity—mechanisms arise to order the lives of the people from a distance. It is the coercive power of the state, of a political jurisdiction, that is vested in the police, who are sworn law enforcement officers with the power of arrest. Any person can take it upon him- or herself to enforce the laws—such as the case of the "citizen arrest"—but because of the increasingly specialized activities involved in the imposition of one person's will against another, it no longer makes much sense for average citizens to invoke these powers except under extreme circumstances. Hence, it is left to the police to arrive on scene when an issue arises, whether called by a victim or some other observer. Sometimes police actually catch persons perpetrating a crime, but for the most part police are a reactive force responding to citizens' calls for help.

Local municipalities pass a plethora of laws—actually ordinances—for ordering the collective lives of the people. These ordinances run the gamut from the mundane to the profound. Some of these, when violated, call forth a police presence. For example, in a parking lot of a fast-food hamburger restaurant is posted the following sign: NO EATING IN THE PARKING LOT. Why was this ordinance passed in this particular location? The restaurant was built within a residential area. Sometimes, especially during the evening, young persons would order their food and congregate outside in the parking lot to hang out and sometimes play their car stereos. Complaints to city hall and the police started being made, and the first thing the city did was build a fence between the restaurant and adjoining houses to reduce both noise and visibility.

But now with fences up, residents in these adjacent houses found no relief simply because they were less visible to those in the parking lot. This led to even more boisterous behavior among the young persons congregating there, so rather than solving the problem, in many ways the fence made things worse. Calls to the police increased, and the police made their presence felt in increasing numbers to send out the message that this law would be taken seriously. When the police were called out, it was usually simply to disperse crowds and drive off troublemakers. Some young persons, though, were arrested, and word spread that the police were "hassling" people simply because of their race (it was a predominantly Black neighborhood).

This concern of racist or biased policing was illustrated recently by an altercation that happened between Harvard professor Henry Louis Gates—who happens to be Black—and Cambridge police officers who were called to the scene by someone in the neighborhood who thought someone may be breaking into a home. It was actually Gates who was trying to get into his own home. He had trouble with the front door and was attempting to force it open, the neighbor saw this, and phoned police headquarters about the suspicious activity. Sergeant

James Crowley—who happens to be White—was one of the first officers on the scene, and when Gates saw him his immediate reaction was one of consternation and fear. Reflecting a long history of rough treatment by law enforcement, as an African-American man Gates was ready to expect the worst, and he let Crowley know in no uncertain terms that he believed he was being targeted simply because of his skin color. The unmistakable position of Gates was that he had become a victim of racial profiling, and he continued shouting at Crowley, egging him on with taunts about being arrested in his own home because he was a Black man.

Crowley did eventually arrest Gates for disturbing the peace, although charges were quickly dropped. At a healthcare news conference a short time later, President Barack Obama was asked about the incident, and although the President admitted that he did not yet have all the facts, he did opine that the Cambridge police acted "stupidly" for arresting a man (Gates) in his own home. This in turn ignited somewhat of a media firestorm, as law enforcement departments and personnel quickly condemned the President's remarks for too quickly assuming the police on the scene, and Sergeant Crowley in particular, had engaged in racial profiling. There was a further irony to this, as Crowley had an impeccable record as a police officer and was even an instructor teaching fellow cops in his department about racial profiling. Finding out about this, President Obama had to backtrack, admitting that Officer Crowley was a superb police officer, and that very likely Professor Gates—a personal friend of Obama—stepped over the line and said some things that contributed to his arrest.

After the dust settled, Officer Crowley suggested that the three of them—Obama, Crowley, and Gates—ought to get together at the White House and have a few beers. And so the "beer summit" was on. Obama tried to play this up as a "teachable moment," again attempting to gain the upper hand on the national dialogue over race. Although the meeting between Gates and Crowley was cordial, they both went away from the beer summit agreeing to disagree. Many in the media and in the general public had lingering questions, however. One of the persistent questions was, "Should Officer Crowley have arrested Professor Gates?"

The answer to this question seemed to have a lot to do with the person's race, class, political affiliation, and occupational status. Democrats tended to think Crowley should not have arrested Gates, Republicans disagreed. Persons of color tended to think Gates should not have been arrested, while many Whites disagreed. And overwhelmingly, those who work in law enforcement or who have relatives in the field, believed that Crowley was justified in arresting Gates, while many outside of law enforcement believed he was not justified. This difference of opinion over the propriety of the arrest of Henry Louis Gates reflects a number of real-world complexities about the nature of police arrests in general. (The complexities of the arrest decision will be returned to in Chapter 4).

BITTNER'S PRINCIPLE

There have been an extraordinary number of scholars over the years who have contributed profound insights into the history and operations of policing in modern society, far too many to list here. The work of some of these scholars has been drawn upon in this book and included in the bibliography. I want to set aside the work of Egon Bittner for special attention, however, as I believe it represents the pinnacle of achievement in the analysis of all facets of modern policing.

Many of his key publications have been brought together in a 1990 collection titled *Aspects of Police Work*, and within this collection Bittner included his original 1970 book *The Functions of the Police in Modern Society*, which is currently out of print and copies of which are exceedingly hard to find. It is *The Functions of the Police in Modern Society* that will be the focus of our discussion here.

Early on Bittner tackles the difficult issue of how to disentangle commonsense notions of what police do and what policing is from the scientific effort to explain policing as a modern, empirical phenomenon. This is a challenge that confronts the social scientist in many areas of analysis. For example, many criminologists and sociologists have been somewhat apprehensive about dealing with the settling of the western frontier because of the way popular media—movies, television, books, and magazines—have glamorized and over-dramatized it with countless versions of "cowboys and Indians" storytelling. The social scientist venturing into this field obviously has to be careful wading through that which is exploitive and sensationalized about the Wild West, and that which contains kernels of truth.[4] However, with due diligence and care a systematic analysis of the rise of policing in the western frontier between 1840 and 1890 is possible, and it is this conviction that guided my own work on the topic, as evident in Chapter 3 and elsewhere.

Bittner discusses three characteristics of police work generally held by the public. First, "police work is a tainted occupation" (Bittner 1990, p. 94). Workers are often judged, fairly or unfairly, by the nature and character of their clientele. Police place themselves among the undesirables of society, including criminals, thieves, scam artists, prostitutes, and informants willing to rat out persons for whatever favors the police may grant them. Police often must enter into unholy alliances with those whom they are sworn to investigate, detain, or arrest (see Chapter 9), and the stigma of working closely with such disreputable characters is bound to taint the policing profession as a whole.

Bittner's second point is that "police work is not merely a tainted occupation" (Bittner 1990, p. 96). Bittner draws an analogy to some types of medical work which deal with filth and grime, such as the proctologist who must gain close and personal familiarity with the patient's rectum and general defecatory system. However, for the most part medical practitioners are handsomely remunerated for their services, whereas police officers typically are not. Also, while attending to the needs of patients doctors rarely work against the needs of others, but this is not the case for the police. In acting in their official capacity to help someone, for example, responding to a burglary call, police must also and necessarily act to the detriment of those who are accused of the offense. Police must not only respond to transgressive acts which are made public by some complainant, they must also be alive to possible unlawful activities residing below the surface appearances of respectability. This means that police officers take charge of subtle areas of human behavior wherever they are defined as actionable by the state, yet the tools at their disposal are rather crude and primitive (for example, the use of force or its threat). The expectation that police are pleasant and carry out their work with attention to professional decorum, all the while being armed with relatively primitive tools to get the job done, embodies Bittner's notion that policing is a mixed bag: part legitimate, part tainted.

Third, police work for the most part is deployed against persons possessing particular characteristics living in particular areas of the city (e.g., the poor and the destitute living in economically-deprived areas with an overrepresentation of racial or ethnic minorities). This gives the impression that police are prejudiced and use their advantage of power to protect the economically privileged (Bittner 1990, pp. 98–99). For example, the police would consider you crazy if you called the station and demanded that they go to Wall Street and arrest someone, right there on the trading floor, for insider trading.[5] Police rarely view their own work as biased or prejudiced, even if the attention they give to people who are "up to something" eventuates in the overrepresentation of certain sociodemographic characteristics in the crime statistics.

These three elements—taint, more than taint, and the ecological distribution of police work—go a long way in describing the realities of police work as viewed from the perspective of the general public as well as scholars working in the field of police studies. Bittner derives a general principle lying behind these various aspects of police work, as he asks the question, "At its most basic level, what allows police to be positioned to carry out the multiple duties assigned to them?" Or rather, "What lies behind this 'impossible' mandate?" (Manning 1978). Bittner (1990, p. 131) responds by offering the following principle, which is

> The role of the police officer is best understood as a mechanism for the distribution of non-negotiably coercive force employed in accordance with the dictates of an intuitive grasp of situational exigencies.

This is an elegant statement which requires only brief unpacking. First of all, because of the broad trend in society away from self-help toward more specialized forms of formal control—legal and medical primarily (see Chriss 2007b)—everyday citizens find themselves in situations where it is simply inadvisable to take matters into their own hands when some conflict arises. For better or worse, in modern society persons may be placed in a position where they feel they have no recourse but to "call the cops." This "trouble" leading to citizen calls for help means that citizens believe that the use of force may be required, and they are unwilling or unable to provide enough of it to deal with the situation at hand. It is the job of the police to arrive on scene and use their professional judgment—that is, discretion whether of the active or do-nothing form—to determine whether or not formal intervention is warranted. Most of the time police *do not* resort to the use of physical force, but the key is that it is always potentially available, and *that's why they are called in the first place*. There is no other occupational role which offers this feature, that is, the potential use of legitimate coercive force, and that is why police are called into so many situations, and also why their mandate is so diffuse and, frankly, unmanageable.

The various operational strategies available to police departments, including crime control, order maintenance, and service, are simply variations on the key distinguishing principle underlying all of police work, namely, the distribution of nonnegotiably coercive force. This means that, ultimately, police legitimation emanates from power seated in the polity, and although newer innovations of policing have attempted to soften up the "iron fist" of potential coercive force in favor of the "velvet glove" of advanced training, community outreach, and citizen participation, there can be no denying this incessant underlying reality.

Since the police do not employ physical force most of the time, it is ironic to note that this first principle lying behind all police work remains invisible and largely occluded. As Bittner stated in an interview with Jean-Paul Brodeur, "The use of force does not characterize police work in the way in which the doing of surgery characterizes surgeons' work" (Brodeur 2007b, p. 111). This singular, penetrating insight is a gift to all those who toil attempting to advance our understanding of policing, and for this Bittner will always receive his just accolades.

AN OVERVIEW OF THE BOOK

The idea of the police is captured well by the Greek word αστυνομία, as we have seen. The police are a modern, urban phenomenon, the embodiment of the coercive power of the state in the enforcement of laws. In this book, although some attention will be paid to the history of policing systems in western society, the main goal will be to develop a conceptual scheme for an explanation of the structure and function of modern or municipal policing. I argue that this reality can be captured within the conceptual schema developed by Talcott Parsons, with some modifications to be introduced throughout the volume.

It should also be noted that policing is a vast topic, far too expansive to cover comprehensively in a single volume. This means that choices have to be made, and here I will discuss the topics I have chosen to focus on in this book. Chapters 2 and 3 are concerned with detailing the historical development of policing in western society, with particular focus on the situation in America. In presenting a typology of three broad eras of policing in Chapter 2, I follow the recommendations of Kelling and Moore (1988) with some later modifications I presented in my book *Social Control* (Chriss 2007b). It is important to understand why formal policing arose in the first place, and how it has changed over time. The three eras of policing—political spoils, reform and early professionalization, and community policing—provide us this glimpse into the structure and function of (largely) municipal policing from the 1830s to the present day. Chapter 3 goes into detail on policing as it relates to the settling of the American western frontier, much more so than is the case for most books on policing. In looking at standard histories of policing, I discovered that there was an overweening emphasis on the examination of American policing as it has arisen in the American northeast, in major urban metropolises such as Boston, Philadelphia, and New York City. This is all well and good, but it tended to leave out for consideration the development of American policing west of the Mississippi River from the 1840s through the 1890s. In some respects, then, this is one of the unique contributions of the volume.

It should also be noted that, from the perspective being employed here, policing per se is not necessarily the thing to be studied, but rather, the focus is on the broader, more general phenomenon referred to as "police and society." Policing as a whole, along with aspects of policing, cannot sufficiently be explained or understood without also analyzing policing in relation to history, culture, economics, and social structure, not only of policing itself, but also of the societies within which policing is located. A program of study referred to as "police and society" would be analogous to what has happened in the sociologically-oriented program of study often referred to as "law and society." In fact, there is an actual professional association which calls itself the Law and Society Association. They also publish one of the leading scholarly journals dedicated to law and society issues, namely *Law and Society Review*. This association, founded in 1964, describes itself as "a group of scholars from many fields and countries, interested in the place of law in social, political, economic, and cultural life" (see http://www.lawandsociety.org). A number of scholarly journals dedicated to policing issues reflect this attention to both policing and society, including such leading journals as *Policing and Society, Policing, Police Quarterly, Police Practice and Research*, and *Ideas in American Policing*.[6]

Chapter 4 is dedicated to examining one particular strategy for battling police corruption, namely integrity testing. Integrity tests are sting operations carried out by police departments against their own police officers, and they may be conducted either randomly or targeted at specific officers who are suspected of wrongdoing. Much of social life reflects the unmistakable reality that any strategy that works, or that provides socially desired results, can also be used against itself either for bad or, in the case of policing, for the good of exposing corruption that would otherwise be difficult if not impossible to bring to light. Specifically, the resource or strategy central to this area of concern is deception, something that is and has been pervasive throughout the human condition. Integrity testing places police officers in situations which appear to be normal and routine but which are carefully staged by police examiners. These fabricated settings provide a field laboratory in which unwitting officers can be observed interacting with the public while carrying out their duties. Many areas of police operations can be examined through random or targeted integrity testing, including of course the single most important set of actions engaged in by the police, namely, use of force. Among all the things that mark the police as unique or special, the power to arrest represents the pinnacle of distinction separating the police from the lay public. The last half of the chapter examines the variety of factors lying behind the police decision to arrest, both those officially authorized (e.g., seriousness of offense, availability of evidence), and those which are informal or "off the books" (such as race of suspect, suspect's general demeanor, or personal considerations of the officer including how late it is in the shift).

Chapter 5 extends the three-era policing model introduced earlier by discussing what many police scholars consider to be an emerging fourth era of policing, namely, post 9/11 policing. This chapter interrogates the title of the book, and asks whether or not post 9/11 policing represents an important or enduring example of "going beyond" community policing. I argue that in many ways it does, although like everything else, policing tends to go in cycles reflecting the saying "everything that is old is new again." The threat of international terrorism has put local police departments on high alert and federal mandates have been put into place which require that municipal police are trained in various forms of counterterrorism and planning in the event of a terrorist attack. Under post 9/11 policing, "security" becomes the operative concept, and although it is as old as informal self-help and the earliest forms of professional policing, it nevertheless must be reexamined in light of the terrorist threat. Even so, this chapter provides merely an introduction, as the full extent of the conceptual rethinking of security will be taken up in the last chapter. The topic of terrorism also serves as a launching point for the full-blown utilization of Talcott Parsons' AGIL schema, whereby functional linkages across all subsystems of the criminal justice system will be specified. Not only is the criminal justice system located relative to the broader social system, the police subsystem is located relative to the criminal justice system. Additionally, various functional elements of post 9/11 policing are identified and considered in light of attempts by professionals in the policing field to make sense of this emerging fourth era of policing.

Chapter 6 returns to the issue of police discretion, picking up from the limited discussion in Chapter 4 regarding the arrest decision. Although I recognize the traditional factors associated with police discretion found in the literature, I also suggest other factors often overlooked by scholars, including openness of horizons, personnel density, and visibility. I also follow the logic of the functional elements of the criminal justice system discussed in Chapter 5 to provide a comparison of the levels of professional discretion of key criminal justice agents. All things considered, police operate with the highest levels of discretion in the criminal justice system, followed by legal agents (prosecutors and judges), and then, much further down the list, correctional agents. I also tie high levels of police discretion to the importance of informal rules and procedures which police officers develop in the course of their professional work. In other words, because of the unique aspects of police work, formal bureaucratic directives are limited as a way of ensuring that real flesh-and-blood police officers do certain things specified in writing during the course of their work. This is not judged as a necessarily negative or positive state of affairs. Instead, it is merely recognition of the levels and forms of discretion available to police officers as they go about their field operations.

Chapter 7 takes a long-term historical approach in seeking to explain how and when the term "proactive" came to prominence in sociology and related social science disciplines, including criminology. Because proactivity—that is, actions which are engaged in to keep bad things from happening (negative proactivity) or to promote a desired future state of affairs (positive proactivity)—is so central in many social science and policy arenas, including social prediction, organizational analysis, public health, and, of course, policing, it is important to trace out the historical development of the concept in sociology and criminology. In the second half of the chapter, I specify the ways in which the concept of proactivity has been applied to policing, both its negative and positive forms.

In Chapter 8, I make the argument that since the 1970s with the rise of community policing, police officers are working more and more like contact men (and women). The contact person is a special role type which emerges in organizations which are concerned with the creation of cultural items which require expertise in the way of judging human potential for creativity. In the arts and entertainment industry, contact persons are assumed to recognize talent and use their personal discretion to hit the streets and make contact with cultural producers, sign them to contracts with the organization, and promote these items (books, films, and music) to the wider public. They must also be able to work with key media gatekeepers in the community, who would then hopefully look favorably on the product and highlight the author's work in appropriate venues (in bookstores, on radio stations, in movie theaters, and so forth). It may appear a stretch to make the analogy between contact men in culture industries and police officers as contact men, yet the analogy holds for reasons described in the chapter.

In Chapter 9 I return to the issues of security first introduced in Chapter 5, but I go beyond the conceptualization of security as it pertains to terrorism and post 9/11 policing. In doing so, in this chapter I discuss the long-held distinction between public and private, and consider how security was originally the responsibility of persons in their community and only later became the responsibility of public police with the rise of the state and that particular configuration known as the service city. This in turn opens an avenue for understanding how private security operates alongside public policing in the modern and postmodern world. Especially in times of economic decline where budgets are tight, governments act more like private businesses with regard to the various programs and services they have provided to citizens especially since the rise of the service city in the late 1700s. It appears that the trend toward increasing privatization of security will be of enduring interest to local govern-ments as they struggle to provide essential safety services—police, fire, and EMS—to citizens, and is well on the way to transforming certain key aspect of police operations and organization.

Finally, in the last chapter I provide a summary, in proposition form, of the key findings discussed throughout the book. These "findings" are of course provisional and subject to further analysis and testing with the continuing scien-tific study of the police and society.

NOTES

[1] Reports on the Greek rioting were gathered from http://news.bbc.co.uk/2/hi/europe/7769710.stm and http://www.cbsnews.com/stories/2008/12/12/world/main4670778.shtml.

[2] Following the distinction made famous by Jean-Paul Brodeur (1983), the Greek police could be described primarily as engaging in "high policing," name-ly, the protection of government through intelligence gathering and national and/or international security. This is contrasted against "low policing," which is the typical operation of local or municipal policing with regard to crime control, order maintenance, and/or service provision. For a critique of the concept of high policing, see O'Reilly and Ellison (2006).

[3] However, during the summer of 2009 Karamanlis was defeated by Papandreou and his New Democracy socialist party. The socialists were successful in cha-racterizing Karamanlis as a corrupt and greedy politician who made questiona-ble deals with industrial giant Siemens. For a summary of the Greek election results, see http://www.cnn.com/2009/WORLD/europe/10/04/greece.elections/index.html.

[4] Paradigmatic of this distrust of the popular narrative of the Wild West is Will Wright's *The Wild West Myth: The Mythical Cowboy and Social Theory*, which rejects much of what has been written about the Wild West because it is satu-rated through and through with the myth of rugged individualism, where cow-boys and settlers worked against great odds to establish lives for themselves and their families in the struggle to tame the western frontier. Authors are of course free to engage with particular subject matter as they see fit, but I believe such wholesale rejection of an area because of its being contaminated by the popular imagination cannot be sustained as a model for good science. This would be akin to rejecting the study of crime scene investigation because of its aggran-dizement in the wildly popular *CSI* television series. Rather than taking this course, I choose not to throw the baby out with the bathwater.

[5] This example was used in a published piece authored by a police scholar, but I do not remember the source.

[6] There are actually two journals with the title *Policing*. Both are published by European publishers but have slightly different aims. The one published by Emerald has the subtitle "An International Journal of Police Strategies and Management," and as the subtitle indicates is dedicated to cross-cultural analyses of various aspects of policing at local, state, federal, and international levels. Even so, many of the articles concentrate on policing in the United States. The other journal is published by Oxford University Press, and although it too publishes papers covering a wide range of national interests, it is more focused on policing in Britain.

2

Three Eras of Policing

Human societies have always attempted to control the behavior of their members. Even among the most primitive tribes, there exist customs and beliefs which everyone accepts and which typically are adhered to, primarily out of fear of punishment for violating them. These systems of control are more or less informal, embodied in the stocks of knowledge members have about their world and how to act within it. Many of the beliefs and practices of early human beings would appall modern sensibilities, but it must be understood that such primitive practices did not emerge out of thin air. Rather, whatever has been reported or discovered about early human behavior is typically reflective of the environments within which these human groups lived. Virtually all acts taking place within human groups are collective attempts to survive given the limitations of environmental resources and the threats to life and limb, whether real or perceived.

For example, as William Graham Sumner (1906) summarizes in his book *Folkways*, in particular times and places in the human past cannibalism was an acceptable practice. Wherever cannibalism was found to be practiced, it was almost always a result of a defect in the food supply. In short, where food supplies are meager—especially when there is a shortage of meat—cannibalism may be practiced. Yet, even if a particular primitive group practices cannibalism, there are rules regarding who can and cannot be eaten, and under what conditions. For example, members of the same tribe rarely eat their own. Instead, they may eat the flesh of enemies or strangers. Under the harshest conditions, however, the males of the tribe may eat other members who are deemed sickly or weak, but almost never will they eat a woman (Sumner 1906, p. 330).

In the condition of the primitive tribe (or the even more remote "primal horde"; see, e.g., Giddings 1896), members of the group police themselves to the extent that the folkways—the norms and customs of the group—are known to all and are expected to be enforced by all. Only when disputes arise over some important event will higher authorities be called to judge the believability

25

of one side or the other in the dispute. Overwhelmingly in primitive human societies, these esteemed authorities are the elders, and they gain their authority and prestige on the basis of tradition and the fact that they have survived to a relatively old age even in a harsh physical environment where average life expectancies are short. In short, even in the most primitive of societies there are typically patterns of association among members dedicated in certain crucial instances or social situations to the regulation of norms and to the sanctioning of members who violate these folkways, customs, or norms.

Good examples of this are various types of association among Native American tribes which serve explicitly political functions. Among the Plains Indians (including the Hidatsa, Crow, Mandan, Blackfoot, Dakota, and Pawnee), the work of government was carried out by associations of male members of the tribe. For example, an important event among these Plains Indians was the communal buffalo hunt, and the association in charge of the hunt was vested with the power to confiscate the kill of any hunter who did not abide by the ground rules (for example, starting the hunt too soon or taking more than his fair share). In extreme cases of malfeasance the offending parties could even be put to death. Buffalo hunt police could not act outside of their narrow jurisdiction associated with the activities of the hunt, and each year typically new members were named to the association (Krader 1968, p. 34).

In the long march out of human savagery, human beings slowly changed the way they controlled and coordinated the activities of fellow human beings. Rather than relying on informal control, whereby clans, families, or associations regulate the behavior of their own members and defend themselves against persons outside of the group, more advanced societies started relying on specialized agents to carry out control functions for the wider society. When societies move to more advanced stages, their populations grow larger and the informal systems of control based upon blood ties and familiarity between all members are rendered less effective. Some of the earliest systems of control in Britain and Colonial America that moved beyond pure informal control, such as "hue and cry," frankpledge groups, and "watch and ward," utilized aspects of law enforcement or policing, although the persons taking on these roles were not professionals nor were they trained in the specific tasks necessary to do the job.

EARLY POLICING IN LONDON

In Britain, for example, even as late as the late 1600s residents of city wards were expected to act as night watchmen if selected, and they were instructed to cry out and send an alarm if they observed anything suspicious. They were expected to provide this service free of charge, and anyone who shirked his or her duty faced heavy fines or other penalties in the Lord Mayor's Court (Fletcher 1850, p. 222). Over time, however, persons started resisting volunteering for watch and ward duty, and this necessitated developing special categories of watch persons, some of which received pay. By the early 1700s Britain passed the Watch Acts, whereby pay was given to night watchmen as supervised and regulated within each ward. This system of night policing stayed relatively intact until the 1830s, at which time, due to various changes in London specifically and Western society more generally—urbanization and industrialization being the two most important factors—the night watch was replaced by a more systematic and professional system of policing.

The early impetus toward modern municipal policing was embodied in Robert Peel's Metropolitan Police Act, which was passed by British parliament in 1829. Concomitant to the establishment of the new police force of metropolitan London, there was also a description of the expansion of police powers. Some of the new regulations specified as enforceable by the new police were as follows:

- The regulation of routes and conduct of persons driving stage-carriages and cattle during the hours of divine services;
- Public houses to remain shut on Sundays, Christmas day, and Good Friday;
- Liquor shall not be supplied to persons under sixteen years of age;
- Power is given to the police to enter unlicensed theatres, and to regulate the activities taking place in coffee houses and cook shops;
- Pawnbrokers who receive pledges from persons under the age of sixteen are subjected to penalties;
- Drunkards guilty of indecent behavior may be imprisoned (Fletcher 1850, pp. 235–236).

Also included was the specification of a vast array of "street offences" for which police could take persons into custody for their violation, including illegal posting of bills or other papers on public buildings, walls, or fences; prostitution, night-walking, or loitering; distribution or exhibition of profane, indecent, or obscene books or papers; and regulation of threatening, abusive, or insulting words or behavior which threaten to or actually "provoke a breach of the peace" (Fletcher 1850, p. 237).

The establishment of a sworn, paid police force in London was symbolic of the new levels of political control and oversight which the city of London was eager to establish, even in the face of opposition among many of its residents who felt, from the very beginning, that the police were either corrupt, inefficient, or simply inattentive to some of their sworn duties, particularly in the areas of "protecting" and "serving." This theme, namely, the ambivalence of the citizenry toward sworn police officers, has resonated and continues to resonate across most societies. In his massive study of poverty in turn-of-the-century London, Charles Booth (1970 [1902–1904]) commented frequently on the role of police in the lives of Londoners and the generally negative views of them shared especially among the poor. Booth quoted one resident of Bethnal Green as saying "[The police] won't interfere to stop the most hideous disorder in the streets." Another Bethnal Green resident complained of the police that there are not "half enough of them, and [they] see as little as possible," and that they are "afraid to assert themselves in a district like this" (Booth 1970 [1902–1904], p. 132).

Even with these negative sentiments, in some rough areas the police are seen by the residents as effective in maintaining at least a modicum of order on the streets, primarily by making a point of knowing "by name and sight" who the "rough" characters are. The police will generally not intervene in activities taking place within homes or other private areas, but if it spills out into the streets, such as a drunken brawl, the police will make a show of corralling the primary aggressors and giving them a good "going over" (Booth 1970 [1902–1904], p. 137). This order-maintenance strategy is still practiced by modern police, as confirmed in Bittner's (1967) study of policing in skid row where police apply a standard of "rough informality" to keep the regulars in line, thereby often avoiding the need to invoke their formal powers of arrest.

THE AMERICAN SITUATION

By the late 1830s American cities began establishing police forces modeled on the London Metropolitan police. The negative effects of urbanization and industrialization that had earlier prodded the development of policing in London were now starting to affect larger American cities in the East. In America, in fact, urbanization and industrialization combined with other factors to produce a unique set of social circumstances that shaped early American policing and made it somewhat distinct from the British model even as it was based upon it. As David Johnson (1981, pp. 22–25) points out, these other factors in America were nativism, racism, social reform, and politics.

Nativism refers to negative treatment or attitudes toward persons on the basis of their being perceived as outsiders, especially those of foreign birth. The influx of Catholics, especially after the 1840s with the arrival of large numbers of Irish Catholics, led to high levels of social and economic discrimination against them. Many riots that occurred—in Boston in 1834, Philadelphia in 1844, and Louisville in 1855—can be traced to these and other forms of nativism.

Racism, against Blacks but also against Hispanics and American Indians (or Native Americans), was a staple of American life not only in the South, where slavery was legal until 1865, but also in parts of the country where Blacks were presumably "free" but nevertheless often mistreated. As Johnson (1981, p. 23) notes, between 1829 and 1850 five major race riots erupted in Philadelphia alone, all of which required military intervention.

Social reform also sparked violence, instigated primarily among those who looked unfavorably on the proposed reforms. The two major reforms leading to social unrest were the abolition of slavery and the temperance movement. The temperance movement caused class antagonisms between social reformers as "do-gooders" who tended to come from the higher strata of society, and middle- to lower-class Americans who viewed the attempt to restrict their drinking as an unacceptable infringement on their freedom. Slavery and the question of its abolition was a source of antagonism in America since its founding, culminating of course in the Civil War and continuing into the era of Reconstruction as freed African-Americans sought better opportunities wherever they could find them, including on the Western frontier.

Finally, these and other issues led to protracted *political battles*, as urban political leaders staked out positions on divisive issues, while opponents became entrenched on the opposite side. This was the beginning of American partisan politics, and by the time of their establishment in each local community, police departments were inexorably shaped by these varied political entanglements.

POLITICAL SPOILS[1]

Following Kelling and Moore (1988) with modifications developed by Chriss (2007b), there have been three eras of American policing, described as political spoils; reform and early professionalization; and community policing (1970s to present).[2]

The first phase of modern policing, running from the 1830s to the 1920s, is referred to as the *political spoils era*. In this earliest stage of development police departments were controlled by city government as well as ward bosses who wielded considerable influence not only on how police were to be used, but also who would be chosen as police officers. There was no pretense of choosing officers on the basis of objective criteria of competence or ability. Rather, officers during the first era were chosen on the basis of political loyalty and ascribed characteristics such as family connections, race or ethnicity, or friendship. Such close relations between city government and police officers produced an entitlement mentality among ward leaders and the administrative staff of the police organization, and because police were poorly paid, all parties tended to look the other way when officers engaged in questionable activities. As a result, patronage abuses abounded and police engaged in many under-the-table or quid pro quo arrangements with various constituents in the community.

As Kelling and Moore (1988) note, policing of the political spoils era was scrabbled together haphazardly and willy-nilly, as there were no organizational mandates yet established for proper police procedures or defining the role of police officers in the community. As a result, the political class within each local community determined goals and activities for the police, thus contributing to the fragmentation of policing and the great variability in police organization from community to community. Police were simply an appendage of the political machine, beholden to those in power at the moment. When a new administration came in, it was not uncommon to see a complete housecleaning take place as the new mayor or city hall put into position "their" men (and women) in policing roles.

During the political spoils era police provided a wide array of services, including crime control, order maintenance, and various social services such as running soup lines, providing temporary lodging for new arrivals to the city, and working with ward leaders to help find work, especially for newly arriving immigrants. Additionally, early police were not as centralized as later more professional departments organized along quasi-military design. This is because cities were divided into wards, and police departments into precincts. Precinct-level police managers worked closely with city ward leaders in hiring, firing, and assigning personnel. This meant that there were lots of quid pro quo arrangements.

Police had tremendous discretion out in the field since all they had to tie them back to the precinct house was the call box.[3] Fire call boxes started appearing in American cities as early as the 1860s (a glass front that any citizen could break to alarm the fire department), but police call boxes appeared about two decades later. Police call boxes were sealed boxes which a patrol officer could access with a key. The patrol officer would enter the call box and flip a switch to notify a central command center that his patrol was proceeding as normal and that no assistance was necessary. Police officers pulled a different box switch on their patrol route every thirty minutes. It also featured a telephone that officers could use to communicate problems to the central command. These earliest patrol routes were called Carney Blocks, named after an officer that devised the system. The police call box was painted blue, and illumination of the light at night provided an officer the location of the box in case of emergency if or when they needed to call for backup. Each box had a number affixed, and policemen quickly identified problem areas in neighborhoods by the unique call box number. All early police boxes were on party lines, so the beat cop would have to pull the box lever to identify which box he was at on the circuit. There was also a pointer in the early boxes for ambulance, paddy wagon, riot, fire, and other safety or order-related issues. The front door had a citizen's key, and any passerby could insert the key and call a wagon for any manner of accident or emergency.

The decentralization of early policing fit in well with foot patrol (walking a beat), and as they were directly visible and available citizen demands focused on them, while ward politicians focused on the organization more generally. Demand for police services appeared at street level, with respect to average citizen calls and encounters, and also at the precinct level, with regard to the local requirements for use of police personnel by ward bosses, city hall, and as directed by police administration.

Aside from the early call box, the primary program or technology for police during this era was foot patrol. A system of "rough informality" (Bittner 1967) was the rule of the day, and much "off the books" activities occurred, including the third degree, widespread use of police informants, and police being at the beck and whim of ward bosses and the political machine for whatever purposes they deemed appropriate. It was not uncommon, for example, for

politicians to use detectives to get dirt on people. In this sense, the earliest polic- |
ing tended to be more person-centered than offense-centered.

Finally, the expected outcomes of police work were crime and crowd control, order maintenance, and urban relief (where police dealt with such issues as poverty, homelessness, and "poor relief" more generally). This sounds much like the basic goals or expected outcomes of more modern policing, and in many ways it is. However, the major difference between policing in this first era and policing in later eras is the level of professionalization: in the earliest political spoils era there were no pretenses that police officers should be trained or that a certain class of individual was necessary to fill these roles. Although relatively well paid because of the real or potential danger of the work, nineteenth-century police were poorly trained, and virtually anyone with the right political connections and an inclination to violence could be lured into police work. With no real training, police had to learn "on the fly" and fashioned their own personal strategies for dealing with whatever or whomever they encountered in their day-to-day rounds (Lane 1992, p. 13).

Even so, police attempted to maintain a precarious balancing act between assuring citizen satisfaction (at the street level) and political satisfaction (at the precinct level). Since there were few if any rules in place to regulate the behavior of police or to recruit new members into the department, police had almost no checks on their personal behavior. Of course, the department could censure or punish members, including suspending or firing officers, but since there was no meaningful reporting of the department's activities, public accountability of the police was nonexistent. Attempts to change this set of conditions would occur in the next policing era.

REFORM AND EARLY PROFESSIONALIZATION

The second policing era ran from approximately the 1920s through the 1960s. This second era of policing, referred to as *reform and early professionalization*, was dedicated to correcting some of the problems associated with first-era policing, especially the patronage abuses, graft and corruption, and brutality which characterized early policing. In order to keep officers in line, more attention was given over to organizing departments along military lines, and the new forms of bureaucracy emerging under Taylorism was also useful in setting up a system of overt checks and balances to ensure that the actions of police met the expectations of the department as well as the wider community. Police were also concerned with gaining more autonomy, and they did this by placing greater distance between themselves and local political influence. And to address the graft and corruption, police moved away from an emphasis on foot patrol to more impersonal relations with citizens.

The impulse toward (early) professionalization resulted in a strategy whereby police felt they should no longer engage in the various activities that marked their work in the earlier era. Instead of running soup kitchens or dealing with runaway children, the police opted to professionalization through specialization, and the special role they chose was that of the crime fighter. With the mass production of the automobile beginning in the 1930s, police departments were able to kill two birds with one stone, in terms of both reform and early professionalization, by shifting the mode of patrol from foot to automobile. This created an instantaneous expansion of coverage for calls arriving through dispatch, but also quicker response times, hence further meeting the goals of professionalism and efficiency.

The other advantage of automobile patrol was that the police placed greater physical distance between themselves and citizens, and in so doing mitigated to some extent the graft and corruption of the previous era. But this professionalism was early, incipient, and provisional because there was not yet consideration given to systematically increasing the amount or content of training for police officers, as up to this time there was still the widespread sentiment that policing was a blue-collar job—a craft, not a profession—which could be filled by virtually any able-bodied person with an inclination to that sort of work. The move toward full professionalization, complete with attention to the educational background of police candidates and implementation of ongoing training, would not be realized until the community-policing era (to be discussed below).

Vollmer, Wilson, and Beyond

Attention to some of the background elements of this second era of police reform and professionalization should be noted. Berkeley, CA police chief August Vollmer was one of the first to push for police reforms during the 1920s and early 1930s. Vollmer saw the police as guardians of societal morality, and the goodness of officers would be judged on the quality and integrity of their work. As chief of the Los Angeles Police Department, Vollmer wrote an annual summary of conditions in the department for the year 1924. Many of the themes of modern policing, including emphases on education, training, specialization, and efficiency were evident in Vollmer's 1924 report. One key passage is worth noting:

> If [police] were thoroughly trained for the service before being appointed, they would soon be able to teach, preach and write concerning the obligation that rests upon every individual in the community to cooperate in creating reverence for law. Accordingly a tentative outline of courses for policemen has been prepared and is on file at police headquarters. It has been found that specialization is necessary in modern police organizations. The duties are too varied and control of the multiplicity of details must be done through a staff of competent experts. Police departments cannot continue to operate as in the past and efficiency will be impossible until highly specialized functions are

placed in the hands of persons who have been trained for their profession (Vollmer 1974 [1924], p. 11).

O.W. Wilson, Vollmer's protégé, wrote explicit texts on municipal police administration, following what J. Edgar Hoover had done at the federal level with the FBI. Hoover professionalized the investigative function of the bureau and pushed for more stringent educational and training requirements for FBI recruits. Although Hoover's FBI was the model of professionalization for state, county, and local policing after the 1930s, Hoover himself engaged in a range of improper behaviors—such as domestic spying on particular Americans for overtly political purposes—which required further reforms of the FBI beginning in the 1960s (Johnson et al. 2008).

Wilson's *Police Planning* stood as the "bible" for police management and organizational training for many decades after it was first published in 1952. Wilson also crafted the Law Enforcement Code of Ethics, adopted in 1956 by the Peace Officers' Association of California. Even today, this code of ethics (see Figure 2.1) is recited by a majority of police recruits newly graduating from their respective programs, albeit with some modifications of language to comport with today's sensibilities (e.g., dropping "God" at the end of the oath).

Law Enforcement Code of Ethics

As a Law Enforcement Officer, my fundamental duty is to serve mankind; to safeguard lives and property; to protect the innocent against deception, the weak against oppression or intimidation, and the peaceful against violence or disorder; and to respect the Constitutional rights of all men to liberty, equality and justice.

I will keep my private life unsullied as an example to all; maintain courageous calm in the face of danger, scorn, or ridicule; develop self-restraint; and be constantly mindful of the welfare of others. Honest in thought and deed in both my personal and official life, I will be exemplary in obeying the laws of the land and the regulations of my department. Whatever I see or hear of a confidential nature or that is confided to me in my official capacity will be kept ever secret unless revelation is necessary in the performance of my duty.

I will never act officiously or permit personal feelings, prejudices, animosities, or friendships to influence my decisions. With no compromise for crime and with relentless prosecution of criminals, I will enforce the law courteously and appropriately without fear of favor, malice or ill will, never employing unnecessary force or violence and never accepting gratuities.

I recognize the badge of my office as a symbol of public faith, and I accept it as a public trust to be held so long as I am true to the ethics of police service. I will constantly strive to achieve these objectives and ideals, dedicating myself before God to my chosen profession...law enforcement.

Figure 2.1. O.W. Wilson's Code of Ethics (circa 1956)

The reform aspects of this second era of policing are tied to several high-profile failures of the political spoils system which eventuated in the passage of the federal Pendleton Act in 1883. In 1865 President Abraham Lincoln was assassinated, largely because his handpicked bodyguard, a federal police officer by the name of John Parker, decided to go off drinking in a saloon while leaving Lincoln unattended next door at Ford's Theater. This gave John Wilkes Booth unfettered access to the president, who took the opportunity to shoot Lincoln in cold blood (Oates 1984). Sixteen years later, in the summer of 1881, a disgruntled office seeker, Charles Guiteau, shot President James A. Garfield, who died in September, 1881 from his wounds (Theriault 2003).

By this time, the political patronage system, whereby persons were given positions of authority and trust without explicit guidelines in place to determine their fitness for the position, was in deep disarray, and the call for meaningful civil service reform was being taken seriously. The resulting Pendleton Act passed by Congress required that those seeking positions in federal government be selected by competitive testing. It was referred to as the merit system, the forerunner to the now well-established civil service examination (Hogenboom 1959). Although originally designed to screen applicants for federal positions, somewhat later state and local governments began following suit, including of course the screening of applicants for municipal policing positions.

By the time of the Progressive Era beginning in the 1890s, then, reformers rejected politics as the basis of local governance in general and police legitimacy in particular. New civil service regulations for hiring, firing, and promotion of public personnel were favored by progressives, thereby presumably eliminating informal "good old boys" networks while championing achievement over ascription. This also served to move police further away from the citizens they served as well as the influence of local politics. This also coincided with a new claim of special police knowledge and expertise, based on knowledge of law and professional responsibilities. As a result of such specialization and professionalization, police were seen as more autonomous and not beholden to city hall, ward bosses, or others seeking to use the police for personal or political purposes.

Additionally, this focus on the law meant that the police started narrowing their agenda to crime control and criminal apprehension. They became law enforcement agencies, rather than safety organizations or peace forces. From the perspective of the organization, there was no need for police to entangle themselves in the political, social, cultural, or economic conditions presumably contributing to disorder and crime. In other words, police should not try to solve root causes of crime because they are neither social workers nor behavioral scientists. They should merely use their technical legal expertise to combat crime. Specialization of this sort also meant that medical and emergency services were shifted to private providers and/or firefighting organizations. In sum, in the second-era police were no longer an agency of urban government, but now part of the criminal justice system.

Further, the organizational design for policing beginning in the early 1900s was influenced by Frederick Taylor's ideas regarding control and efficiency within large, formal organizations (Bendix 1947). Within this formal organizational or bureaucratic model, the assumption is that workers are not all that interested in work, so economic incentives are the key. Conceptualizing police organization in this way implies that worker productivity is linked to employees' rewards. To achieve control of this process a specialized, well-regulated division of labor is required. The military command-and-control model of hierarchical, top-down, supervision of lower-level personnel was useful for these purposes, where emphasis is placed on a chain of command and explicit rules are designed for each officeholder. There is also an attempt to reduce officer discretion by holding up the universality of the criminal code applied to all persons equally (rather than specificity). This further implies a legalistic rather than a service orientation. Further refinements in the police division of labor give rise to specialized units such as vice, juvenile bureaus, drugs, tactical/SWAT, gangs, and the like.

And just as J. Edgar Hoover used propaganda methods to sell the public on the growing problem of urban crime and the need to invest more resources and trust in law enforcement at all levels of government, so too did police reformers discover that public relations and increased use of media could be effective in publicizing police activities and related public concerns, whether good or bad. The second era of policing established public relations as an integral aspect of police practice, and it grew in importance into the third, community-policing era. The group image that was presented was that police are first and foremost crime fighters. Foot patrol was deemed outmoded and inefficient, which also served to keep officers at arm's length from citizens. This also led to the increased reliance on the use of the squad car for routine police patrols. Additionally, centralization is an organizing element in second-era policing, insofar as citizens are expected to contact police headquarters rather than individual cops on a beat.

As mentioned above, during the reform and early professionalization era police claimed to be specialists in crime control, and it was also upon this basis that police professionalization was assured (Kelling and Moore 1988). August Vollmer initiated the development of a uniform system of crime classification, which was later codified by the International Association of Chiefs of Police (IACP) in 1930. This early attempt by the IACP to codify crime statistics was seen as so promising that the FBI took over the collection and reporting of crime statistics a year later, eventually becoming the Uniform Crime Reports (Mosher et al. 2002). Since then all police departments have measured their effectiveness against this standard, especially in terms of such key measures as the crime rate, clearance rate, response time in patrol and other field operations, and so forth. This was an effective reform strategy during the relatively stable 1940s and 1950s, but was somewhat rigid and inflexible in the face of rapid social changes occurring during the 1960s, especially with regard to rising crime rates during the decade, fueled largely by the baby boom (1946–1963; see Cohen and

Land 1987). As defenders of the status quo, police could not adjust rapidly enough to the sweeping cultural and social changes occurring during the 1960s.

COMMUNITY POLICING

As mentioned above, the third era of policing, running from the 1970s to the present, is known as community-oriented or problem-oriented policing. Community-oriented policing (COP) or simply *community policing*, along with the closely-related problem-oriented policing (POP), emerged out of the social transitions of the 1960s. With new challenges to the status quo in the form of social movements such as feminism, civil rights, gay rights, as well as war and campus protests, the police were forced into high-profile and sometimes violent clashes with these and other groups, and as defenders of a status quo under siege they were easy targets for protests and demands for reform beyond those of the second era. It seemed that the professionalism upon which the police staked their claim in the previous era was badly out of touch with the realities of a new and rapidly changing urban landscape. Out of this came the impetus towards real reform, such as developing explicit guidelines for improved training and education of police, as well as attempts to recruit police candidates who matched more closely the sociodemographic characteristics of the populations they served, especially in the areas of gender and race.

Coming out of a tumultuous period of sometimes violent clashes with social movement actors, the police were certainly eager to retool their image and show themselves to be committed to solving problems besetting communities with a spirit of collaboration and mutual respect. This also meant that police would relinquish the claim of specialists in crime control and start taking on a variety of roles in the community, being especially keen to bolster their positive presence in the community through order maintenance, service, and a more scientific approach to studying and solving community problems. To pull off this new ability to take on multiple roles, urban policing became committed to improving educational requirements of their officers, not only in the area of "hard" skills (the newest police technologies) but also with regard to "soft skills" (training in human relations where police act like counselors, psychologists, social workers, and sociologists if need be).

To reiterate, in the third era of community policing police departments made a concerted effort to be more "user friendly," including the downplaying of automobile patrol in favor of foot patrols, bike patrols, and other "slower" forms of police response and presence. Police endeavored to get more information to citizens about the nature of police operations and of crime and disorder in their community. Police started taking an overt interest in fear of crime, studying ways to reduce or eliminate it. This led to a thriving "fear of crime" industry, in effect launching a partnership with higher education to conduct studies/surveys about citizen fears and wants. In sum, there was a push to work more closely with citizens to address issues of the community (Renauer 2007). Indeed, this problem-solving or problem-oriented focus of community policing is embodied in the SARA acronym, which represents the elements or stages of police work aimed at identifying and resolving problems in the community. SARA stands for:

- **Scanning**—Initial identification of community problems to be addressed;
- **Analysis**—Collecting information and analyzing the data;
- **Response**—Developing a strategy to address the underlying condition;
- **Assessment**—Evaluating the effectiveness of the intervention or response (White 2007, pp. 96–98).

This problem-solving methodology assumes that citizens are prepared to work alongside police in a collaborative effort to solve community problems. A recent meta-analysis of a number of published evaluations of problem-oriented policing initiatives found that, for the most part, the SARA method is effective in helping police respond to and alleviate the various problems they and citizens of the jurisdiction identify (Weisburd et al. 2010). Nevertheless, it is important to examine more closely not only this but other assumptions which underlie community policing. Riechers and Roberg (1990) have summarized this bundle of assumptions, which include:

- **Fear of crime**—Beyond the obvious problem of crime, police should also be concerned with citizen fear of crime and set up monitoring systems (such as citizen surveys) to measure it;
- **Active shaping of community norms**—In collaboration with citizens, police can and should actively shape community norms and standards;
- **Demand for police services**—The public demands that police be more involved in the issues of interest to them, and that these citizen demands can be measured and defined;
- **Initiation not domination**—Although police spearhead and initiate community services and programs that citizens want, police neither dominate nor dictate community standards (although they *do* shape and guide them based upon feedback from the citizenry);
- **Value-neutrality**—Police can act in a value-neutral way, consistent with the professional orientation of the previous (reform and early professionalization) policing era;
- **Organizational change**—The old top-down, command-and-control, quasi-military organizational structure can be transformed into a flatter, more organic, more user-friendly form, including increased use of citizens within the organization (or so-called "civilianization");
- **Higher-quality personnel**—With increased educational requirements and more stringent screening systems, a better class of people can be recruited into policing who are more attentive to community needs and demands;

- **Police as community leaders**—Although a complex and difficult undertaking, the project of community restoration and safety is one that the police are in the best position to fulfill (see also Reed 1999).

For the most part these are assumptions generated from the perspective of law enforcement practitioners themselves, and as such at least some of them may play more of a rhetorical function than reflecting the perspectives of actual citizens. For example, one of the assumptions above is that citizens "demand" community-policing programs and services, but the reality is that many citizens are at best apathetic about these services and at worst don't trust the police or simply want to be left alone (see Buerger 1994; Herbert 2006a).

Themes in Community Policing

Whether merely rhetorical or grounded in the actual operational realities of policing citizens in a community, and acknowledging the great diversity of community-policing programs taking place in particular communities (Skogan 1994), it is nevertheless possible to produce an even more narrowly focused view of the essential elements of community policing. Mastrofski (1998, pp. 162–166) argues that community policing can be distilled down to four fundamental themes: debureaucratization, professionalization, democratization, and service integration. Early in its history municipal policing adopted a quasi-military, bureaucratic model of organization which emphasized political control (especially in the first, political-spoils era), rules, strict adherence to proper communications and a chain of command, centralization (such as command-and-control imperatives emanating from police headquarters), and specialization (especially beginning in the second era of policing). By the 1970s and the emergence of the community-oriented policing era, there was a feeling that the legal and technical requirements of the old bureaucratic model of policing should give way to a more humanistic and *debureaucratized* organizational model. Rather than being distant from citizens and coldly efficient "snappy bureaucrats" (Klockars 1980) specializing in crime control, police are now expected to work side by side with citizens and other stakeholders in the community to solve community problems collectively.

The second theme, *professionalization*, actually began in the second policing era of reform and early professionalization (as summarized above). Yet, professionalization of the third era does not come by way of organizational rules or centralization of command, but by increasing educational requirements for police recruits and training officers in the newest technologists as well as in the vagaries of human behavior. Under this model, police are given even more autonomy to act, since their training is grounded not only in the technical aspects of police work but also in the scientific knowledge base of sociology, psychology, and other pertinent disciplines teaching human or "soft" skills. Indeed, under problem-oriented policing the police are rewarded more for taking initiative to formulate and solve problems in the community rather than the traditionally valued outcomes, namely the "good pinch" (i.e., arrests).

The third theme according to Mastrofski is *democratization*. Community-oriented policing could be described as a sort of democratic policing to the extent that there is an explicit attempt to get citizens more involved in the day-to-day operations of the police department. This appears not only with regard to the emergence of a number of community-policing programs which invite higher levels of citizen participation, but also citizen review boards as a crucial source of external accountability for police departments. Additionally, community policing coincides with the trend of civilianization, namely, the continuing increase in the number of civilians employed in police departments (Crank 1989). These civilian employees are said to act as important bridges or intermediaries between citizens of the community on the one hand and sworn police officers on the other.

A fourth theme of community policing is *service integration*. If police are now taking the approach of solving problems via collaboration with stakeholders in the community, they must do so under the condition that all key community resources should be brought to bear on these problems and that they should be integrated into a seamless whole (this is a concept borrowed from therapeutic practices such as drug-addiction counseling, child services, or clinical social work, namely, helping the client in need with the provision of all-encompassing "wraparound services"; see, e.g., Toffalo 2000). Hence, more than ever before police have developed organizational linkages not only with other city safety forces, but also with schools, social service agencies, housing services (especially in the case of housing authority police), businesses, and colleges and universities in the local area. In addition, police service provision is being made in increasingly intimate settings, as police are now spending more time in people's homes, whether for domestic violence or calls for assistant for family issues such as runaways, delinquency, abandonment, child support and custody cases, or missing persons.[4]

All of these ideal aspects of community policing—debureaucratization, professionalization, democratization, and service integration—are evident in one of the biggest and most ambitious experiments in community-policing implementation, namely, Chicago Alternative Policing Strategy (CAPS). As described by Skogan (2006a, p. 3), who has studied the program extensively, CAPS "features extensive resident involvement, a problem-solving approach toward tackling chronic crime and disorder problems, and coordination between police and a wide range of partner agencies." There are always operational realities impinging on the implementation of community policing, in that under certain conditions some aspects of the program are muted or less apparent than under other conditions. For example, like other large urban areas, Chicago has distinct areas of town that are predominantly White, Black, or Hispanic. Skogan (2006a) found that community-policing implementation and effectiveness varied along sociodemographic characteristics of the community, and race was one of those significant sociodemographic variables. Indeed, Skogan's (2006a) study of community-policing implementation in Chicago is subtitled "A Tale of Three Cities."

The short story is that, although community policing-implementation and involvement of the citizenry went well in White and Black communities, there were significant barriers to CAPS implementation in Latino communities. Why was this? First, Latinos were the youngest of the three groups, and as a rule young people do not participate in community-policing programs. Second, home ownership and length of time at residence was one of the strongest predictors of involvement in community-policing programs. But out of the three groups, Latinos had the lowest level of home ownership, and were more likely to move and hence possessed lower stakes in the program. Third, Spanish-speaking Latinos especially, even more so than their English-speaking counterparts, tended to retreat from involvement with the police because of immigration concerns. What this illustrates is that more needs to be understood about the conditions and factors which reduce or enhance citizen involvement in and commitment to community-oriented policing programs. We will return to this topic shortly.

Beyond Community Policing?

Notice that there has been a shortening of the length of policing eras over time. Political spoils ran a full century (1830s to 1920s). Reform and early professionalization ran about fifty years (1920s to 1960s). The third, community-oriented policing, has had about a forty year run, from the 1970s to the present. And there is talk of the emergence of yet another era of policing, so-called post 9/11 policing (to be discussed in Chapter 5). These collapsing eras may simply be a function of the pressures to remain new and fresh, both from the perspective of police practitioners out in the field as well as scientists observing the police. It may indeed reflect the sort of modernist myopia which Lester F. Ward (1903) referred to long ago as the "illusion of the near." We "modern folk" are fond of talking about how, due to advances in technology as well as other factors, the pace of life is quickening. In policing as well as in many other areas of life, there is the idea that a newfangled "next big thing" is just around the corner, nurtured along by continuous improvement, best practices, and the sheer growth of knowledge. This reflects the idea that innovations and improvements in both technology and everyday life are happening so rapidly that things that used to be considered the "cutting edge" rapidly become obsolete.

There does seem to be some truth to the notion that modern societies continue to place an overweening premium on quickness, speed, and efficiency. Just the other day I plunked down an extra five dollars a month for a quicker DSL connection for my home Internet. In fact, French cultural theorist Paul Virilio made a nice career for himself placing this emphasis on speed and efficiency front and center in his writings. Virilio (1986) refers to his own study of speed as dromology (the science of the journey; see Haggerty 2006). One point Virilio makes in his dromological studies worth briefly noting is that high social status also brings with it the ability to have things literally at your fingertips. Those with money, power, and the right connections can speed up access to goods and services that the average person either could never access or would have to wait in line for for a very long time. And just as is the case for many other things, the wealthy and powerful are looked up to by those further down the status ladder, and they covet those things that they do not have. In effect, the middle and lower classes have a tendency of adopting and striving for the objects, resources, signs, and symbols that characterize the well-to-do.

Savvy entrepreneurs pick up on this, and set up marketing campaigns promising to give speedy access to things persons covet even if they can't afford them. The credit system functions as much as anything to allow mere commoners to keep up with the Joneses, and to maintain the outward appearance of a middle-class lifestyle. Lester Ward (1893) made note of this phenomenon in a general sense, which he called "the principle of deception." Influenced by Ward, a few years later and more famously economist Thorstein Veblen called it "conspicuous consumption." This emphasis on speed and quickness, which operates on both the consumption and production sides with regard to goods and services, is now a generalized phenomenon across society. This means that the police, too, are judged on how well they are keeping up with current trends, and how quickly and efficiently they make available to the public their various goods and services.

Rather than a passing fad (although granted it has been around for some forty years now), Wesley Skogan (2006c) believes community policing is pretty much here to stay. In fact, in many ways the argument made by proponents of community policing is that local governments, city leaders, and police administrators should resist temptations to give in to new fads, because presumably the major elements of community policing (described above) represent the way policing in a modern, industrial, and culturally diverse society ought to be done. This temptation is made even more palpable when tight budgets challenge the delivery of services and programs community-policing departments think they should be providing (Skogan 2006c).

Stephen Mastrofksi (2006) wonders how community policing, as a process or programmatic orientation, should be measured. Perhaps much of what passes for community policing is more rhetoric than reality. If indeed local communities decide for themselves which kinds of services and programs community-oriented policing departments should provide, how do we make sense of this massive diversity? There are ways of indirectly measuring such things as the level of citizen participation in community-policing programs, the extent to which local police departments are moving toward decentralization, and whether or not problem solving by the police, in collaboration with the citizenry, is really going on. Presumably research teams could go to local communities and survey residents about their needs and their view of the effectiveness of police services, as well as conducting on-site observations of the police in action (Mastrofski 2006, p. 49). Of course, the limitation of such approaches is the limitation of the case method in general, in that it is difficult to produce generalized knowledge about community policing from individual cases. Local communities have their own unique histories, needs, and resources, so implementation of community policing in any of these locations will likewise be limited by such realities.

Measuring the Implementation of Community Policing

Yet even in the face of these difficulties, research continues to move forward regarding how to understand and conceptualize what community policing is doing, and to what extent it is being implemented community by community (Roberg 1994). Jeremy Wilson (2006), for example, has undertaken an ambitious effort to develop an empirical model for actually measuring the level of community-policing implementation in American cities. Wilson's (2006) review of the existing literature (e.g., King 1998; Maguire 2003; Maguire and Mastrofski 2000) led him to posit three broad factors that could explain the level of community-policing implementation (as measured in 1999):

- Organizational context, including such factors as size of the police department, the department's task or goal orientation (e.g., legalistic, service, or watchmen-oriented), demographic characteristics of the community being served, levels of funding for COP programs, and region;
- Organizational structure, including two main subvariables: *structural complexity* (e.g., number of stations or precincts, level of specialization within the department) and *structural control* (e.g., degree of centralization, degree of formalization, and administrative weight, or the proportion of total employees within the police organization assigned to administrative and technical support tasks; Wilson 2006, p. 64);
- Level of community-oriented policing (COP) implementation as measured in 1997.

After running appropriate statistical tests, Wilson (2006) found that some of these factors were significant in predicting community-policing implementation, while others were not. For example, with regard to organizational context, neither size of the department nor task scope affected COP implementation. Additionally, police chief turnover negatively affected COP implementation (that is, as police chief turnover increased COP implementation decreased). This seems to indicate that continuity of leadership of the police organization is important in creating a commitment to community policing over the long term.

One community characteristic affected COP implementation, and that was population mobility. Specifically, as population mobility increased COP implementation increased. Presumably high levels of population turnover creates more uncertainty within the police organization, as its planners and leaders may be uncertain about which services or orientations are appropriate for the community. In such a condition of uncertainty, police organizations may be more open to COP implementation. The funding variable was also significant: police departments which receive greater funding for specifically community-oriented programs and orientations are more likely to implement community policing. Region was also significant: police departments located in the western United States were more likely than departments in other regions to move toward COP implementation. Perhaps given the uneven and peculiar history of policing in the West (to be covered next chapter), western police departments are more progressive, innovative, and aligned with the philosophical orientation underlying COP implementation.

What about the organizational structure variables? First of all, structural complexity was insignificant: the number of stations or the degree of task specialization was not related to the level of COP implementation. The findings regarding structural control were mixed. On the one hand, neither centralization nor administrative weight affected the level of COP implementation. However, formalization did influence COP implementation: formal directives regarding COP implementation had a positive effect on actual COP implementation.

Finally, and no big surprise at all, the level of COP implementation in 1997 significantly predicted the level of COP implementation in 1999 as measured in the Law Enforcement Management and Administrative Statistics (LEMAS) survey. However, although statistically significant, the strength of the relationship was weaker than expected. This may have to do with the fact that police departments are not consistent, or that procedures vary from department to department, with regard to identifying community-policing programs, services, and orientations and reporting these in the LEMAS survey.

Informally Embedded Formality

It would seem that the positive relation between formality and the level of community-policing implementation is a somewhat counterintuitive or unexpected finding. Standard professional policing is driven by a top-down bureaucratic model shot through with formalized rules and operating procedures concerning how police are to act and which goals are to be pursued. Indeed, the highly formalized nature of policing of the second era viewed the police as "snappy bureaucrats" who pursued the goal of crime control and who, as highly-trained professionals, did not need "mere" citizens to help carry out their duties. Indeed, under traditional professionalization everyday citizens were barely tolerated, as they were described as "know-nothings" according to Van Maanen's (1978) famous typology. The third era of community policing was supposed to cut into this heavy formality, by the creation of flatter organizational hierarchies and the sincere effort to incorporate citizens of the police district into police planning, organization, and provision of services. This seemed to indicate that informality would be favored over stiff or mechanical formality, and therefore the number of rules in place guiding police activities would be minimized in favor of the human element and a more organic organizational structure, which would thereby also be open to negotiation, dynamism, and flux as conditions on the ground dictated.

But finding both higher formality *and* higher levels of community-policing implementation—as Wilson's (2006) research indicates—can be explained if we take into consideration the work of Arthur Stinchcombe (2001), who wrote a book on when and how formality works. Stinchcombe is correct to note that, traditionally, formality has been viewed negatively because of the perception that it somehow distorts and unduly restricts the agency and creativity of real flesh-and-blood human beings. The idea is that if an extra set of guidelines has to be developed to steer certain types of activity—as in the case of the myriad laws, ordinances, policy initiatives, and governmental regulations characteristic of modern living—then this is an *ipso facto* admission that the mere informal norms and rules of everyday life have somehow broken down and are no longer effective in generating social order or the "good life" more generally. From this perspective, the formalizations of law or bureaucratic regulation are seen at best as "necessary evils" but, if left unchecked, can eventually lead to an "iron cage" of stultifying routine and harsh rules which are enforced as ends in themselves (Weber 1978).

Although an important starting point, the Weberian tradition of bureaucracy, rationalization, and formalization has typically not been concerned with a fine-grained analysis of what these terms actually mean beyond common-sense understandings, or what the analytical connections are between formality and informality. Formalization is an abstraction which dictates a set of rules or procedures for carrying out some type of work in some human social setting. But all formalizations have some unstated or tacit elements which allow human beings who are carrying out the directives to use their professional judgment—otherwise known as discretion—to complete the task at hand. For example, Stinchcombe notes that the highly formalized procedures embodied in the blueprints for constructing a building leave certain bits of information out. Blueprints tend to be very precise about planning and construction, and graphical representations are provided concerning configuration of space and materials to be used. The size and location of the foundation, the load points, the nature of the subsoil upon which the building is to be erected, and the amount and type of concrete needed by building contractors are some of the many points formally designated and enumerated within blueprints. But much of the smaller details are left to the craft workers—plumbers, carpenters, stone masons, etc.—and these are not part of the blueprint. Stinchcombe (2001, p. 59) describes the types of informality that creep into the discretionary work of construction craftpersons as follows:

> The actual floor [as constructed] may be easily an eighth of an inch off; a plumbing connection between a toilet and a waste line that is an eighth of an inch off can put a lot of sewage on the floor. Neither the exact location of the plumbing in the walls nor the exact location of the fixtures is described in the blueprints, and both are designed with ad-

justable connectors…so that they can be adapted to the building as built.

Likewise, drawing on the work of Llewellyn (2008), Stinchcombe notes that although the great majority of appellate decisions are based upon the technical aspects of law embedded in the procedures taking place in the lower court as well as general principles of precedent—indicating of course that judges maintain a high level of fidelity with the formalizations of law—about 9% of cases are decided on the basis of *obiter dicta* or "other reasons." This means that in about 10% of the cases, rather than relying on the formalizations of legal procedures and precedents, judges go "off the books" and use their professional discretion to decide these cases based upon hunch, instinct, a sense of fairness or social justice, mitigating circumstances, their training, or a whole host of additional possibilities. This is a condition Stinchcombe (2001) refers to as "informally embedded formality."

Returning to the case of Wilson's finding of the correlation between formality and the implementation of community policing, if we take the concept of informally embedded formality seriously, then what we see is that the rather abstract and elusive configuration of activities described as "community policing" are made better sense of by real flesh-and-blood human beings when a set of guidelines—a "connect-the-dots" for community policing if you will—are put into place, and clear paths are illuminated with regard to "how to do" community policing and recognizing it as such. Where such guidelines are lacking, all that is left for police practitioners to do is to rely on their standard understandings of traditional policing—which is done according to the formal dictates developed for such policing—while any attempts at community policing likely "slip through the cracks" because they are not anchored effectively within the abstractions of the formalities necessary to pull off this type of work.

CONCLUSION

In considering the work of Wilson (2006), it is clear that the project of identifying community-policing components and measuring to what extent they are being implemented in communities is an exceedingly complex undertaking. As thorough as Wilson's model is, it explains only about 28% of the variance in the relationship between the various variables he considered (organizational context, organizational structure, and level of prior COP implementation) and the outcome to be explained, namely later implementation of community policing. This is not the fault of Wilson, for there are a host of other variables which were not measured or which could not be brought into the model, and these missing or unmeasurable variables surely play a large part in reducing the robustness of the model's explanation. As is the case for research in most other areas of sociology and criminology, the issue of community-oriented policing and the factors

associated with its level of implementation will require further analytical refinement and research out in the field.

NOTES

[1] This section and later sections discussing the three eras of policing draw in part
from Chriss (2007b, pp. 96–98).

[2] There are several anomalies not adequately addressed in the Kelling and
Moore (1988) three-era model of the history of American policing. First, there
were slave patrols in the American south, stretching as far back as the 1740s,
which took place well before the alleged first era of municipal policing beginning in the 1840s. These police forces acted to maintain the racial and social
status quo of the southern slave system (see Hadden 2001; Williams and Murphy 2006). The second anomaly is the uneven development of municipal policing that took place west of the Mississippi, in what is known as the western frontier, beginning in 1857 in San Francisco, presumably the first western police
department, as defined by the date of adoption of police uniforms (Monkkonen
1981). Although the story of policing in the Wild West is just now beginning to
be told, there are several scholarly studies (see, e.g., Dykstra 1968; Gard 1949;
Prassel 1972) of the more individualistic lawman versus gunslinger model which
has, of course, been so widely depicted in movies and other popular accounts.
Chapter 3 is devoted to studying the transition from the solitary lawman to the
establishment of police departments across the western frontier. Nevertheless,
even given these caveats and blind spots, as far as the three eras of policing are
concerned, the Kelling and Moore (1988) typology is a useful approximation of
how policing emerged over these periods.

[3] For the history of the call box in particular and early police patrols in general, I
draw upon Thale (2004). Another source of information on this topic was
gleaned from Kelsey and Associates, an organization dedicated to the architectural history of Washington, DC. Part of this project involves a careful docu-
mentation of the history of fire and police call boxes in DC. This information
can be found at http://www.washingtonhistory.com/Projects/CallBox/index.
html.

[4] Interestingly enough, the recent case of Anthony Sowell in Cleveland has
brought the issue of police response to missing persons into the critical spotlight.
Upwards of eleven bodies were discovered in and around Sowell's house, all
African-American women living in poverty and who were either drug addicts or
prostitutes. Some had gone missing for months or years, and although missing
persons cases had been filed on most of them, police investigations came to a
dead end. The implication here is that Cleveland police did not take these missing cases seriously because of the race of the missing persons. Hence, we also

have another example of the ease with which criminal justice officials in general, and the police in particular, can be accused of biased or even racist actions.

3

Policing in the Wild West

As was discussed last chapter, the story of the development of policing in America through three eras—political spoils, reform and early professionalization, and community policing—is somewhat inadequate because of how historians, sociologists, and criminologists have tended narrowly to focus on the northeastern and southern Atlantic United States as the model for the development of American policing in general. This focus on the American northeast and south is understandable, as the original thirteen American colonies were located in this geographical region.[1] Because of the historical pattern of settlement of the United States, the frontier was always located to the west, and because of this later developments occurring west of the Mississippi River were often overlooked.

This continuing westward movement of the frontier is illustrated in the case of Virginia, America's first colony (founded in 1607). Before 1730 very few settlers lived west of the Rivanna River, located in eastern Virginia. For all intents and purposes, those parts of Virginia lying to the west of the Rivanna were considered by Virginians to be wild, unsettled, and inhospitable to civilized society (Turner 1996 [1920], pp. 92–95). These westward points became acceptable, in fact, only after Thomas Jefferson made his mark on American politics. He was born in 1743 in Monticello, a former frontier town which was not highly thought of at the time of his birth.

The history of the settlement of America is a huge and expansive topic, far too vast to be handled adequately in a book about policing. As Otterstrom and Earle (2002) argue, the United States has gone through three distinct periods of settlement: (1) settlement of Eastern regions between 1790 and 1840; (2) settlement of Western regions from 1840 to 1910; and (3) more general settlement patterns between 1910 and 1990. Because I am interested in filling in the gaps on the missing story of the development of policing in the Wild West, I obviously will be concentrating on the second period running from 1840 to 1910. This discussion brings together three interrelated literatures: the history of policing, the history and development of the American western frontier, and more general literature on the settlement of cities and towns.

When President Thomas Jefferson acquired the Louisiana Purchase from France in 1803, the United States doubled its size literally overnight. The Louisiana Purchase encompassed more than 800,000 square miles extending from the Mississippi River to the Rocky Mountains (Nobles 1993). From the perspective of American state building, such a vast expanse of land reflected the immediate concern with land management, hence, from 1840 onwards the American military was deployed throughout the West to provide safe passage to settlers as well as deal with the so-called "Indian problem."[2] In 1849 the Department of the Interior was established ostensibly to oversee the orderly expansion and settlement of the western frontier, which also meant using the American military—primarily the Army—to enforce treaties with Native Americans and to deal more forcibly with those tribes which were resistant to being relocated from their native lands.[3]

The Indian wars were a conflict between two people—White settlers and Native Americans—whose values were wholly incompatible. Some Indians were sedentary and claimed lands, but most were nomadic and roamed freely, searching for food and shelter wherever they could be found. As Russell (1963, p. 195) has argued, "The Indians inhabited this country, but they did not occupy it. They wandered over it." Americans did indeed take lands from the Indians, but the Indians also had a bloody history of battles and conquests among warring tribes.

Nevertheless, the treatment of Native Americans by the United States in order to achieve her "manifest destiny" of continuous Euro-American expansion and settlement was oftentimes horrendous. Even though early on American government policy was officially one of paternalism and support toward Native American tribes—especially as established in the seemingly amicable fur trade decades earlier (see Morgan 1963)—in reality over time Native Americans increasingly were viewed as a roadblock toward progress. Especially after the Civil War, as Native American resistance became even more intense, state-sanctioned violence against them escalated accordingly (Ball 2001, p. 206). The continuing heavy presence of Army regulars on the western frontier through this period also effectively suppressed the establishment of cities and towns along with the social services typically associated with them (such as fire and police departments), and this at least partially accounts for the ad hoc and zigzag pattern of development of policing in the West.

Although there have been a very large number of important and influential studies of cities written in the fields of sociology, history, anthropology, political science, and economics (see, e.g., Mumford 1961; Schwab 1992; Sennett 1990), for the most part these writings are not directly relevant to the particular case of the western frontier and how cities west of the Mississippi developed from 1840 onwards. Much of the research in urban sociology, for example, has focused on the early history and development of such urban metropolises as New York City, Boston, and Philadelphia. Likewise, one can find a number of useful studies of the development of police departments in these and other northeastern cities. This discussion of policing in the Wild West aims at least partially to fill this lacuna.

As mentioned above, in America the frontier tended to move westward over time, and as cities started being established west of the Atlantic coast from the 1750s onward, the frontier moved and was identified and understood in relation to these newer settlements. For example, writers from the east who ventured west were apt to refer to Pittsburgh (writing in 1828) and Cincinnati (writing in 1827) as the first "urban" frontier towns (McKelvey 1969, pp. 138–148). Shortly thereafter, attention turned to such cities as St. Louis, Indianapolis, and Chicago. By the 1840s St. Louis was the premier "western" city, whose population grew from 16,000 in 1840 to over 310,000 by 1870. Although Chicago lagged behind St. Louis in both prestige and population during this period, by the turn of the century Chicago had become the new premier Midwestern city, having attained a population of close to two million by that time (Monkkonen 1988, pp. 44–45). Because of its extreme population growth among other factors, Chicago became the most studied city alongside those of the metropolitan northeast.

As important as Chicago was and still is today in terms of the analysis of population growth, class structure, ethnic diversity, migration patterns, municipal governance, and the historical nature of its criminal justice system—for example, the first juvenile court was established in Chicago in 1899—Chicago will not be a major focus here for the simple fact that it lies east of the Mississippi River. Because the western United States is vast, attempting succinctly to explain the rise of cities and police departments within this region from the 1840s onward is a daunting task. What is needed is a general theory which can explain the rise of towns and the development of police departments within them, and which can capture the empirical details among this great diversity. In this book I will be utilizing the grand theory of Talcott Parsons, and I will spend some time describing the major concepts of the theory. Once the theoretical framework is established, we will then be in a position to explain why and under what conditions police departments developed west of the Mississippi. Yet, police departments come into existence only after settlements appear, and the western frontier was settled in a pattern not altogether consistent with patterns of settlement characteristic of the eastern United States. Hence, there is an interconnected set of issues that must be addressed in this chapter: the concept of the frontier in general; the historical particulars attending to the settlement of the western frontier; the problem of social order in these western settlements; the rise of cities across the west, even amid chaos, disorder, and violence especially during the period 1865 through 1880; and the emergence of police departments in these western cities.

THE CONCEPT OF THE FRONTIER

The first thing to establish is the general concept of the frontier, as well as the specifics of the western frontier from 1840 through the early 1900s. The earliest and most influential study of the American western frontier was written by Frederick Jackson Turner in 1920. Even today, nearly ninety years later, anyone dealing with the frontier must at least come to grips with how Turner conceptualized it. I would suggest that for the most part, the "Turner thesis" is still valuable, although later writings have modified some aspects of the thesis and have introduced more nuance into its conceptualization.

Following Turner, the simplest statement about the frontier is that it is the "meeting point between savagery and civilization" (Turner 1996 [1920], p. 3). With the continuing westward movement of settlements, those leading the charge westward—pioneers and frontiersmen—became successively more American and less European than those who originally settled on the Atlantic coast.[4] For Turner, then, the movement into the western frontier made America what it is today, more so even than the founding of America as it gained its independence from the British much earlier. When men and women first confront the frontier, the frontier environment is at first too strong for them. In other words, they must accommodate themselves to the stark physical and geographical realities of this unknown, wilderness area. Most of the men and women venturing out to the western frontier did so voluntarily, seeking opportunities and willing to take risks in an environment that offered no sure bets.

Even given this hearty pioneer spirit of striking out to make a better life in a condition of high uncertainty, the United States government occasionally provided incentives for persons to venture forth to the western frontier. The single most important inducement spurring settlement and population growth in the West was the Homestead Act, signed into law by President Abraham Lincoln in 1862.[5] For a relatively small filing fee, those who could prove American citizenship were given 160 acres of land with the expectation that they would farm it or engage in some other money-making activity (Richardson 2007, p. 25). (This was also seen by Lincoln as an expedient way of raising money for the war effort.) Areas that were sparsely populated up to that point, specifically the Dakotas, Minnesota, Nebraska, and Kansas, enjoyed rapid increases in population as a result of the act. For example, Nebraska's population was 29,000 in 1860, but then jumped to 123,000 in 1870 and 452,000 by 1880.

The Homestead Act worked in combination with several other factors to promote growth in population west of the Mississippi. Considering the case of Nebraska again, a key factor was the construction of railways through the state, such as the Union Pacific, Central Pacific, and Burlington. This allowed more widespread settlement of Nebraska away from the original settlements concentrated around the Missouri River in the easternmost part of the state. There were also push or expelling factors, both from the eastern United States as well as from Europe, which sent persons in search of opportunities on the frontier. By the middle of the nineteenth century, some cities in the northeast—Boston, New

York City, and Philadelphia to name a few—were already experiencing problems of industrialization, crowding, and urban unrest from which at least some residents of these cities were hoping to escape (Olson 1966, pp. 154–165). The third factor contributing to the stability of settlements was the increased presence of the U.S. military across the western frontier ostensibly to control, subdue, and contain the remaining Native American population.

The western frontier was the setting for the convergence of growing numbers of persons across space and time, from diverse background and walks of life, for purposes of starting new lives and new human settlements. The settling of the frontier follows an importation model, in that those seeking to settle the frontier always arrived from somewhere else that was likely already settled. In others words, these settlers and pioneers had already lived in and been exposed to modern service cities—whether originating from the eastern United States or overseas—and they carried in their heads ideals about how life should be organized. In the sparsely populated and relatively open horizons of the frontier, even though persons had a notion of propriety and social order, there was only so much new arrivals could do to make these ideas a reality. This is because human society requires the cooperation of others to build the social structures that could support a city way of life.

Daniel Elazar (1996) conceptualizes the frontier as a chain reaction, linking persons newly arriving to the frontier to those formations and human collectivities existing before and outside of it. In other words, collective settlement of land by human beings by necessity has a beginning, and concentration of persons in that beginning area mark everything outside of it as foreign or untamed. There is typically a direction to the exploration of the uncharted, since most human settlements are constrained on one side or the other by natural features, typically mountains, rivers, and/or different soils. Natural geography, at least initially, also dictates the modes and styles of transportation available to human settlement, and cities tend to be established along these transportation routes (Cooley 1930). But whole areas are not settled all in one fell swoop. Parts are settled, leaving some other parts to be defined as the frontier. But later, typically more explorations into remaining frontier areas are initiated, and the nature of the previous era of settlement influences how the next phase of understanding and dealing with the frontier will be done. Elazar (1996) provides a list of key characteristics of the frontier, including:

- The exploration of that which was previously unknown, wild, or undeveloped;
- New organization of the uses of space and available resources;
- A growth economy based on application of existing and developing technologies;
- Within a particular geographical area labeled the frontier, there are always unique frontier projects within the whole with their own logics, goals, interests, and resources (hence, frontier experiences were

different and occurred at different times in the Southwest, the Midwest, the upper Midwest, the Rockies, and the Far West);

- The frontier brings together elements of opportunity and growth as well as risk, danger, and uncertainty;
- There must be reasonably free access to the frontier for maximal development; hence the western frontier attracted Americans from the east, recently freed slaves from the south, and foreigners seeking a new life;
- Persons seeking to make a new life in the frontier are endowed with a special "frontier spirit," including elements of freedom, courage, and equality.

These and other factors should be kept in mind as we trace, however briefly, the history of the American western frontier and the eventual settlement of cities and towns within and across it. After this is established, we can then explore the factors within these settlements that set the stage for the development of modern policing.

LEWIS AND CLARK, AND BEYOND

In 1804 the Lewis and Clark expedition entered the Missouri River to begin explorations. Meriwether Lewis, William Clark, and other members of the expedition first encountered Indians, and promptly engaged in trade with those who were willing or able (Morgan 1963). The explorers founded Fort Mandan, named after an Indian tribe roaming the area. Moving to the west, toward the Rockies and beyond, the exploration team ran into fur traders. Soon more trading posts were established, even as far east as St. Louis. With these establishments the marketplace for furs expanded, and not only independent businessmen were setting up trading posts, but the U.S. Army added to the mix with the establishment of military forts throughout the West beginning in the 1840s. Most of the earliest forts were built along rivers and major tributaries, and these locations are also where a number of cities began appearing as well, but only after the earlier appearance of military forts to provide safe passage to traders and settlers, as well as to suppress Indian hostility.

As early as 1817 St. Louis had been visited by an early steamboat, the *Pike*. These were used in the fur trade along tributaries of the Mississippi. St. Louis was the center of western steamboating during the rush of settlers to Oregon and miners to California. Just up the river, trips were made to Franklin, Missouri, the place for loading wagons moving westward on the Santa Fe Trail. The Santa Fe Trail was first opened in 1821, running from St. Louis to Santa Fe, New Mexico.

Wagons also got their start in St. Louis, and by 1843 long wagons trains were being organized for the long haul west (Winther 1963, p. 108). River crossings were treacherous, and these difficulties eventually led to the large-scale construction of bridges. Heavy migration to Oregon during the 1840s

opened the Oregon Trail. Combined with the heavy migration to California beginning with the 1848 gold rush, entrepreneurs, seeing a demand, established
overland coach services. This was the birth of the stagecoach business. This was
also used by the government to move the mail, such as Butterfield's Overland
Mail Coach starting from Atchison, Kansas in the 1850s (Winther 1963, p. 121).
The demand for speed intensified, however, and a single rider on horseback
could move the mail quicker, thus giving rise to the Pony Express in 1860, the
route running from St. Joseph, Missouri to Sacramento, California (the San
Francisco to Sacramento leg was often by boat, however). But exhaustion, both
on the part of horses and riders, attacks by Indians, and bad weather hampered
operations. As famous as the Pony Express was, it lasted only one year because
of these problems.

GROWING POPULATIONS, ARMY INTERVENTION, AND
TERRITORIAL POLICING

U.S. military policy in the Trans-Mississippi West passed through three phases.
Phase one (1804–1845) was concerned with maintaining a line of posts in advance of settlements west of the Mississippi (Frazer 1965). As mentioned previously, this meant not only protection from Indians, but also protecting Indians
from depredations from settlers and con artists, the latter of whom often targeted
Native American tribes which were receiving cash reparations as part of reloca-
tion treaties.

    The second phase (1845 into the 1880s), which followed immediately
upon the annexation of Texas, saw the early establishment of Forts Brown and
Polk ostensibly to deal with continuing hostilities with Mexico. Forts were also
established along most of the overland routes to the west from Texas and the
Great Plains. Between 1868 and 1880 the number of military posts expanded
greatly. The reasons included the Indian Wars, but also securing resources such
as agricultural operations, gold and silver mining, the cattle industry, and providing safe passage for settlers (although heavy military presence also at times
hindered local city development, as too much meddling by the federal government often prompted citizen protests). As transportation routes and technologies
proliferated as well—first by river, by horse and coach on land, and then by the
building of railroads that connected settlements in the South and Midwest to
points further west—the military along with government surveyors continued to
explore new routes of travel (Atwood 2008).

    In 1864 President Abraham Lincoln signed acts for the building of a
rail line to the Pacific. The railroad would be built from Omaha, Nebraska on the
eastern end to Sacramento on the western end. Railroad companies—some privately owned, some federally chartered—included the Central Pacific, Union
Pacific, Northern Pacific, and Pacific. By the end of the Civil War many miles
of railroad track had been laid down. For example, in order to overcome its relative isolation, Minnesota built 122 miles of track within its borders by the end of

the Civil War (Winther 1963, p. 127). Other rails that linked the Great Plains states to points further west, especially Kansas and Nebraska, were the Kansas Pacific; the Atchison, Topeka, and Santa Fe; the Southern Pacific; the Texas Pacific; and the Illinois Central (Winther 1963, p. 128). The Union and Pacific railroads eventually met in Promontory, Utah in 1869.

The third phase resulted from the growth and ultimate stabilization of the reservation system for remaining American Indians. This occurred at different times at different places across the West, but most happened during and after the 1890s. By 1912, with the entry of New Mexico and Arizona into the union, this last phase of military operations, and hence the closing of the frontier, was considered complete (Frazer 1965).

As we see, then, the nature of the frontier shifted over time with increasing pressures to expand the areas of White settlement, often at the expense of the indigenous Indian or Native American population. This became especially acute between 1865 and 1880, when the chief operational goal of the U.S. Army was to subdue Indians in the American West (Nacy 2000, p. 4). Military forts were set up in key locations across the West as a visible reminder to the Indians that they were being watched, and that ready military responses were available if needed. During this time the West became particularly chaotic (after the end of the Civil War) because there were fears that southerners along with surviving members of the defeated Confederate Army would be able to spill into the frontier and seize control of it. There was already talk of secession among Southern states, and Texas as well as the Great Plains states—Kansas, Nebraska, and up to Minnesota, but also Missouri—became battlegrounds of a sort during this chaotic transition. Towns that either were established, or attempting to become established, were also thrown into disarray, and cities could not hope to establish charters that would allow their own development independent of the military forces and presence necessitated by (1) the Indian problem, and (2) secessionist concerns at the end of the Civil War. Ball (2001, p. 207) states that:

> The resistance of indigenous peoples to United States sovereignty presented only half of the frontier threat to the nation's internal security. Euroamerican social unrest and political riot also challenged the rule of law on the western frontier and triggered the intervention of regulars to aid federal and county law enforcement officers. The scale of such operations ranged from expelling a single family trespassing on an Indian reservation to quelling organized mass resistance such as that practiced by free-soilers in Kansas, Mormons in Utah, and Hispanos in Texas.

Later, the Sioux tribe went on the warpath beginning in Minnesota in 1862 as a reaction to continuing buffeting and oversight by the U.S. Army as the Civil War was coming to an end. What precipitated this explosion of violence in Minnesota and elsewhere during this time? For a long time several Sioux Nation tribes had inhabited and roamed over the areas of northwestern Iowa, western Wisconsin, southwestern Minnesota, and what was known at the time as the

Dakota Territory. Flora and fauna were readily available, as were herds of buffalo. These features also attracted White settlers, and it was only a matter of time before violence would erupt according to the U.S. manifest destiny of the opening of the frontier. These lands also, at least initially, were never considered to be opened to White settlement. Since the 1820s the assumption was made that this region stretching down through the Great Plains was inhospitable to settlement, and for awhile anyway Indians were given free reign. All this changed as White settlers pushed into these regions. By 1858, a series of treaties had pressed the Sioux Nation Indians into a small strip of land along the bank of the Minnesota River (Jones 1961). The Sioux uprisings threatened small settlements and towns at the mouth of the Yellow Medicine River near Ft. Ridgley, which had been established in 1853, and which was abandoned in 1867 (Frazer 1965).

After Lincoln was inaugurated, Union forces withdrew from the north and west to prepare for the Civil War, and in their place, many local militia and state law enforcement agencies—for example, the Texas Rangers in Texas—as well as local volunteers assembled to help out on the frontier (like the Fifth Minnesota Volunteer Infantry in 1862). During all these military perturbations, there was simply not much time for social services to develop within western frontier towns. The conditions of stability were absent. Domination by federal and territorial military exigencies retarded the development of towns, and hence police forces, in these areas. But the Sioux uprising grew worse, and more military units had to be redeployed, and abandoned forts were repopulated. This great Sioux War lasted until 1877, exacerbated by General George Custer moving troops into the Black Hills after gold was discovered, and suffering mass casualties in what has become known as Custer's Last Stand. The Sioux considered this area their sacred ancestral homeland (Richardson 2007, p. 160).

Much of the action on the western frontier during this time was concentrated in the Great Plains, a vast area extending from what is now Austin, Texas to the south, and northward through Oklahoma, Kansas, Nebraska, South Dakota, North Dakota, and most of Saskatchewan, Canada. The area also encompasses parts of Colorado, Wyoming, and Montana running along the eastern edge of the Rocky Mountains. When I refer to the Great Plains, I will generally be referring to Kansas, Nebraska, and the Dakotas. Texas had had a history of violence as a former territory of Mexico and the conflicts that continued from the 1830s onward with White settlement. Indeed, there was a triadic structure of conflict between Mexicans, Anglo settlers, and Indians. Nevertheless White settlement in Texas was a rousing success: "In 1870 Anglos accounted for more than 550,000 of the state's 818,000 people" (Graybill 2007, p. 11).

Because of this history of struggle and violence, the Texas territory established early on a mounted constabulary police force, the Texas Rangers, founded in 1835. They acted basically as "citizen soldiers" until their formal institutionalization in 1874. They gained expertise in fighting Mexicans and Indians, and acting as bounty hunters, they roamed sometimes even outside of the territory to round up lawbreakers. The Texas militia, by contrast, was limited to dealing with civil unrest.

However, the Rangers also played a large part in shepherding along the development of the Texas cattle and ranching industry, especially after 1865. By that time feral longhorn cattle had grown in prodigious numbers and were roaming the south Texas countryside. There were new northern and eastern markets for beef with the outbreak of the Civil War, and the longhorns filled the bill nicely. They were a hearty stock, with short gestation periods so that birth rates were high, and immunity to many of the tick-bearing diseases that afflicted so many other cattle breeds. But because of this immunity, longhorns were eventually banned along the Chisholm Trail whose endpoint was Wichita, Kansas, because they were causing death and sickness to other cattle breeds which were not immune to these ticks.

FRONTIER TOWNS, INSTABILITY, AND LAWLESSNESS

Across the frontier, the highwayman, the horse thief, and the cattle rustler were all characters that were internal threats to settlers, in addition to dealing with Indians, and the unknowns of open plains and prairies. Most who moved into the frontier had noble ambitions, namely, to get a piece of land of their own, to settle and build, to farm or ranch, to drive cattle, to invent, or to work in whatever occupation they were capable. But wherever humans beings gather together to forge collective activities, there will also be those who are out for no good, who want to profit off the hard work of others without having to do their own, or take what is not rightfully theirs simply because there is no one there to tell them otherwise. In the frontier, oftentimes might makes right. Many years ago Herbert Spencer (1872 [1850], p. 450) aptly described this state of affairs:

> ...we have the fact that men, partially adapted to the social state, retrograde on being placed in circumstances which call forth the old propensities. ...The back settlers of America, amongst whom unavenged murders, rifle duels, and Lynch law prevail—or, better still, the trappers, who leading a savage life have descended to savage habits, to scalping, and occasionally even to cannibalism—sufficiently exemplify it.

This meant that with lawlessness, or the perception of the inadequacy of law personnel—typically the lone sheriff or marshal who would call on a posse of men if he needed them—men and women on the frontier took the law into their own hands. They were often armed, and ready to fight if challenged. Among all social types occupying the frontier, the one most vilified was the horse thief, and the noose was reserved for such persons of ill repute (Gard 1963). The horse was oftentimes the only form of personal transportation for the frontiersman, and especially the cowboy (Denhardt 1947). The cost was $50 and up for a good steed, which at that time was quite a bit of money. They had to pay more if the horse was already broken (or tamed). Breaking a wild horse was dangerous and time consuming. Acquiring and maintaining the equipment necessary to ride a horse—saddles, bits, snaffles, headstalls, reins, quirts, blankets, and for cowboys, all the additional equipment necessary for riding—spurs, chaps, boots, hats, scarves, and bandanas, as well as guns, bullets, and holsters—was cumbersome and costly (Adams 1963).

There was something of a "gentleman's agreement" regarding leaving an unattended horse alone. If a cowboy went into town to take a break from the trail, whether to go drinking at the saloon or to visit lady friends at the brothel, or to purchase something at the local store, he would tie his trusty steed loosely to whipping posts positioned just off the streets in front of these establishments. It would be very easy for anyone with a mind to do so to steal a horse. The reason more people did not engage in horse theft was that the price was high if caught, typically death. From 1840 through the 1890s, across the western frontier lynch law was in effect, an informal code of justice which allowed the victim to act as judge, jury, and executioner if that person caught up with someone who stole his or her horse. Lawmen either were absent or would be complicitous in the hanging if the facts as alleged by the victim seemed plausible, and especially so if there were witnesses to the theft and identification of the suspect was verified. The horse thief was the lowest of the low, and a "necktie party" was often his or her fate. Indeed, the horse was the central focus of an unstable social system, and many unattached males were brought together for various purposes across the frontier. Within this random scattering of humanity, there was not much way of determining who was "good" and who was "bad." Hence, the assumption was that persons were "bad" unless they were known to be "good" through personal acquaintance or unassailable reputation.

Vigilance committees were also formed around the broad sentiment that law enforcement was inadequate and did little to deter crime (McGrath 1984). These vigilance groups originated in California—San Francisco specifically—as a result of the lawlessness and crime which arose after the discovery of gold in 1848.[6] Vigilantes took the law into their own hands to control and punish those who were accused of jumping stakes. Even if a lawman had captured one of the thieves, the vigilance group might very well storm the jail, overpower the guards, and hang the criminals themselves, representing yet another version of the so-called necktie party. This was lynch law.

Another type of lawlessness was the frontier feud. These were especially likely to break out in sparely populated areas where law was either absent or sporadically enforced. In essence, feuds between groups were simply a version of self-help (informal control). One of the bloodiest took place in Arizona's Pleasant Valley between the Graham and Tewksbury families. The feuding began in 1884. These families had built cabins about ten miles apart. Children of both families were working at the Stinson ranch, and both sides accused the other of stealing cattle from the ranch. In 1886 a Stinson ranch foreman accused Ed Tewksbury of stealing a horse, and Ed shot him. Later more feuds erupted between sheepmen on one side and cattlemen on the other—a common type of range war—and more shooting and violence occurred. Tewksbury killed Billy

Graham, and fled to a fortified house in the mountains (Gard 1963, p. 288). By 1888, as the feud continued, at least eight more persons were either shot or hanged.

Yet another type of feud was the so-called fence cutters' war. The cattle drives that started in Texas—the Chisholm trail, for example, started in San Antonio, extended northward through the Indian territory (latter day Oklahoma), and terminated in Wichita, Kansas—were along trails that were always considered to be free land or open range. What cowboys wanted was enough open space to drive their cattle through. This activity expanded greatly after the Civil War. But by the 1870s barbed wire began appearing, and many of the areas of open range were being fenced in by settlers and ranchers. (Barbed wire was patented first in De Kalb, Illinois in 1874, and by this time much of the West was being fenced, further damaging the ability of cowboys to drive cattle.) Did capitalism kill the cowboy? Large landowners now were able to place local lawmen in their back pocket, and the lawmen did what they could to disrupt cattle drives that came through the area. This included scattering the herd through spooking them, a technique picked up from the Oglala Indians in Nebraska (the cattle town Ogallala, Nebraska was named after this tribe). Many cowboys did not take the situation lying down, and engaged in fence cutting and other forms of vandalism. By the late 1880s the cowboy era of the open range had come to an end, and the era of the rancher began. Barbed wire changed the West dramatically, and had a stabilizing effect on the entire social system, in terms of making life more sedentary and controlled, as rowdy elements—cowboys and other unattached males—were slowly reduced as the work became economically unfeasible (McCallum and McCallum 1965).

THE CODE OF THE WEST

On the frontier, tenacity, masculinity, and rugged individualism were all favored personality traits. For example, a man challenged to a duel would likely accept the challenge simply to save face, even if it meant sure death going up against someone quicker to the draw. Those who refused duels typically slinked away from town on their own, their shame too much to bear.

This ethic of rugged individualism, combined with the perception of the ineffectiveness of local law enforcement, meant that if the sheriff or constable did effect an arrest and bring up an alleged outlaw or cattle rustler on charges, there was a chance that members of the community, acting as a jury or in a more informal capacity, would not even deliver an indictment against the perpetrator. One of the most notorious western peace officers was James Butler "Wild Bill" Hickok, whose reputation as a marksman sometimes prodded foolish men into testing his mettle. Hickok is a prime example of the distortions and the outright mythologies which can arise around men whose pioneering spirit and commitment to frontier life made them larger than life. Born in Illinois in 1837, Wild Bill Hickok was rumored to have killed upwards of seventeen men during his lifetime, but the reality is closer to five men killed, most in self-defense, and at least two while serving as a peace officer in cow towns like Abilene, Kansas during the early 1870s. Hickok was a man big of stature and an imposing presence wherever he traveled, as most of the time he sported twin handguns and carried a large hunting knife prominently displayed on his belt (as seen in Figure 3.1). Hickok once quipped that "It's me for the West. I would be lost back in the States" (Rosa 1996, p. 12). It is fitting that this sometimes outlaw, sometimes lawman, sometimes Army scout, sometimes government detective, and most of the time heavy gambler and drinker, would be killed in a Dakota Territory saloon over a gambling debt in 1876. This points to the fluidity of the role of the marshal or sheriff, in that there was not a clean dividing line between the just and the unjust, between the outlaw and the lawman. Many who became lawmen on the western frontier were at one point considered outlaws or vice versa (such as was also the case of Wyatt Earp; see Gard 1949).

At least up through the 1880s, there was in operation what John Hallwas (2008, pp. 30–31) describes as the "code of the west."[7] The code of the west was an informal system of justice that prescribed violence in response to perceived or real slight or offense. Indeed, this willingness to perpetrate violence was a badge of honor in defense of manliness. As Hallwas (2008, p. 31) goes on to explain:

> But beneath that obsession with honor was insecurity—as men strove for acceptance and stature in a new and turbulent social environment where masculine identity was always at issue.

Yet along with these traits, there was also optimism. This was the optimism of the Gilded Age, which suggested that through hard work and a hearty pioneer spirit, one could overcome the obstacles of an unsettled territory and the unknown of Indians and even fellow travelers. This was the optimistic doctrine of inevitable social progress, and it fit well with social Darwinism. Indeed, the typical frontier town in the West was an extraordinary illustration of this idea. As Haywood (1991, p. 34) explains,

> In a matter of a few years, sometimes months, a collection of temporary buildings and a disorganized population with the simplest of social, political, and economic structures progressed to a town flourishing with trade, expanding in population, and supporting a complexity of institutions, government, churches, schools, courts, laws, transportation systems, boards of trade, utilities, and social services.

Although the development of settled towns and social services (especially police departments) lagged behind the model of eastern development, since the eastern model was already in place, many pioneers who ventured onto the frontier had ideas about what to do once they got there. This is the importation model mention earlier. Battling the natural elements as well as the indigenous population

Figure 3.1. James "Wild Bill" Hickok (circa 1869)

and fellow travelers meant that the rough spots had to be worked through and allowed to play out before "civilization" could take hold and flourish. It was a question of rooting out the "bad" elements of towns, and one of the biggest sources of disturbance was the single, unattached, typically male cowboy. Kansas cattle towns were a microcosm of this broader attempt to civilize and tame the frontier.

Admittedly, western frontier literature is heavily biased toward male violence, and with good reason. In most human societies where sex ratios are high, that is, where males significantly outnumber females by a wide margin, there will tend to be higher levels of deviance and especially violence perpetrated by males against other males (Melbin 1987). Reporting on this particular aspect of life on the frontier, however, does not negate the fact that violence was not only male-on-male, although it was indeed largely so. Within this vast enterprise called science, there are always opportunities to analyze aspects of a phenomenon that have traditionally been underreported or overlooked, and such studies remind us of other ways of telling the story of the Wild West as we seek to understand the various configurations of policing which developed within in. One could, for example, concentrate on the fact that women and children were observers of male violence on the frontier, and sometimes were also its victims. One such study of "gendered justice" on the western frontier can be found in Butler (1997).

These and other such studies are worthwhile contributions to the broader project of explaining the emergence of policing and justice systems in the West, but my coverage of these alternative approaches must stop here, at least for now. This is justifiable on the basis of the selectivity which is endemic to all scholarly studies which carve out a particular object of study from a particular perspective or frame of reference. In the next section we will take a look at the case of Wichita, Kansas, and see a living, breathing example of just how rapidly a city can come into existence, and the kinds of challenges this poses for law enforcement.

THE CASE OF WICHITA, KANSAS

There was a twenty-year period on the Great Plains—primarily in Kansas but also Nebraska—of a tremendous burst of activity in town building. Most of this was due to the burgeoning of the Texas cattle industry, and the need to move heads of cattle northward to new markets, especially after the Civil War and during the period of Reconstruction. Many of the cowboys on these cattle drives were single and unattached, and they were concerned with defending their manly honor (Miller and Snell 1963). Many were young and inexperienced. An August 1871 edition of the *Kansas Daily Commonwealth* newspaper described the typical cowboy as "unlearned and illiterate, with few wants and meager ambition" who seemed content to live on "a diet of Navy plug and whiskey" (Rosa 1993, p. 100).

64   *Chapter 3*

The most famous cattle or cow towns were in Kansas—Ellsworth, Wichita, Caldwell, Abilene, and Dodge City. Some colorful outlaws and lawmen were part of the history of these cattle towns, including Wyatt Earp, Doc Holliday, Wild Bill Hickok, Bat Masterson, and Bill Tilghman to name a few. Wichita, Kansas traces its history to 1868. In that year the U.S. Army established Camp Davidson (later Camp Beecher) ostensibly to quell hostilities and potential threats from the Wichita Indians. A trading group which had been working in the area noted that present-day Wichita possessed ideal characteristics for the establishment of a frontier town, including:

- Location near a river or stream;
- Location near an established trail; and
- Because of this location, it would be in line to be selected as a county seat or have a railway run through it (Williamson 2001, p. 4).

Along with the establishment of military forts, Indian trader Jesse Chisholm established his own commercial trading site in the area with the help of several entrepreneurs. Chisholm also established a trail that was used for driving cattle from San Antonio, Texas up through to Wichita and beyond, and by 1870s the Chisholm Trail was the major route by which Texas cattle were moved to northern and eastern markets. Indeed, the key to incorporating Wichita as a city was a congressional act which forcibly moved the Osage Indians off the land that was to become Wichita. Six days after the act was passed and put into effect, Wichita became a city on July 21, 1870 (Dykstra 1968).

By 1871 Wichita was rapidly becoming a major trading center, but it was not until a year later when the Santa Fe railroad connected to the Wichita and Southwestern lines near Newton that it became a major cattle town. With this additional influx of people and resources, there were concerns that rowdy elements—specifically cowboys taking a break from the trail—were imperiling the continuing growth of the city. Between 1970 and 1972, three different town marshals were appointed, and all eventually resigned or left town (Miller and Snell 1963, p. 344). One of the first city council acts involved attempts to prohibit the carrying of deadly weapons within the city limits. There were also attempts to ensure that the town marshal had a few capable men around to help quell disturbances, and hence the marshal was given the power to deputize citizens and give them badges as needed. A city jail was built in 1871, and an ordinance was passed to tax profits from the local saloons. Indeed, during this time through the late 1870s, Wichita had one of the highest per capita concentrations of saloons in the entire country.

What we see in Wichita in the decade of the 1870s is an accelerated case of the transition from informal to formal social control. This entire chapter has been concerned with tracing out how human settlements were scrabbled together west of the Mississippi River after 1840, and how once a critical mass of stable population is achieved—roughly 1,000 persons is considered to be the benchmark—there will then be put into place attempts to fashion a formal system of control and law enforcement to augment the informal systems of control and order that occur naturally within human populations. In Wichita by 1872, we see the precarious transition from informal to formal social control, as the city was lurching forward toward the establishment of an official, sworn police force, but in an accelerated fashion not typical of the longer-range and slower development of police forces in the northeast.

By 1873 Wichita was well known as a haven for drinking, gambling, vice, avarice, corruption, and lawlessness. An unidentified paper wrote that:

> Wichita especially is a most abandoned place—a sort of pandemonium where the offscourings of humanity have congregated, as harpies to feed upon the moral and physical being of Texas shippers (Williamson 2001, p. 12).

In response to such rowdiness and disorder, a small police force was established in Wichita, which consisted of the town marshal and a coterie of men who on any given day might be deputized to carry out law enforcement duties for the city. A shooting of a Black man by a White Texan in 1874—described as Wichita's first drive-by shooting—further raised the ire of the community, and increased anti-cowboy sentiment to a near fever pitch. In response to this, a vigilance committee was set up to augment the meager police force, and by 1875 additional lawmen had been hired on to help the city maintain order, including Wyatt Earp. When Earp was appointed as a Wichita police officer in that year, his starting pay was $60.00 a month, while the marshal was paid $91.66 a month. This was actually good pay, primarily because the work of a western peace officer was dangerous and demanding (Prassel 1972).

Earp lasted only one year on the force, however. It was discovered that Earp had collected money from saloon and prostitution activities in the city. It was this kind of graft and corruption, whereby law enforcement personnel felt emboldened to push the boundaries of the law and sometimes break it, even as they were being paid to uphold it, which characterized the struggle of the transition from informal to formal control. More attempts by the city council to subdue the more lascivious aspects of life in the city, including prostitution, drinking, and gambling, appeared in the form of requiring police officers to be uniformed, which occurred in Wichita in 1877.

CONCLUSION

This is an extraordinary burst of activity in a short time. Wichita went from being incorporated as a town in 1870 to the establishment of a uniformed, sworn police force in 1877. The establishment of sworn police forces and criminal justice systems occurred in a zigzag fashion across the western frontier as local circumstances—and sometimes more distant forces or factors—dictated. If we follow Eric Monkkonen (1981) in marking the establishment of a municipal police force as the year of uniform adoption, then San Francisco was the first police force established in the West, in the year 1857. The police departments of both San Francisco and Wichita were instigated by concerns over rising crime rates connected with specific local activities (Texas cattle drives in Wichita, the gold rush in San Francisco). Not all cities establish a police force because of real or perceived crime, however. Monkkonen (1981) has suggested at least four distinct patterns in the establishment of police departments.

The first, and perhaps most prevalent, reason for the establishment of local policing is citizen concerns over rising crime rates (as we have seen in the cases of Wichita and San Francisco). A second factor may be a perception of general civil unrest or social disorder that may not rise to the level of criminal activity, such as the yellow fever panic in New Orleans or civic unrest in Omaha, Nebraska. A third factor instigating the establishment of formal policing is an influx of poor immigrants to the area, sparking local concerns with the "dangerous" or "defective" classes (Monkkonen 1981, pp. 20–23). Finally, a fourth factor may be simple competition and imitation between cities, especially those which are geographically close and are competing to attract new residents. For example, in Minnesota the city council of St. Paul passed an ordinance to pay for uniforms for their local police in 1872, and in response Minneapolis uniformed their police officers two years later (Monkkonen 1981, pp. 59–61; Wingerd 2001). There were no special circumstances precipitating this, as neither city was dealing with crime or perceived dangerous classes or even civil unrest during this period. In this case, the police are showcased as a selling point, to show prospective residents or settlers just how "civilized" the town is, and that the safety of its citizens is a top priority.

NOTES

[1] The original thirteen colonies were Connecticut, Delaware, Georgia, Maryland, Massachusetts, New Hampshire, New Jersey, New York, North Carolina, Pennsylvania, Rhode Island, South Carolina, and Virginia.

[2] Much of the literature published before the 1980s on Native Americans in the West during the period of interest (1840–1910) refers to these people simply as "Indians." In this book the terms Native American, Indian, and American Indian should be considered to be synonymous, although since the 1980s the more preferred literary term has been Native American. But notice how awkward it is to change historical terms like "the Indian problem" to the "Native American problem." My rule for dealing with this semantic difficulty is to follow the usage of the authors being cited, and so earlier works are likely to use Indian while later works are more likely to use Native American. One further terminological issue concerning how Native Americans are discussed in this book must be addressed. Some early writers occasionally referred to Indians pejoratively as "savages," "brutes," "ignorant," "superstitious," "uncivilized," and so forth. As far as pos-

sible I will avoid referring to the various Native American tribes in this way, even when drawing on sources which do.

[3] Ironically, many parts of the Far West were settled before points further east, such as the Great Plains. This is because of the early influence of Spain across the Southwest and Far West—indeed, Mexico and what is now the American Southwest including California was originally known as "New Spain" (Russell 1994; Lewis 1980)—and later as a result of the immediate aftermath of the Mexican–American War (1846–1848), which itself was ignited by the annexation of Texas from Mexico a year earlier. After the war a flood of emigration to the Oregon County ensued, typically by way of the Santa Fe and Oregon–California trails (Ball 2001, p. 13). This illustrates that although the settling of the American frontier typically moved westward, the line of settlement was neither perfectly uniform nor unbroken.

[4] Although pioneers, frontiersman, cowboys, marshals and sheriffs, Army personnel, and Native Americans garner the bulk of attention when discussing the western frontier, before human settlements even have a chance to emerge, there were the unsung surveyors working the public lands to mark off boundaries and establish tracts of land for later use. For an excellent summary of the importance of surveyors in the establishment and opening of the western frontier, see Atwood (2008) and Bartlett (1962).

[5] The Homestead Act was designed to attract frontier smallholders, but knowing a good thing when they saw it, a number of wealthy investors took advantage of provisions of the act for their own ends. Many of the wealthiest members of St. Paul, Minnesota, for example, benefitted immensely by staking spurious claims under the act (Wingerd 2001, p. 34).

[6] The topic of vigilantism will be returned to in Chapter 9.

[7] Hallwas's "code of the west" is similar to Elijah Anderson's (1999) "code of the street." Both are informal systems of justice which prescribe violence to defend masculinity and honor in social environments where both are in short supply. The only difference, of course, is that the code of the west applies to life on the American western frontier, while the code of the street applies to life among the urban poor concentrated in the inner cities of the modern metropolis (Chriss 2007b).

4

Integrity Testing and the Decision to Arrest

A widely accepted notion within police scholarship is that police are effective only to the extent that citizens perceive the police to be fair, impartial, and honest in discharging their duties. The reason that police must operate with high levels of transparency and accountability is that they are vested with the coercive power of the state, and hence carry a special burden to utilize the power granted to them in a responsible way. The broadest term designated for ideal police conduct is "integrity." Webster's defines integrity as "the quality or state of being of sound moral principle; uprightness, honesty, and sincerity." Although there is nothing wrong with this definition, for purposes of talking about *police* integrity per se, there is no better definition than the one provided by Klockars et al. (2006, p. 1). According to them, police integrity is "the normative inclination among police to resist temptations to abuse the rights and privileges of their occupation."

How do we ensure that police operate in ways covered by this definition of integrity? We have already seen that police carry out their duties without much overt supervision, and that they are often placed in situations where temptations—money, drugs, sex, you name it—could very easily lead them astray. After all, police officers are not supermen and superwomen. They are fallible human beings who occasionally give in to temptations and make wrong decisions even when they know what they are doing is illegal or unethical. Attempting to ensure police officer integrity is complicated to the extent that police officers are held to standards of conduct not only in relation to the general public, but also to the police organization as a whole, as well as to fellow officers and employees of the police organization.

As a result of this complexity, there are at least three types of integrity dilemmas that police departments may be faced with. Kaptein and van Reenen (2001, pp. 286–289) describe these three issues of police integrity as (1) the entangled hands dilemma; (2) the many hands dilemma; and (3) the dirty hands dilemma. These three integrity dilemmas are more nuanced and sometimes indirectly evident than is the case for overt or obvious police misconduct which typically involves gaining some personal advantages (money, sex, psychological satisfaction, etc.) in the misuse of one's position. The issue of police corruption for personal profit will be dealt with after an examination of these three integrity dilemmas.

The *entangled hands* dilemma involves a conflict between the personal interests of employees and the interests of the police organization. Organizations promulgate rules for achieving goals that the organization is set up to achieve. Although created at the organizational level, these rules and goals are enforced and pursued by the human beings employed by the organization. As a formal bureaucracy, a police organization is organized on the basis of offices or statuses, that is, every position in the organization has a formal set of rules and descriptions regarding what each officeholder should be doing. A status (for example, patrol officer) specifies a range of ideal activities for the person incumbent to that role. But statuses typically have multiple roles, or role-sets (Merton 1957), attached to them. A patrol officer has formal responsibilities as a member of the organization, but he or she also is simultaneously a private individual who may encounter circumstances where the formal requirements of the position may be brought to bear, illegitimately, in the role of a private person. For example, although many police departments allow police officers to moonlight, or work extra hours in some other capacity outside of the organization, that outside work must not conflict with the requirements of the position. Hence, a female police officer who poses for a men's magazine may be fined, placed on unpaid leave, or perhaps even fired.

The *many hands* dilemma involves a conflict between the functional interests of various persons or units within the organization. In a formal organization, different offices or statuses are designated as fulfilling particular functions for the broader organization (Parsons 1951). This reflects the increasing levels of task specialization characteristic of the modern division of labor (Durkheim 1984 [1893]). But with specialization, employees or whole units may operate with blinders, focused on their own narrow set of functional tasks, and as a result may lose sight of the broader goals of the organization (embodied in such organizational pathologies as red tape or goal displacement). In effect, "many hands" in the organization contribute to pathological conditions in the operation of the organization. Units within the police organization may come into conflict in various ways, for example, between patrol and communications, investigations and patrol, or administration and field operations. In whatever way it is configured, the many hands dilemma has the potential to imperil the integrity of police organizations.

Finally, a third integrity dilemma is the dilemma of *dirty hands*. This is sometimes referred to as "noble cause" corruption, namely, the use of illegal or unethical means to achieve a legitimate or valued end (Klockars 2006). The dirty hands dilemma is endemic to those in positions of power, for persons in such positions are expected to use their power to get things done in the world. Power-ful persons are expected to follow the rules, but as a result of having such power, they may also resort to illegitimate or corrupt means, always at their dis-posal, to achieve good ends. In this sense, police officers share much with politi-cians. Indeed, William Muir (1977) was not far off when he described police officers as "street corner politicians."

As the frontline agents of the criminal justice system and through their conduct, police illustrate the vivid and living tensions between two competing models of the criminal justice system, namely, due process and crime control (Packer 1968). In other words, we want police to get the "bad guys" and to pro-tect us from harm, but we also want them to do their work within the limits of the law and treat suspects correctly. Alan Barth (1961, p. 45) has described this tension well:

> Zeal leads policemen, at times, into dangerous disregard of individual rights for the sake of what they believe to be the protection of society. This is why nothing is more fundamental to freedom than a recognition that the police—in any time and place and under any circumstances and no matter how conscientious and well-intentioned they may be—must always be kept under careful scrutiny and subjected to exacting judicial supervision.

WHY INTEGRITY TESTING?

Given this tension inherent in the operation of the criminal justice system, inte-grity testing is merely the latest in a long line of attempts to control and/or reduce the problem of police corruption, misbehavior, or deviance. Traditional techniques of investigating police misbehavior through formal procedures involving the interviewing of witnesses and the gathering of data—usually oc-curring after the fact and in response to police deviance—have met with limited success. This is because police often act alone or with a partner who is loyal to the other partner, even when illegal behavior is involved. In its examination of police misconduct in the New York City Police Department, the Knapp Com-mission (1973) noted that although outright and overt misbehavior on the part of police officers was relatively rare (so-called "meat eating"), there was a wide-spread culture of "grass eating," namely, police officers who weren't directly involved in bad behavior looking the other way and not reporting the deviance of fellow officers.

Soon after the release of the Knapp Commission report more police de-partments began conducting sting operations against police who were suspected of various forms of illicit activity. These were and still are overwhelmingly car-ried out by internal affairs divisions within police departments. Although the earliest impulse was to identify officers involved in corruption and punish them (a largely reactive approach), later variations have become more proactive and are concerned with corruption *prevention*, including various ingenious sting operations carried out against officers while at work or even as private citizens (Girodo 1998).

Integrity tests fall into two broad categories, namely targeted and random. In whatever form they take, though, integrity tests "involve simulated events that place an officer unwittingly in a monitored situation with an opportunity for unethical decision making" (Prenzler and Ronken 2001, p. 321). Integrity tests use deception to ferret out information about officers in much the same way that officers use various forms of deception to ferret out information about suspects. For example, one form of legal deception widely used by police investigators is lying to a suspect under interrogation that a witness has placed him or her at the scene of a crime, or that an accomplice under police interrogation has implicated the suspect in some criminal activity when in fact no such confession has occurred (see Alpert and Noble 2009).

With *random* integrity testing, simulations are directed at various police officers on a rotating or random basis. If structured properly, all officers in a department would be equally likely to come under the scrutiny of a random integrity test. Although specific officers are not targeted, whole units within the department may be exposed to simulated opportunities for misconduct under random integrity testing. As such, various operational units can become the focus of attention whether uniformed patrol, undercover operations, or even internal affairs officers themselves. Random testing may well be initiated if there is a perception that anticorruption measures within a department have broken down (Prenzler and Ronken 2001, p. 322). A traditional indicator of such a collapse of integrity is citizen complaints about illegal or unethical police behavior, especially in the case of citizens who have been arrested or simply suspected of criminal activities.

A study of random testing in the New York City Police Department found that the amount of corruption uncovered as a result of the simulations did not seem to justify the expense of the testing (KPMG 1996). For example, if there is a concern that patrol officers are accepting bribes on routine traffic patrol, a random integrity testing strategy that could be implemented would be to send out drivers (usually undercover internal affairs officers) who are instructed to intentionally violate traffic laws (such as speeding, running red lights, not using turn signals, etc.) and see what happens when they are pulled over. The fake drivers would further be instructed to offer a bribe to the officer, asking something to the effect "How much would it take to make this go away?" This sort of random testing, however, produces very few "hits" or "failures," because the reality is that most police officers most of the time abide by the law and are not involved in such overt misbehavior. In the NYPD experiment mentioned above, in 355 tests involving 762 officers there were zero criminal failures and only seven "procedural failures" (Prenzler and Ronken 2001, p. 323).

In light of the limitations of ferreting out police misconduct through randomization, there is also the possibility of targeting specific police officers who may be suspected of corruption but about whom the department lacks adequate legal proof for successful legal prosecution (Prenzler 2006, p. 395). *Targeted* integrity testing focuses in on specific police officers acting alone or in a group setting (such as an anti-gang unit) and the simulations may cover an extensive range of the police officer's activities, even those undertaken as a private citizen. If complaints have been made that a police officer is acting in a biased or even racist manner, it is possible to set up integrity tests to prove such is the case. For example, the department will likely have information about where the officer likes to hang out in his off time, and so undercover personnel posing as, say, a mixed-race couple could be sent to that location. There would be an attempt to interact with the officer and elicit a reaction from him, and if racial bias or animosity is evident, appropriate steps could be taken within the department to address the officer's misconduct.

EXAMPLES OF INTEGRITY TESTS

Although we have seen that integrity testing can take the two broad forms of targeted or random, it would be instructive to take a look at some living, breathing examples of integrity testing in action. This simply provides concrete insights into this particular anticorruption strategy above and beyond those approaches mentioned briefly above.

As originally reported by Marx (1992) and later relayed by Prenzler (2009), there is the story of two members of an anti-burglary police unit who were setting off store burglar alarms and then, upon gaining access to the store, would set about to pilfer valuables (usually electronics equipment). After a tip from an FBI informant, the police department set up a fake burglary situation and caught the two crooked cops in the act. After their arrests, a later search of their homes found a truckload full of stolen electronics equipment.

Newham (2003) provides examples of several random integrity tests as well as one targeted test. In one random test the police department staged a car wreck where one of the drivers needed medical attention and was taken away by emergency personnel. Officers were assigned to guard the vehicle and charged with inventorying its contents. A hidden camera was installed in the vehicle, and if any of the officers assigned to guard the vehicle were to take any of the inventory, he or she would be caught red-handed. This would be done on a random basis over a period of time, thereby establishing a baseline for officer conduct in each of the precincts included in the test.

In another random test, a police department discovered that an unexpectedly high number of property-related thefts were occurring near a hospital located in one of the department's precincts. An integrity test was set up to see if any police officers were involved. An undercover police officer dressed as a nurse presented a bag which, it was explained, was left in a hospital room of a recently discharged patient, to an officer passing by the hospital on routine patrol. The bag contained an assortment of things including a newspaper, a book, some shopping coupons, and cash. Once the officer took possession of the bag presumably for safekeeping, it was easy to determine later whether he or she had in fact acted lawfully regarding the bag and its contents.

The following is an interesting targeted integrity test reported by Newham (2003). Several police officers suspected of wrongdoing were set up in an ingenious sting. The police department rented an apartment and placed two undercover police detectives acting as a married couple newly taking up residence there. After several weeks of living there the couple started getting into verbal arguments loud enough to be heard by neighbors. They finally made a call to the police department, and when the police responded they were able to defuse the situation relatively easily, perhaps issuing a warning against receiving any further calls as their sole formal action. But later another, more serious domestic disturbance call is made to the police, and when the police arrive they find that the woman has been injured in an assault and the man has fled the scene. Amidst the commotion the woman finds an excuse to leave, thereby leaving the officer or officers alone in the apartment. The "couple" just happened to have a number of expensive items—including cash—lying about the apartment, and unbeknownst to the officers cameras are recording their every move. And as mentioned earlier, although police officers are trained to be suspicious, carefully planned and executed targeted integrity tests such as these have a good chance of being successful because corrupt officers will have little reason to suspect they are being videotaped.

ETHICS OF INTEGRITY TESTING

Although targeting officers for a wide range of actions and attitudes may be successful—certainly more so than random testing—this still raises the question of just how far integrity testing can go in ferreting out illegal or even unwanted behavior on the part of police officers. For better or worse, today police officers are held to a very high standard of conduct both on the job and with regard to their private lives, and if malfeasance is found anywhere along this continuum—from public to private—it could be grounds for sanctioning, dismissal, or even arrest (Huberts et al. 2003; Schafer and Martinelli 2008). Most police administrators welcome the use of targeted integrity testing for police officers suspected of serious misconduct, but there are concerns that such testing may be ill-advised or possibly even a violation of the civil rights of officers when it involves relatively minor misconduct, behavioral or lifestyle issues, or attitudes (Girodo 1998).

The fact that police officers are held accountable for their personal or private conduct as well as their professional conduct is evident in the case of the "Stillwater Slap." In 1996 a Stillwater, Oklahoma police officer arrived home one evening and caught a teenage boy having sex with his daughter on the couch. Heated words were exchanged, and at some point the officer slapped the boy, striking him on the nose. The officer was charged with assault and demoted by the department. With criminal charges pending, the officer, with help from his legal team, fought hard to exonerate himself and have the incident removed from his record, which he did successfully. As media attention spread about the case, public sympathy moved in the direction of support for the officer. Indeed, at a press conference the officer stated that "I was acting as a father in my own home," and the governor of the state weighed in as well, stating "I would have slapped him a lot harder" (Rosenfeld 2009, p. 27).

Police departments have always had to contend with the fact that policing is an all-consuming job, and because of this it is difficult for police officers to segregate their public, professional duties from their private lives. Indeed, in most departments even when off duty police officers are on call and in communication with their supervisors. And even more so than the average person, police officers carry heavy burdens in their private lives. The stress of policing is real and palpable, and as a result police run a much higher risk of committing suicide, battling depression, lapsing into destructive drug and/or alcohol use, and having marital or relationship difficulties (Miolanti 1996). The latter was gravely illustrated recently when a married couple, both Detroit police officers, ended a long and stormy marital conflict when the husband fatally shot the wife and then turned the gun on himself.[1]

Because of the high levels of discretion characteristic of police work, there are opportunities for a variety of extralegal factors to contribute to police decision making. According to the bureaucratic, rule-driven model of policing, the police are expected to adhere to their standard operating procedures (SOP) manual and broad professional training when discharging their duties. Of course, the reality is that it is impossible to eliminate informal, unofficial, or "off the books" police actions. Integrity testing is one of the methods available to check the extent to which such extralegal factors play a part in police officer decision making, especially when actions cross the line into unethical or illegal conduct.

How do police departments ensure that integrity testing is fair? Let us consider some of the ethical questions pertaining to integrity testing. For the most part, targeting specific officers typically runs into fewer legal, ethical, or moral entanglements than does random integrity testing. Random integrity testing is conducted to establish baseline behaviors of officers—that is, ascertaining what percentage of police officers randomly selected did or did not engage in corrupt activities. But there is no—and there can be no—presumption or suspicion of guilt of any particular officers since no one is being targeted. On the other hand, stings against officers suspected of misconduct are easier to justify on legal or moral grounds to the extent that integrity testing is seen as merely one tool available to dig out an elusive truth.

Nevertheless, just as is the case for any undercover or sting operation, integrity tests targeted at police officers could run into the problem of entrapment. Prenzler (2006) has discussed some of the special issues with entrapment police departments must take into account when utilizing integrity tests. First, targeted integrity tests are concerned with stopping the future crimes of specific officers, and they are utilized in most instances because there is no solid record of current or past misbehavior on the part of suspected officers. But is it either legally or ethically defensible to go after officers in this way, that is, to catch them in some orchestrated scam requiring heavy doses of deception and artifice? If the testing "works," the department might feel confident that indeed the targeted officer had been corrupt all along, and the sting merely served to confirm suspicions. Entrapment always concerns the potentially ethically questionable practice of placing temptations in front of someone who may not usually succumb to such temptations.

Another objection to integrity testing is its cost. Especially in times of tight municipal budgets, some question the diversion of financial resources from legitimate police operations such as traffic control, law enforcement, or service provision to integrity testing, the effectiveness of which is unclear. However, as discussed earlier, targeted testing tends to provide higher returns on investment—that is, a higher failure rate—than random testing, because the staged scenarios can be fitted to the particular profile of the officer being targeted.

Another issue worth considering is the fact that whether or not the integrity testing is random or targeted, most police departments do not inform officers that they have unwittingly participated in an integrity test, and certainly not whether they have passed one (Newham 2003). (Of course, they would be informed if they failed an integrity test.) This requires operating with a level of deception that runs much deeper than is the case in most other areas of life. For example, in order to get good data in social experiments, research subjects are given a cover story so that they will not know the specific goals of the experiment (see Willer and Walker 2007). However, after completing the experiment the ethics of social research require that research participants are given a debriefing where they are told exactly what happened and why they were asked to participate in the experiment. The decision not to inform police officers that they have participated in an integrity test is a practice which does not recognize the ethics of debriefing.

In the next section we will examine the array of factors—some legal and official, many extralegal and not officially recognized or endorsed—contributing to police officers' arrest decisions, and contemplate to what extent the extralegal factors can be reduced or eliminated. Some of the extralegal factors in the decision to arrest reside on the borders of ethical conduct, and for that reason could become objects of investigation for police departments, including the use of integrity tests.

THE DECISION TO ARREST[2]

One of the first systematic studies of police arrests was Donald Black's "The Social Organization of Arrest," published in 1971. In this paper Black (1971) listed the major determinants of arrests by the police, which were as follows:

- Suspect's race;
- Legal seriousness of the alleged crime;

- Evidence available in the field setting;
- Complainant's preference for police action;
- Social relationship between complainant and suspect;
- Suspect's degree of deference toward the police;
- Manner in which the police come to handle an incident.

Notice that many of these factors are not connected to the legal or technical aspects of the officer's role as a law enforcement agent per se. Two clearly *are* legal factors: the seriousness of the alleged crime, and the evidence available at the scene. It could also be argued that the manner in which a police officer comes to handle an incident is reflective of the legal basis of his or her position, namely, whether the incident was citizen-initiated (which represents the overwhelming majority of cases) or police-initiated. Black (1971, p. 1104) found that arrests are more likely to occur through citizen initiative rather than police initiative. Black attributed this to the fact that citizen complaints act as a moral filter, in essence providing strong justification for formal police actions in such cases given the presence of supporting factors (e.g., seriousness of offense, evidence available at the scene, and suspect's previous record).

Among the strongest extralegal factors in arrest, Black found that non-whites were far more likely to be arrested than Whites in comparison to their representation in the general population. But controlling for legal factors across all cases, Black also determined that there was no evidence of police bias, prejudice, or racism in the higher arrest percentages of blacks. How could this be? This happened because suspect race intersected with another factor which strongly predicted arrest, and that was the amount of deference shown to police officers at the scene. As Black (1971, p. 1109) explains,

> The police arrest blacks at a comparatively higher rate, but the difference between the races appears to result primarily from the greater rate at which blacks show disrespect for the police. The behavioral difference thus lies with the citizen participants, not the police.

The issue of deference to police authority is murky, and needs to be approached carefully. As an operational reality, police officers have legitimate reasons to be alive to suspects' level of cooperativeness and deference. Because of the uncertainties of everyday life, police officers always face the risk of danger, and one strong sign of danger, from the perspective of a police officer, is an uncooperative, fidgety, or defiant suspect. One of the most alarming things a police officer confronts is suspect resistance to his or her authority (Belvedere et al. 2005). Citizen resistance, of course, exists along a continuum from very minor (verbal resistance or nonresponsiveness) to extremely serious (running from the police or threatening with a weapon). Likewise, police are trained in the so-called "continuum of force" (see Garner et al. 1995) whereby (ideally) they apply an appropriate amount of force to counteract corresponding levels of suspect resistance.

Although the conceit is that a formal and unassailable science of force exists which police utilize in the course of their dealings with suspects, the reality is that there are evaluative and interpretive—that is, extralegal—components which are inexorably intertwined in this work. Police are concerned with how citizens behave or intend to behave, and this concern is defensible, but isn't it also possible that police do not read suspects exactly the same way? Due to cultural differences between White officers and nonwhite suspects, isn't it possible that police, at least on some occasions, read nonwhite suspects as more defiant or noncooperative than White suspects? For example, the typical urban street attire of young black males—baggy pants with underwear showing, team sports logos, and perhaps nylon skull caps—is likely to attract more acute police attention because of the overrepresentation among arrestees who dress this way. Indeed, some communities have gone so far as to pass Baggy Pants Laws, because of the association of this style of dress with criminal activities. Such laws provide various forms of punishment, including warnings, fines, or even jail time, for violating guidelines concerning the wearing of pants below the belly button. Of course, many of these proposed or enacted Baggy Pants Laws are under scrutiny because they may very well be unconstitutional, in that they may violate individuals' rights to free expression as guaranteed under the First Amendment. Some critics have gone so far as to charge that such laws are blatantly racist.[3]

Nevertheless, from the police officer's perspective, even mere appearance or presentation of self on the part of suspects or potential suspects can color the way officers evaluate their propensity toward violence. Interestingly enough, not only are police officers affected by potential suspects' demeanor and dress, everyday citizens are also affected by the appearance of police officers. Controlling for officer's race and gender as well as the circumstances of police–citizen contact, Ernest Nickels (2008) found that citizens are more respectful and deferential toward police officers who wear darker uniforms. In fact, black uniforms elicited the most positive impression of the police by citizens. Contrary to the well-known phrase, perhaps it is more accurate to say "good guys wear black."

Even given the discussion so far, we have hardly begun to scratch the surface of the myriad factors that contribute to police officers' decision to arrest. Black (1971) laid out an early framework for making sense of how officers go about doing the work of arrest, and since that time there has been a continuing interest in this issue. The scientific literature, therefore, is vast, and here I can only touch upon the highlights of the findings and recommendations that have emerged since Black's 1971 study.

Chappell et al. (2006) examined the organizational determinants of police arrest decisions. Their work keyed off an earlier and influential work by James Q. Wilson (1968), which argued that police organizational styles inform the way police officers carry out their daily business, including that of arrest. According to Wilson, police agencies can be classified into three general styles:

watchman, legalistic, and service. The *watchman* style of police organization is characterized by police officers overlooking cases where arrests could be made in favor of order maintenance solutions. For example, an officer operating in a watchman-style organization might not arrest an intoxicated citizen for violating an open container ordinance, but instead, offer to give the person a ride home. The calculation here is that enforcing the technical letter of the law would not be as effective as simply taking the man home and getting him off the streets. In the watchman style, officers are afforded high levels of discretion, especially in the form of "do-nothing" discretion, where specific aspects of the case at hand may be considered more important than what the legal code says should be done in such cases.

In direct contrast to the watchman style, some police departments are characterized by a legalistic style. Police officers operating within a *legalistic* framework use the legal codebook as the ultimate principle guiding their choices for action, and if a technical violation is observed, no matter how seemingly minor, they invoke their formal powers of intervention and possibly arrest. As opposed to the particularism adopted by the watchman style of policing, the legalistic police officers choose universalism, that is, treating all cases sharing the same basic legal elements similarly regardless of persons, places, or situations (Parsons 1960b). The legalistic style reduces discretion, as police actions are based on the legal aspects of their work as law enforcers, and as a consequence, arrest rates are higher in comparison to the watchman styles. Although police officers working in departments characterized as legalistic may indeed gain the reputation of being "hard asses," they also readily point out that bias and discrimination are reduced as well, since all similar cases are treated equally. It does not matter if you are John Doe or the mayor of the city; you will be treated equally under the law regardless.

Finally, Wilson suggests a third organizational style for policing, namely, service. In *service* organizations, police act in a professional manner similar to the legalistic organizational style, except that they expand their mandate beyond crime control per se into all manner of sanctioned activities, all for the avowed sake of upholding public order. As a consequence, in service organizations police emphasize "training, recordkeeping, and education" (Chappell et al. 2006, p. 290). The service style becomes especially prominent under community policing, where police have to deal with an increasingly diverse citizenry who make demands on police services on a variety of issues touching upon peace and order, family and personal issues, community and business issues, fear of crime, and so forth. Similar to the watchman style, under the service style police reserve arrest for only the most serious cases.

Wilson's typology of police organizational styles has been the standard for decades for conceptualizing the operational side, particularly the goal-structure, of police organizations. And of course it has been the subject of a number of empirical tests over the years, most of which have attempted to ascertain which features of police organization and operations are associated with particular outcomes (for example, arrest rates, citizen complaints of unfair treatment, level of corruption, and so forth).[4] Chappell et al. (2006) studied a number of police organizations and noted the organizational characteristics associated with police arrest rates. Specially, the authors examined the number of violent arrests per officer in relation to various organizational and situational characteristics. The factors significantly correlated with violent arrests per officer are as follows:

- The overall violent crime rate (positive);
- Number of officers per 100,000 population (negative);
- Member of a police union (positive).

These findings are rather sparse. It makes sense that the number of violent arrests officers make would be correlated positively with the overall violent crime rate. Another thing to note from above is that as police per capita increases the number of violent arrests per officer decreases, which simply indicates that when there are more police officers in a department total arrests are spread out more evenly across all arresting officers (hence the negative relationship). And finally, police departments with strong union membership have higher average numbers of violent arrests per officer than nonunion departments (a positive relationship). Additionally and somewhat surprisingly, there were no significant relationships found between violent arrests per officer and several organizational factors traditionally considered to be important, such as the percentage of the population that is black; whether the departments were community-oriented policing (COP) or problem-oriented policing (POP); the ratio of male to female officers; departmental residency requirements; or a college education.

Another study by Terrill and Paoline (2007) examined nonarrest decision making in police–citizen encounters. Nonarrest decisions among the police are synonymous with "do-nothing" discretion mentioned above. Police are indeed vested with the coercive power of the state, but they also have the ability to do nothing even in cases where they could take some formal action. Black (1971) found that police officers arrest far less often than could be the case based upon many of the factors discussed above. And when it comes to deciding on the ultimate use of coercive power, that is, drawing a weapon and firing, police refrain from doing so even when it is legally justified far more frequently than popular notions of the "trigger-happy" cop would lead us to believe (Klinger 2005).

One of the clearest examples of do-nothing discretion is the case of enforcement of moving traffic violations. The reality is that if police officers stuck to the technical letter of the law, virtually all vehicles could be pulled over for any number of minor violations (whether speeding, not using turn indicators, changing lanes in an intersection, tailgating, illegal turns, and so forth). If universalism were invoked by patrol officers, the effect would be to bring traffic to a virtual standstill. For practical purposes, patrol officers almost always invoke particularism in the enforcement of traffic ordinances, and as a result they open themselves to the charge of biased enforcement especially when it involves persons of color.

Terrill and Paoline (2007) and a team of trained researchers observed police field operations in police departments in Indianapolis, Indiana, and St. Petersburg, Florida. The observers noted any face-to-face interaction between officers and citizens. These observers also were able to interview the observed officers to note how officers interpreted these situations. In the two cities the researchers observed 2,472 nontraffic encounters between police and citizens. This total was reduced further to exclude cases where arrest was not a possibility (due to lack of evidence, lack of complainant, lack of probable cause from the perspective of the police, and so forth). Applying this threshold, the final total stood at 729 cases where arrest was possible.

The dependent variable, that is, the variable to be explained, is the arrest decision (arrest or nonarrest). The following independent variables were included to ascertain which if any were significantly related to the decision to arrest or not arrest:

- Seriousness of the incident;
- Victim request not to arrest the suspect;
- Citizen initiated or officer initiated;
- City within which incident occurred;
- Presence of weapons;
- Level of suspect resistance;
- Suspect's level of disrespect;
- Indications of drugs and/or alcohol at the scene;
- A range of suspect characteristics (gender, race, age, socioeconomic status).

All of these predictor variables are consistent with the previous literature from Black (1971) onward. The city variable was useful because the Indianapolis department practiced a type of "broken windows" policing associated with more aggressive, street-level patrols, while the St. Petersburg department emphasized a less aggressive problem-solving and community-organizing approach. All things being equal, then, the researchers hypothesized that St. Petersburg police would be less likely to arrest.

The findings are consistent with much of the previous literature. Of the 729 nontraffic cases, arrests occurred only 27.2% of the time (about one out of four). Consistent with Black (1971), the findings suggest that officers were unlikely to make an arrest. Which of the situational variables listed above were significantly related to the decision not to arrest? First, nonserious problems were four times more likely to lead to nonarrest than serious problems. Second, city was a significant factor. Cases in St. Petersburg were more than three times more likely to lead to nonarrest than cases in Indianapolis (consistent with the hypothesis). A third significant factor was that citizen-initiated encounters were less likely to lead to nonarrest than police-initiated encounters. Fourth, as suspect resistance increases, the likelihood of nonarrest decreases. Fifth, suspects who treated officers with respect were less likely to be arrested than suspects who were disrespectful. Sixth, suspects who showed no signs of drug and/or alcohol involvement were less likely to be arrested than suspects who did.

Further analysis shed light on the reasons officers gave for not arresting a suspect in these cases. The most often cited reason given for nonarrest was *officer uncertainty* over the illegality of the alleged act. For example, transit officials made a call to the police of trespassing at a bus stop, but when the police arrived they discovered that it was a homeless person possibly living near the bus stop. Faced with the difficulty of having to determine whether a trespass actually occurred, the police on the scene simply instructed the man to move along (Terrill and Paoline 2007, p. 322). A second reason given for nonarrest was the officer's determination that an *arrest would be too severe*. In such cases, the officers decided to threaten or warn, or on occasion hand out a citation (for example, in the case of a noise complaint). A third reason given was that *an arrest would serve no useful purpose*. For example, a suspect could have been arrested for a misdemeanor marijuana violation, but the bond for such an arrest is only $50. The suspect had $50 on his person, so the officers decided that an arrest in this case would simply be a waste of both time and limited resources. Other reasons included practical considerations (e.g., the officer was outside of his or her jurisdiction); the suspect was nice, cooperative, or honest; and at least in some cases officers deemed that the victim was as blameworthy as the alleged offender (such as in the case of interpersonal disputes even where an assault is alleged).

Recent work by Edith Linn (2009) highlights yet another set of factors which contribute to police officers' arrest decisions. Linn developed a survey which was administered to patrol officers operating within departments of several New York City boroughs. Eventually, out of the much larger initial sample a core sample of 506 participants was chosen, selected according to the following criteria: "officers who performed regular uniformed patrol, alone or with a partner, with relative autonomy, at least three out of five days a week" (Linn 2009, p. 37). Linn's (2009, p. 9) research focuses on police officers' *adaptive arrest behavior*, namely, "the seeking or avoidance of arrest in furtherance of personal interests." Adaptive arrest-making among police officers occurs because of two factors: (1) the high levels of discretion uniformed patrol officers enjoy out in the field, and (2) the limitations of formal organizations. With regard to the latter point, although formal organizations certainly promulgate a set of rules for discharging one's position in compliance with organizational training and mandates, the organization cannot possibly encompass every facet of a police officer's existence. In other words, there are numerous opportunities for police officers to escape the clutches of organizational mandates and operate "off the books," as it were, to further their own interests, even if they conflict on some level with the bureaucratic rules specifying ideal conduct.

Some of the more interesting findings of Linn's (2009) study have to do with police officers' arrest-seeking and arrest-avoidance adaptations. Some officers may seek to increase the number of arrests they make during their patrol tour, and this would most often be done for personal financial reasons.[5] Specifically, an officer can increase the amount of overtime he accrues if he is able to make arrests in the second half—or better yet, near the end—of his shift. Arrests entail a potentially lengthy series of events, due primarily to the time it takes to make the physical arrest, book the suspect, and complete the arrest paperwork. Officers who make arrests near the end of their shift can tack on two to three hours of overtime while they complete the necessary paperwork. Linn (2009, p. 85) provides a list of the most often employed strategies among arrest-seeking officers, with the top five being:

- Trying to arrive faster at crimes in progress in second half of tour;
- Patrolling in areas known for easy arrests in second half of tour;
- Trying hard to find suspects who left scene in second half of tour;
- Making more mobile computer checks or car stops in second half of tour;
- Asking fellow officers for their unwanted arrests.

The last strategy—asking an officer for his or her unwanted arrests—points to the collusive aspect of arrest-seeking behavior, in that there is a tacit understanding that if an officer needs arrests, he or she can get them from other officers. Linn (2009) found as well that the most questionable strategies for seeking arrests, such as making a questionable stop or focusing on minority individuals who might be perpetrators, are also the least common.

Sometimes patrol officers engage in arrest-avoidance strategies, and these are usually justified on the basis that the police officer has a personal issue which requires that he finish his shift on time. In such cases, overtime is not sought, as the more important consideration is to leave work as expeditiously as possible. Although personal reasons for leaving on time are important, there are of course other, work-related reasons which sometimes come into play in officers' arrest-avoidance behavior. Simply put, there are times when police officers do not wish to face the onerous task of arresting suspects, processing the arrest, or having to deal with prisoners. Just as for the arrest-seeking strategies, Linn (2009, p. 89) lists a number of arrest-avoidance strategies engaged in by patrol officers. The five most common are:

- Conducting few or no stops or frisks of suspects;
- Making few or no computer checks or car stops;
- Ignoring minor violations;
- Avoiding patrol areas where arrests are likely or available;
- Asking fellow officers to take arrests that the officer may get stuck with.

It may strike the reader as rather extraordinary that police officers manipulate arrests in this way. It is one thing to take into account suspects' demeanor within the interaction situation, or to be influenced in arrest decisions on the basis of organizational mandates (as in the legalistic/service/watchman distinctions of Wilson). Maximizing arrest opportunities during the latter half of a patrol shift for purposes of garnering overtime is the sort of behavior which may become the target of integrity testing. Actually, it is more likely the case that officers who accumulate large amounts of overtime are likely to come to the attention of Integrity Control Officers (ICOs) regardless of the underlying reasons for the excess overtime (Linn 2009, p. 111). But in the specific case of officers delaying arrests until later in their shifts, more police departments are keeping explicit records not only on the number of each officer's arrests—which has always been tracked—but also on the distribution of arrests over officers' shifts.

CONCLUSION

Police officers have an intuitive grasp of just how different their work and their everyday lives are from other persons, and this is why it makes sense that they often refer to average citizens as "know-nothings" (Van Maanen 1978). Rather than being purely derisive, however, the term know-nothing simply reflects the fact that most persons have no comprehension of what police work is really like. Among the various elements of the police subculture (see Westley 1970), the extreme isolation endemic to police work contributes to police seeing themselves as the guardians of an exceedingly fragile social order (the "thin blue line"). As Bittner (1970) argued, police understand—or at least assume—that the public sees policing as a tainted profession, and sensitive to such public resentment they sometimes return the favor in kind, including engaging in various forms of "off the books" or unsanctioned activities which can become the focus of targeted or random integrity testing.

In order to stay out of trouble, police seek off-duty venues where the people they are likely to encounter are of roughly the same mindset. This means even in their leisure hours police commiserate with fellow police officers or others who are sympathetic to their plight as they struggle to find their place in a world hostile to their very existence. One longtime police officer, Mitch Librett, now a professor of Criminal Justice, reports on the fact that before becoming a police officer he was a member of a motorcycle club. Librett goes on to suggest that in some ways both types of groups—one marginal or illegal (an outlaw motorcycle gang in the latter case), the other legal (police officers)—share a similar orientation toward "edgework." Edgeworkers are persons who derive pleasure from living "on the edge," largely through participating in various voluntary risk-taking activities. Librett explains this connection based upon his experiences in both worlds, suggesting that the thrill of speeding down an open highway at 80 mph trading beers with fellow bikers, for example, is the same as the thrill of holding a terrified suspect at bay with weapon drawn and ready to fire. As Librett (2008, p. 267) concludes, "But the feeling is the same. It is the overwhelming rush of power." It is this, the ready availability of coercive power to intervene in people's lives, which is both the bulwark of policing as well as its potential downfall.

NOTES

[1] This was reported at http://www.foxnews.com on September 22, 2009, the story titled "Married Police Officers Shot in Apparent Domestic Dispute outside Michigan Library."

[2] This particular focus on discretion in arrest decision making will be expanded in Chapter 6 where police discretion will be dealt with in general terms.

[3] For a discussion of the Baggy Pants Law of Flint, Michigan, and some of the controversies that have ensued, see http://www.asdlabs.com/blog/wp-content-uploads/asdlabs-baggy-pants.jpg.

[4] One of the more comprehensive tests of Wilson's theory published in the past five years is Zhao and Hassell (2005). The authors suggest that Wilson's observations concerning the extent to which local politics shapes operational decision making by the police are no longer valid. Wilson's typology of police organizational styles was written in the 1960s, a time in which policing was changing dramatically on the way to a third era of community policing. Zhao and Hassell (2005) note that compared to then, today's police departments are much more shielded from political influences.

[5] This finding is consistent with Peter Moskos' (2008) personal accounts of policing in the ghettos of Baltimore's eastern district.

5

Post 9-11 Policing:
A Functional Analysis

In 2005 a document titled "Post 9-11 Policing: The Crime Control–Homeland Security Paradigm" was released by the International Association of Chiefs of Police in cooperation with other professional law enforcement organizations and the U.S. Department of Justice.[1] This represents a serious and sustained attempt by professional law enforcement to provide not only a position statement but also a set of recommendations for the operation of municipal policing in the post 9-11 environment. As important as this document is, however, it cannot be accepted at face value, but must undergo independent scholarly scrutiny by persons not affiliated with the organization which produced it. This is not to suggest that law enforcement has an ax to grind or cannot be trusted insofar as its findings or recommendations are concerned. Far from it. All professional organizations seek to maximize whatever economic and/or social benefits may accrue to its members through their collective actions (Chriss 1999b). This means that the interests of professional organizations, including those of law enforcement, must be balanced against the interests of the general public.

This chapter will concentrate on key provisions or elements of the Post 9-11 model, to be discussed more fully below. Once delineated, we will be in a position to apply Talcott Parsons' AGIL schema to help organize the multiple position statements and recommendations of the task force. For reasons to be delineated below, I will argue that institutionalism, the theory that is currently invoked most often to explain policing and police organizations, is inadequate when compared to Parsons' functionalist theory, primarily because Parsons' systems theory is both more parsimonious and much broader in scope than is institutionalism.

AN OVERVIEW OF FINDINGS AND RECOMMENDATIONS

The terrorist attacks of September 11, 2001 profoundly altered not only American society in general, but also the operation and management of law enforcement at federal, state, and local levels. With the establishment of the Department of Homeland Security, there was a new urgency to bring into alignment the previously fragmented and more or less autonomous operation of law enforcement organizations at the various levels (see Brodeur 2007a; Clarke and Newman 2007; Manning 2006; Marks and Sun 2007). This represents, in effect, the beginning of a new merger between federal law enforcement—so-called "high policing" typically involved in political surveillance—and local or municipal law enforcement—so-called "low policing" more directly concerned with crime control and order maintenance (see Brodeur and Leman-Langlois 2006).

New concerns with regard to establishing police priorities, harnessing the newest technologies to combat terrorism—including most importantly information technologies—and facilitating greater agency cooperation across and within levels (federal, state, and local) were at the core of the impetus to create a new template, both cognitive and operational, for police practices. These and other positions were generated from data in the form of feedback collected from major stakeholders within law enforcement. For example, CEO roundtables were held consisting of a diverse group of professionals including sheriffs, police chiefs, and Federal Bureau of Investigation personnel. There was also a CEO survey mailed to a stratified sample of approximately 500 law enforcement chief executives.

One goal of this data collection was to select promising practice priorities for police operations. A few of these promising practices included:

- An emphasis on *intelligence-led policing*, which requires a new collaboration between intelligence and law enforcement agencies from the federal level down to the municipal level;
- Consistent with this, *multijurisdictional* agreements and partnerships between police, fire, EMS, public health, military, and other governing bodies;
- An emphasis on policing terrorism *locally*, to the extent that terrorists go after specific targets that are necessarily in some specific police jurisdiction, thereby requiring meaningful preparedness and participation of state and local police.

Stakeholders at the municipal or local level of policing are faced with the reality of greater accountability to higher level (federal and state) authorities as a result of 9-11, including such federal mandates as counterterrorism training and emergency preparedness and response in case of an attack, while facing flat or shrinking local budgets. The promising practices summarized above amount to a rhetorical ploy of sorts, the sentiments of which are: if such demands are going to be placed upon local policing, then by all means make higher-level operations and functionaries transparent to those street-level law enforcement personnel who after all will be the ones dealing with possible terrorist activities. The idea of not only vertical but also horizontal integration of operations, namely ensuring that a variety of "safety forces" including police, fire, and EMS are on the same page and can act with unanimity in the case of a terrorist event, provides more leverage to municipal governance vis-à-vis federal-level command-and-control mandates.

COMMUNITY POLICING AND BEYOND

On a broader or more general conceptual level, major stakeholders settled on an evolving paradigm, which was referred to as the post 9-11 policing model. The assertion of the emergence of a new policing paradigm in the wake of the 9-11 attacks can only be understood in relation to earlier models of municipal policing which have existed since the 1830s. These are the three eras of policing which were discussed in Chapter 2.

Of concern here is the transition from the latest community-oriented policing era to a new post 9-11 policing era. Oliver (2000) argues that community policing has evolved through three generations. The first generation (1979–1986) was innovation, representing the earliest transition from the reform era whereby a select number of police departments began experimenting with community-policing programs and initiatives. In essence, the innovation involved a transition of the police role from specialist in crime fighting to generalist in community outreach, order maintenance, and service provision in addition to crime fighting.

The second generation of community policing (1987–1994) is characterized as diffusion, whereby "best practices" from early and successful experiments with various community-policing programs were adopted by more and more departments, thereby informing public policy across the law enforcement community. Finally, the third generation of community policing (1995 to the present) is described as institutionalization, meaning that not only have the larger, urban police departments implemented the community-policing model, but virtually all smaller city as well as rural police departments have also. Because it has now become so broadly accepted, the institutionalization of community policing has forged linkages to the federal level; for example, the availability of federal grants for local communities to implement a number of community-policing programs (such as G.R.E.A.T. or D.A.R.E.).

It is this third generation of community policing that provides the bridge to what the framers of the Post 9-11 document are referring to as a new paradigm of policing (to be discussed below). This has eventuated not only in more meaningful linkages being forged between federal and local law enforcement, but also the sense that even newer approaches need to be tried given the extreme instability of the environment within which law enforcement must operate as a result of the 9-11 terrorist attacks.[2]

A LOOK AT THE NEW PARADIGM OF POLICING:
THE POST 9-11 MODEL

For many years prior to the 9-11 attacks, it was the FBI that played the lead role in information gathering related to domestic counterterrorism operations.[3] After the World Trade Center bombing of 1993, however, efforts were launched to reform the use and dissemination of information across law enforcement jurisdictions, including better information sharing between federal agencies and local law enforcement. Indeed, this "wall" that had been in place between criminal and intelligence investigators prior to 9-11 certainly was one of the factors contributing to the government's failure to identify the perpetrators or thwart the attacks.

This is the reason the Post 9-11 position paper places so much emphasis on the harnessing of information technologies and, concomitant to this, the more meaningful inclusion of local law enforcement in the federal counterterrorism effort. In light of the greater emphasis being placed on the terrorism dimension as it relates to municipal policing, the suggestion has been to go beyond the current paradigm of community policing toward a newer Post 9-11 model. Conceptually, this would represent a fourth era of municipal policing (Oliver 2006). There are fourteen dimensions or aspects comprising the paradigm, all of which are briefly summarized below.[4]

1. **Terrorism Dimension** (discussed above);

2. **Mission Reconfiguration**—Transition from community-oriented policing to a domestic security model;

3. **Federally Led Response**—Directives are promulgated from the top and disseminated downward, although feedback from the ground level (local law enforcement) is crucial for assuring operational success;

4. **Leadership**—Chief law enforcement officers must interpret federal mandates and lead their implementation at the local level against terrorist threats;

5. **Readying for Action**—Local law enforcement must deal with turbulent operational environments and fashion and ready responses to terrorism utilizing the best and latest information and intelligence;

6. **Business as Usual Mindset**—Must overcome the sentiment that terrorism is only a "big city" problem, or that it is perpetrated by a readily identifiable class of individuals (Middle Easterners or Muslims, for example). The reality is that homegrown or domestic terrorism is a continuing threat as well, and it can be carried out in virtually any locale (Carlson 1995);

7. **Financial Paradox**—Municipal police are being asked to do more with dwindling financial resources, yet must still prepare an effective response to terrorist threats;

8. **Federal–Local Crime Control Partnerships** (discussed above);

9. **Federal–Local Homeland Security Partnerships**—Follows from 8, but emphasis here on specific and well-organized cooperation with the Department of Homeland Security regarding local threat levels and appropriate responses;

10. **Patriot Act**—State and local law enforcement uniting to support reauthorization of the act; revisions are suggested with regard to fuller reimbursement of costs incurred to local governments for carrying out federally mandated counterterrorism measures[5];

11. **Preserving Public Trust**—Must maintain the gains in public trust realized by way of community policing, and must reassure citizens that in the fight against terrorism their civil liberties will be protected;

12. **Changing Leadership Requirements**—In the volatile operational environment of post 9-11 new missions and issues mean that leaders must be open to new knowledge and better practices to supplement core or traditional law enforcement missions;

13. **Promising Practices**—Local law enforcement is particularly anxious to assemble proven assets and approaches for addressing terrorism, but most importantly prevention assets;

14. **Issues Hierarchy**—Issues most critical to law enforcement CEOs include:

- Budget and financing
- Homeland security and terrorism
- Recruitment, retention, and staffing
- Crime and disorder
- Crime prevention
- Public trust

In the next section I briefly review the currently fashionable theory of policing and police organization, namely institutionalism, and illustrate why it is inadequate compared to Parsons' systems theory, the latter of which will be covered in detail in the section afterwards. Much more so than any other theory currently available, the general systems theory of Talcott Parsons, which will be used to organize the fourteen dimensions of the Post 9-11 model, will also further clarify the role municipal policing is playing or could play in the war against terrorism.

INSTITUTIONALISM VERSUS FUNCTIONALISM

Probably the single most influential theory of the organization and development of policing today is institutional or neo-institutional theory. As Crank (2003, p. 187) explains, contemporary institutional theory traces its origins to Meyer and Rowan (1977). In that paper Meyer and Rowan take to task theories of organization grounded first in Weber and then as extended by one particular tradition of functionalist theory, namely that of Talcott Parsons. Another tradition of functionalism, initiated by a student of Parsons, namely Robert K. Merton (1968), has not been as heavily criticized by institutionalists because Mertonian functionalism shares with them a critique of Parsonian functionalism for, among other things, its alleged conservatism; its inability to adequately explain social change; its overweening emphasis on the problem of social order and the importance of shared norms and values in the production of that order; its favoring of structure (or statics) over action (or dynamics); and its high levels of abstraction which often lost sight of the empirical social realm altogether (for a summary of such criticisms of Parsons, see DiMaggio and Powell 1991, and Giddens 1984).

Further, Weber and Parsons have been criticized for assuming that formal organizations arise around technical problems existing in and across organizational or institutional environments. That is to say, from the Weber–Parsons line of theorizing, whatever an organization is in the business of doing— building planes, trying to find a cure for polio, or fighting crime, for example— that and similar organizations learn through trial and error what works and what doesn't, along the way developing technical and formal approaches (structures, rules, etc.) that in the long run improve the efficiency and operation of the organization. Yet, Meyer and Rowan (1977) go on to argue that the formal features per se of the organization—the rules and structures in place that presumably arise as technical solutions to the dilemmas organizations face in pursuing stated goals—are as much as anything myths, created by organizations themselves to legitimate their existence.

Institutional theory arose, then, as a corrective to purportedly naïve theories by Weber and Parsons who saw the rise of bureaucracy as simply a technical and rational solution to the problems of modern work organization. Take, for example, the quasi-military structure of the typical municipal police department, or the bureaucratic regulations in place geared ostensibly toward making more transparent and accountable the actions of patrol officers out in the field. From the critical, institutional perspective, these would be viewed not so much as functional elements crucial to the survival of police organizations, but rather as myths shot through with social values that comport with public perceptions of what constitutes good or legitimate police practices, procedures, and/or operating principles.

This gets us back to Merton's more acceptable version of functionalism, at least as interpreted from the perspective of institutional theory. In opposition to Parsons' (1951) tendencies toward grand theorizing, Merton (1968) called for middle-range theory. This meant that Merton espoused research questions that were much narrower in scope, and he taught a large number of his students at Columbia University—especially an important coterie of organizational theorists in the 1940s and 1950s such as Alvin Gouldner, Peter Blau, and Philip Selznick—to always keep in sight the empirical realm and to practice organized skepticism toward prevailing theories pertinent to those areas of study (for a summary of these studies, see Chriss 2001). Most pertinent to this discussion is the dissertation of Philip Selznick (1949), which was a case study of the Tennessee Valley Authority (TVA), an organization that was widely heralded at the time as one which embodied democratic values such as decentralization of authority and citizen participation. Yet, Selznick found that for all its high-minded talk of democratic citizenship and participation, the TVA was characterized by the fact that both organizational actors and clients dealing with the organization were often put in a position of having to abdicate their actions to bureaucratic directives. This is a recapitulation of Weber's "iron cage."

This would seem to indicate that Merton's approach to middle-range theory was really not that different from Parsons' version of functionalism after all. Both seemed to have a structuralist bias which neutralized even the best intentions of organizational actors. Yet, a few years later Selznick (1957) wrote that much organizational work is "infused with value beyond the technical requirements of the task at hand" (see also DiMaggio and Powell 1983, p. 148). Here was the value or extra-organizational element which had been overlooked for so long in traditional structural accounts of formal organization. This singular insight served to distance Merton and his students from Parsons, and also set the stage for what later would become institutional and later neo-institutional theory, as summarized by Crank (2003) and Crank and Langworthy (1996).

Yet for all of this talk of divergence between Parsons and institutional theory, the differences are more rhetorical than substantive (see Hirsch and Lounsbury 1997). By the 1960s and into the 1970s, while Parsons was being increasingly dismissed for the alleged inadequacies of his theory, institutional theory was gaining steam as a viable alternative to both Parsons and Merton. But during this time, Parsons' theory was evolving as well, and his later, more mature AGIL schema contained the very same value elements, including attention to real-world actors operating within the constraints of organizational and institutional environments (Parsons' so-called "institutionalized individualism"), which institutionalists had earlier rejected as inadequate. For example, police scholars (see, e.g., Chan 2007; Ericson 2007; Van Maanen and Pentland 1994) argue that police records keeping—especially police incident reports or forms—

are not simply a technical record of "what happened" out in the field or internally within the police department. Rather, police records serve a rhetorical or value function, namely, to give an impression to those on the outside that police are competent social actors who are capable of following a prescribed set of regulations which ultimately benefits society as a whole. As Van Maanen and Pentland (1994, p. 55) note, the legitimizing function of records

> ...may, of course, be of more value than whatever instrumental role records play in directing activities within the organization. Good record keeping, for example, may enhance the reputation of the organization by suggesting that managers have at their fingertips information useful to guiding intelligent choices, and, by implication, are using it.

Although this insight is informed by institutional theory, it is not inconsistent with the way Parsons would explain these very same organizational processes. This is because Parsons' later AGIL schema—which will be delineated below—places culture at the top of the cybernetic hierarchy of control, and because of this values are overtly acknowledged as crucial elements in the organization of human activities, including of course work organization. Because institutionalist theory contains many elements of Parsonian functionalism, it is not "wrong" per se. In fact, it is inadequate only to the extent that it has failed to acknowledge how much it has borrowed from Parsons' and Merton's variations of functionalism, and hence its rejection of Parsons reflects a misguided attempt to appear "new."

All things considered, however, Parsons' theory does have several advantages over institutionalism. Where institutional theorists self-consciously restrict their subject matter to formal organizations and those institutional environments which are the source of extra-organizational factors in the production and sustenance of those organizations, Parsons' functionalist theory is not similarly restricted. One advantage Parsons has over both institutionalism and neo-institutionalism, then, is that Parsons' theory is much broader in scope, aspiring as it does to explain anything and everything connected with the human condition. A second advantage is that, in delineating four functional elements existing at all levels of the social system, Parsons attained a conceptual consistency across all levels of analysis—micro, meso, and macro—the parsimoniousness of which has never been matched by institutionalism. In sum, the great strength of Parsons' theory is that it employs an elegant and parsimonious four-function schema which is able to explain not only organizations per se—including both its instrumental and expressive or value elements—but everything else that could be construed as social.

A potential third advantage of Parsons' AGIL schema is that it could serve as a model for the Human Factors Division, one of six program areas within the Science and Technology Directorate of Homeland Security. In particular, within the Human Factors Division, there is an area of ongoing study and research dedicated to Human Systems Research and Engineering. This is the project of integrating "human factors into the development, use, and acceptance of homeland security technologies" (Rausch and LaFree 2007, p. 3). The analysis presented here could be construed as fitting the broader aims and ambitions of this particular program.

It should also be pointed out that I have taken liberties to apply Parsons' schema to some areas that heretofore have never been covered by Parsons or later researchers. For example, the conceptualization of the criminal justice system and linkages of its subsystems to other systems (including that of the police) is new and, admittedly, provisional. These and other aspects of the analysis will begin in the next section.

INTRODUCING PARSONS' AGIL SCHEMA

Talcott Parsons (1902–1979) was an American sociologist who over the course of a long career developed a systems theory which aspired to explain society in its totality. This meant that Parsons approached social explanation with the assumption that societies are social systems, with identifiable parts and well-established boundaries which distinguish not only the system itself from its external environment, but also the various units or parts within the system that constitute the whole (see Hamilton 1996; Kinkaid 2007; Parsons 1951).

Parsons further argued that all social systems must solve four functional problems if they are to maintain equilibrium and hence persist over time. The most pertinent aspect of Parsons' systems or functionalist theory for our purposes is the so-called AGIL schema. The fully developed AGIL schema, which was still evolving in the year of Parsons' death in 1979, is quite technically elaborate, and it would be well beyond the scope of this book to get into the full complexity of the theoretical system.[6] Hence, for purposes of this discussion, we will begin at the level of the system Parsons referred to as the social system. At the level of the social system, the AGIL schema identified specific social institutions which specialize in fulfilling functions for the social system more broadly understood. Exactly what AGIL means, and how various social institutions go about fulfilling particular functions for the social system, will be the focus of this section's discussion.

Although the AGIL or four-function schema was introduced briefly in Chapter 1 (see Figure 1.1, p. 8), it would be helpful to reintroduce it before beginning further analysis. Each letter of AGIL stands for a particular functional problem that social systems must solve in order to remain viable and healthy. The A stands for *adaptation*, which refers to the problem of securing sufficient resources from the environment and distributing them throughout the system. Parsons (1991, p. 14) states that adaptation "concerns the processes by which conditions imposed on a system by the situation external to it are met."

The economy is the specialized structure fulfilling the function of adaptation for the social system in that external resources, such as land or raw materials, are gathered and brought into a production process which creates income or other consumables for use within the system as a whole. Societies vary, of course, in their ability to adapt to external conditions and, hence, in their ability to secure resources that can be utilized or consumed by societal members. For example, modes of adaptation (or subsistence) and levels of complexity of economies vary with the stage of development of societies as a whole (e.g., primitive hunter–gatherer, horticultural or pastoral, agricultural, modern industrial).

The second letter, G, stands for *goal attainment*. This is the problem of mobilizing internal resources and energies to attain broader system goals and to establish priorities among them. In essence, it is the problem of directing resources to specified, collective ends. Just as the economy fulfills the societal function of adaptation, the polity (or government) is the specialized structure or social institution fulfilling the function of goal attainment. The major resource emanating from this subsystem that circulates throughout the broader system is power. Whether through concentration of power into the hands of the few (such as in monarchies or dictatorships), or through dispersal of power throughout the citizenry (as in democracies), societal goals are established and pursued largely through the political institution (Parsons 1967a).

The I function should be next, but because it is a somewhat involved discussion we will first discuss the L function. L stands for *latent pattern maintenance* (or simply *latency*). Latency serves a twofold function for the broader society: to make sure that actors within the system are sufficiently motivated to play their parts, and to provide mechanisms for internal tension management. This is the problem of keeping the value system intact, as well as guaranteeing the conformity of the members of the system by transmitting societal values and by invoking value commitment. This is an internal systems problem, and the operative mechanism is culture and the values, norms, symbols, rules, and roles constituting it. The central question to be addressed, then, is moral commitment to shared values. The institutions of family, religion, and education, all of which are contained within the subsystem referred to as the fiduciary or socialization system, are the primary structures which fulfill the latent pattern-maintenance and tension-management functions for society as a whole.

The letter I stands for integration, which is the problem of coordinating, adjusting, and regulating the relationships among various actors or units within the system. Both latent pattern maintenance and integration are functional problems which are internal to the system. As societies become more populous and, hence, more structurally differentiated and complex, the function of integration becomes increasingly crucial, as the proliferation of parts and structures creates the possibility of mutual interference between the units of the system. A key issue, then, is the implementation of norms, and the generalized medium circulating throughout the system is influence.[7] The major subsystem fulfilling the I-function for the social system is the societal community. Modern industrial societies have inexorably moved toward structural differentiation of religious, economic, and government systems, and all these also attempt to maintain the integrity of a distinct societal community—the informal places constituting everyday life, where informal pressures are brought to bear to act in ways that conform to group expectations—which operates alongside the other subsystems of the social system (Parsons 1977; Parsons and Platt 1973).

Where power is the generalized medium of the polity and money is the generalized medium of the economy, the societal community's generalized medium is *influence*. As a generalized medium, influence consists in a specialized type of performative capacity. As Lidz (2001, p. 161) explains, influence "...involves an actor's capacity to invoke relationships of solidarity with other actors as means of affecting their decisions regarding present or future courses of action."

The generalized symbolic medium of influence anchored in the societal community is to be understood as concerned primarily with the enforcement of norms, but in the sense of using persuasion within the context of small groups and other aspects of collective solidarity (that is, informal control). Another sort of norm enforcement, reflecting the workings of formal control, emanates from the polity, and seated here is the generalized medium of *power* (Parsons 1966, 1967b). Influence as a medium of informal control works as an appeal to conscience within the context of solidarity relations. On the other hand, the legal system specifies a range of formal norms (laws) which are *binding* on citizens, in that violation of laws may generate negative sanctions such as fines, imprisonment, or even death. Regulated enforcement of laws is left to specialized agents of formal control, hence the specialized institutions fulfilling the goal-attainment function for the polity—in the special case of enforcement of legal norms—are the criminal justice system (with its subsystems of courts, corrections, and police) and the juvenile justice system.

Figure 5.1 provides a graphic illustration of our starting point, namely Parsons' social system, which is the biggest box at the top of the figure. The box is actually a two by two table which splits into four distinct subsystems. The four subsystems are the economy (A), polity (G), societal community (I), and the fiduciary system (L). The functional designations of these subsystems are located at the four corners of the bigger box (the social system). It should be noted, however, that subsystems may be broken down further into their own four functional subsystems. In the example provided in Figure 5.1, the dashed lines that appear in the G subsystem of the social system (namely the polity) indicate that this box will be broken down into its own four subsystems. Since it becomes unwieldy to continue writing in boxes that are becoming smaller and smaller as we trace out the subsystems at each descending level, I use the convention of placing a brace next to the appropriate subsystem and an arrow from the brace which points to a smaller box below containing its four functional subsystems. Hence, in Figure 5.1 the four subsystems of the polity are the administrative system (A), executive system (G), legislation (I), and constitutional–judicial system (L).

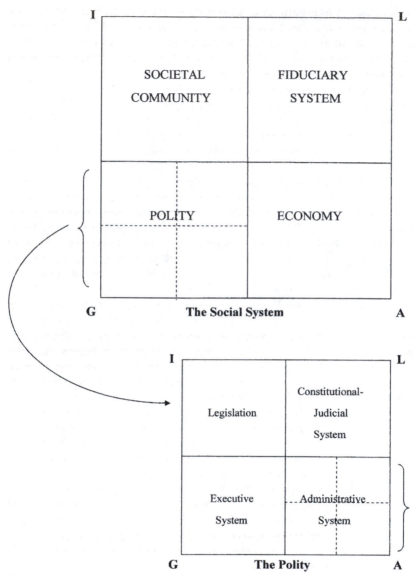

Figure 5.1. The Social System and the Polity Subsystem

These designations are taken with modifications from Parsons and Platt (1973, p. 428) and the justification for assignment of functions to the four sub-systems of the polity will not be gone into here. We will, however, focus further attention on the administrative system, which is the subsystem that serves the adaptation function for the polity. It is crucial to decompose the administrative system one further level down, and this decomposition begins in Figure 5.2. The larger box at the top of Figure 5.2 is the administrative system. There are several types of administration carried out at this level of operation of government, namely the administration of justice (the adult and juvenile justice systems running along the adaptation–integration dimension), the administration of public health (L), and the administration of business both private and public (G).

The L- and G-functions of administration will concern us no further. The administration of the juvenile justice system is seen as fulfilling the I-function for the administrative system insofar as this system represents the admittedly uneasy merger of compassion (or the workings of influence from the societal community) and coercion (or the workings of power from the polity) in the attempt to deal with youthful offenders. On the other hand, the criminal justice system operates by bringing to bear the coercive power of the state to hold adult defenders accountable. Although goals of rehabilitation and restorative justice may be pursed within the system, the primary circulating medium here is power not influence. Use of power at the administrative level in this way functions more or less in an adaptive capacity, in that system resources are geared toward adapting to prevailing environmental conditions, which in this case is represented by potential offenders as raw resources moving about in space and time within the social system.

To reiterate, social systems may be described as consisting of various parts which fulfill particular functions for the wider society. We have already seen that social institutions—government, economy, education, religion, and family to name a few—are specialized structures which solve functional problems whether adaptation, goal attainment, integration, or pattern maintenance. The criminal justice system is a specialized institution for the enforcement of legal norms (laws), hence its functionaries (police, court, and corrections personnel) act as agents of formal control, utilizing the power vested in their institutionalized roles. This means that the criminal justice system is the adaptive subsystem of the administrative system, which in turn is the adaptive subsystem of the government or polity, and the salient medium circulating throughout its operations is power. Yet as a subsystem of political administration, the criminal justice system may be further broken down into its functional subsystems or components. This means at the subsystem level that the criminal justice system acts as a system in its own right, albeit with important linkages to other subsystems of action as well as environments. Before specifying the subsystems of the criminal justice system, however, we must first cover one final crucial analytical issue, namely cybernetics.

CYBERNETICS AND THE CRIMINAL JUSTICE SYSTEM

Parsons argued that the four functions—adaptation, goal attainment, integration, and latency—stand in a cybernetic relation to each other at all levels of the social system. The cybernetic dictum states that "things high in information control things high in energy" (see Fararo and McClelland 2006). For example, a thermostat, which is high in information, controls the energy of the room within which it operates by activating heating or cooling systems to maintain desired temperatures. Likewise the helmsman of a ship or the rider of a horse directs the tremendous energy of the boat or horse, respectively, steering them toward desired goals or end states.

As far as the four functional problems are concerned, the cybernetic hierarchy of control always goes in the direction of L => I => G => A. What this means is that within any system the L-function is highest in information relative to the other functions, hence it "controls" or "directs" the lower-level functions of I, G, and A. Notice also that besides being the lowest in information, the A-function is also highest in energy, and provides the groundwork or "conditions" for the other functions within the system or subsystem. For example, at the level of the social system, the normative elements—namely the norms and values that establish institutionalized patterns of understanding (or culture) via socialization (in the family, religion, and education for example)—are "more directive for social change than the material interests of constitutive units" (Parsons 1977, p. 234), such as is the case with regard to the operation of the economy at the social-system level.

Thinking of the cybernetic information–energy nexus in this way directs us toward the identification and explanation of the functions of the subsystems of the criminal justice system.[8] As we have seen, the polity is the major institution fulfilling the goal-attainment function for society, and a major subsystem of government (by way of the administrative system) is the criminal justice system. These linkages are illustrated in Figure 5.2.

Three readily identifiable subsystems of the criminal justice system are police, criminal courts, and corrections. Thinking along the lines of the cybernetic relations between these three, the courts seem to be highest in information, to the extent that judges are interpreting the law. The police appear to be next in line, and that would leave corrections at the lowest level of the cybernetic hierarchy of control. Because corrections is concerned with the meting out of sanctions against offenders, this subsystem is highest in energy and lowest in information. Corrections serves largely a custodial function, insofar as these institutions merely hold bodies and are told what to do with them by legal authorities. Hence corrections fulfills the adaptation function for the criminal justice system.

What about police? Police are the first line of contact for most persons within the criminal justice system, and they are the agents carrying out the goals or demand structure for police departments, as well as forging contacts with citizens under community policing. This means that the police fulfill goal-attainment functions for the criminal justice system. And with the court's primary role in interpreting preexisting law, it would appear that courts fulfill the criminal justice system's integrative function.

This leaves an empty box at the L or pattern-maintenance position. Law cannot go here, to the extent that law is an abstract set of formalized norms that, analytically, is distant from the more concrete operation of the criminal courts and the criminal justice system more generally.[9] Something less generalized or

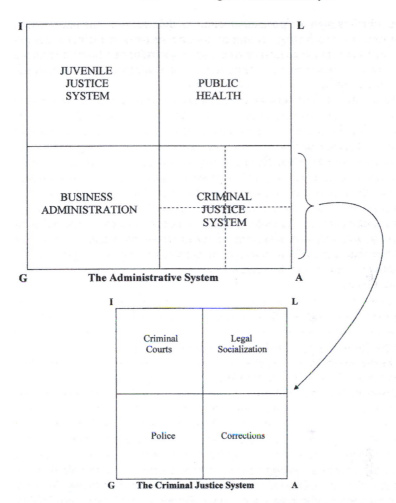

Figure 5.2. The Administrative System and the Criminal Justice Subsystem

abstract than the law, operating at a concrete level just below law but serving a function that is obviously related to it, is what is needed for the L box. The best candidate meeting this description is legal socialization. Because the fiduciary system is already filled to the maximum by other institutional concerns which provide socialization functions to the wider society (namely family, religion, education, and civil society), legal socialization cannot go there. It must, there-fore, be designated as fulfilling the latent pattern-maintenance function for the criminal justice system. Indeed, the mass media are part of culture, and police organizations are more and more concerned with public relations and getting the word out that their mission is righteous, important, good, and so forth.

Further, through the workings of legal socialization parents are urged to teach their children to have respect for the law, and schools attempt to teach this to their students as well. Although as agents of the polity police are armed with the coercive power of the state, since they also operate within local communities, there is an attempt to draw upon the generalized medium of influence from the societal community, whereby (ideally) police are looked upon and respected for their positions of authority. Although under community policing there is an attempt to secure the police's institutionalized positions by way of the medium of influence, in the final analysis power from the polity always trumps influence from the community. Nevertheless, we see how the criminal justice system is linked through inputs and outputs to a variety of other systems and subsystems, including the polity, the societal community, and the fiduciary system, much of it facilitated by the work of legal socialization.

Remembering that functions stand in a cybernetic relation to all other functions whereby L is highest in information while A is highest in energy, we are now able to illustrate all the functional linkages from the social system down to the criminal justice system (see Figure 5.3).

THE POST 9-11 MODEL IN RELATION TO POLICE FUNCTIONS

In order to understand the ways in which local law enforcement articulates with the problem of international terrorism, we now must bring the analysis down to the level of the police or law enforcement subsystem itself. As we have seen, the police fulfill the goal-attainment function for the broader criminal justice system. Yet according to the logic of Parsonian systems theory, each subsystem in turn may be broken down into its own AGIL components. The fourteen elements of the Post 9-11 model summarized above may now be organized according to the functional requirements of the police subsystem.

Insofar as the question concerns municipal policing in relation to the new operational environment of Homeland Security and potential terrorist threats, we may begin with the function of latent pattern maintenance, which as we have seen sits at the pinnacle of the cybernetic hierarchy of control. The following dimensions or aspects of the Post 9-11 model speak specifically to major value elements within police operations which must be addressed as it relates to terrorism in particular. Since these are highest in information with regard to informing an orderly and patterned police response, as well as to creating the new organizational infrastructure for local policing in light of terrorist threats, they must be "worked out" before other considerations involving integration, goal attainment, and adaptation.

The L-Functions

Three of the fourteen dimensions of the Post 9-11 model—numbers 6, 10, and 11—reflect issues of latent pattern maintenance within policing as it relates to

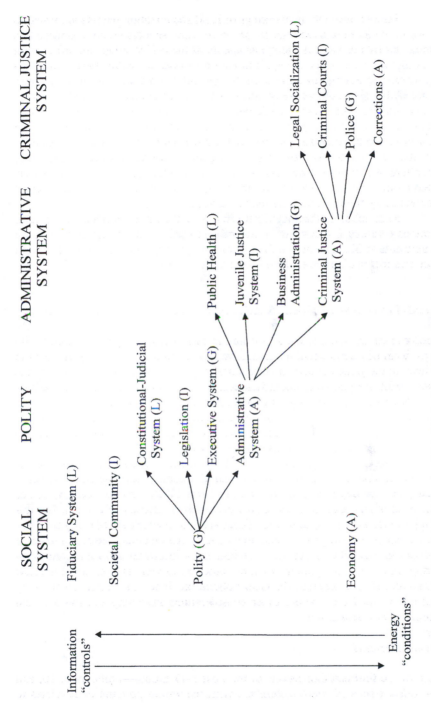

Figure 5.3. Cybernetic Flowchart View of the SocialSystem—Criminal Justice System Functional Linkages

the terrorism question. The first, "business as usual mindset," speaks to the work that local law enforcement must do, primarily with regard to their internal organizational cultures, to ensure that all personnel—from the higher administrative levels all the way down to line staff and even lower-level functionaries—understand the true nature of operational environments as it relates to terrorist threats. Although directives regarding values training can be and are being promulgated from the federal level, they must ultimately be implemented at local levels.

The second dimension is number 10, the Patriot Act. As public law, the Patriot Act puts into motion sweeping legal requirements to which local law enforcement must accommodate itself. That is to say, at many levels of operation of local law enforcement as it pertains to the terrorist threat, the directives and regulations documented in the Patriot Act represent perhaps the single most significant source informing pattern maintenance of not only norms and values, but also of actions of personnel across law enforcement organizations.

The third dimension is number 11, namely "preserving public trust." The specialized activities of the police in this regard are consistent with the broader function of "legal socialization" which is carried out at the L level of the general criminal justice system. The perilous juggling act municipal police face in this regard is attempting to meet the goals of Homeland Security and the Patriot Act with regard to assuring public safety and crime control, but also protecting the civil liberties of citizens as counterterrorism operations are carried out. Police are especially concerned with this issue, and rightfully so, because it reflects the extent to which citizens see local police organizations as legitimate or illegitimate with respect to the treatment of suspects in the name of public safety.

The I-Functions

Three of the fourteen dimensions of the Post 9-11 model—numbers 8, 9, and 13—concern the integrative function of municipal policing. Numbers 8 and 9 are concerned with the new partnerships that must be forged between local police and other entities at the federal, state, and local levels. For example, in order to avoid duplication of effort, law enforcement operations at all levels must be clear about which actors and agencies will take precedence in relation to terrorist threats. So-called Joint Terrorism Task Forces (JTTFs) are attempting to schematize linkages and responsibilities of law enforcement organizations at the three levels of operation. Yet, from the perspective of local law enforcement, looking out at the social system from their vantage points, the operational stage must be clearly delineated and planned in order to maximize effectiveness of personnel in the fight against terrorism. This means that plans drawn up at the federal or state level with regard to more general Homeland Security schemes must pay attention to the realities of multiple local operational environments.

This is where the task of integration, informed by the perspective of local policing, plays a crucial role in the overall development of a coherent counterterrorism strategy. Finally, as various departments compare notes on best or promising practices regarding terrorism or other emergency situations, they are in effect integrating their efforts through information sharing. This information sharing on best practices not only flows horizontally between various police departments, but also vertically up and down through the federal, state, and local levels.

What are the information sources that local and state law enforcement agencies rely on with regard to the threat of terrorism, and how much integration between various levels of government, as well as cooperation across spheres of operation outside of the immediate purview of government (e.g., business, service organizations, and the private sector) is evident? Representatives of law enforcement agencies were asked what sources of information on terrorism they either used or did not use, and if they did use a particular source, were asked how useful they found the mentioned sources. With regard to the perceived utility of these information sources, responses among survey participants were categorized as Never Used, Not at All Useful, Somewhat Useful, or Very Useful. The information sources that scored highest on the Very Useful response were as follows:

- Law Enforcement Professional Association (21% of local law enforcement agencies)
- FBI JTTFs (20%)
- State ATTF (17%)
- FBI Classified reports (15%)
- Other local jurisdictions (15%; Riley et al. 2005, p. 19)

Local police departments rely on a mix of federal-level and state-level sources of information, but given the focus on local communities, there is also a relatively strong network of contacts developed within the local jurisdiction. Here, there is already evidence that integrative capacity for local law enforcement agencies in the fight against terrorism is in place and/or being developed. This is evidenced by the view among intelligence officers that police out on routine patrol—so-called "beat cops"—are an excellent source of information about potential terrorist threats (Riley et al. 2005, p. 39). Officers who work with citizens are thought to be especially useful in this regard, and here we see a potential bridge between community policing and post 9-11 policing insofar as the former stresses closer contact between police and citizens, which could also be useful as a source of information in the war on terror (Bayley and Weisburd 2009).

What about state police departments? Which sources of information on terrorism do representatives of these law enforcement organizations find most useful? The top five Very Useful responses were as follows:

- FBI JTTFs (38% of state law enforcement agencies)
- Other state agencies (36%)
- State office of Homeland Security (35%)
- Internet (31%)
- FBI classified reports (26%; Riley et al. 2005, p. 20)

These data indicate that although state police departments rely on federal-level terrorism information, they also rely on state-level information as well as the Internet. Notice also that the percentage of agencies responding that particular sources of information are Very Useful are somewhat higher than is the case for local law enforcement. This is because there are many more police agencies at the local level, and because of variable local practices and operational exigencies, there simply will not be the level of unanimity of opinion that exists among the much smaller number of state law enforcement agencies.

The G-Functions

The greatest number of items in the Post 9-11 model—namely numbers 2, 3, 4, 7, 12, and 14—reflect problems of goal attainment. What started out as a chaotic and extremely turbulent operational environment for local policing in the immediate aftermath of 9-11, has now settled down at all operational levels, spearheaded of course by the federal-level Department of Homeland Security. The key has been and will continue to be the development of appropriate goals for local law enforcement within the broader counterterrorism effort. The functional problem of goal attainment, then, encompasses a wide assortment of issues pertinent to operational environments of local law enforcement, including shifting mission configurations, the linking of federally-led responses with state and local law enforcement assets, the sorting out of leadership and financing issues, and the development of goal or issue hierarchies from the perspective of local law enforcement.

The A-Functions

Adaptation is the most elemental of all the functions social systems must solve in order to maintain viability, and societies which do not adapt well to the threat of terrorism are particularly vulnerable to decline or, in the worst-case scenario, death (Feucht et al. 2009). There are two issues pertinent to the police function of adaptation, and these are numbers 1 and 5 of the Post 9-11 model. The most basic adaptation dimension for local police is terrorism itself. Notice that adaptation involves merely the cognitive complex, that is, the simple process whereby organisms or organizations adapt to new or novel stimuli in the environment. Nothing at this point is worked out regarding how to go about adapting to a new situation. All of that is worked out at higher levels of functioning, whether at the level of the motivational complex with regard to goal attainment, organizing the units of the system into an integrative whole, or putting mechanisms in place for the stable operation of the system over time.

Another aspect of adaptation is readying for action, that is, assembling or taking stock of the energy and resources that are available for responding to new conditions. Such things as threat assessment and taking inventory of assets and personnel at all levels of field operations are part of this battle readiness. For a summary of these police functions as they relate to elements of the Post 9-11 model, see Table 5.1.

Table 5.1. Elements of the Post 9-11 Model Grouped by Police Functions

Police Functions	Post 9-11 Model Elements
Latent Pattern Maintenance	• Overcoming "business as usual" • Institutionalization of Patriot Act • Preservation of public trust
Integration	• Federal-local crime control partnerships • Federal-local Homeland Security partnerships • Promising "best" practices
Goal Attainment	• Mission reconfiguration • Federally-led response • Leadership imperatives and requirements • Issues hierarchy • Financial paradox
Adaptation	• Terrorism as a new operational reality • Readying for action

IMPLEMENTING POST 9-11 POLICING

The crime control–homeland security paradigm delineated in the "Post 9-11 Policing" report (International Association of Chiefs of Police 2005) provides a perspective on the role of municipal policing in combating terrorism from the perspective of the local law enforcement community. The major contribution of this chapter has been the ordering of the fourteen dimensions of this new paradigm or model along the lines of policing functions as informed by the systems theory of Talcott Parsons. Like any professional organization, municipal police organizations seek to protect and extend their own self-interests as well as the interests of the communities that they serve (see Thacher and Rein 2004). Although no necessary conflict may exist between these two sets of interests, often there are conflicts. With regard to the role of municipal policing in the struggle against terrorism specifically, the Post 9-11 policing document exhibits no major examples of policing self-interests compromising or imperiling the interests of the community-at-large. Perhaps the greatest sources of strain in this regard is the potential and sometimes real conflict that emerges as police attempt to strike a delicate balance between, on the one hand, assuring public safety and preventing terrorist attacks, while on the other hand maintaining proper police procedures so that citizens' due process rights are not violated. It is the sincere belief of police personnel that federal mandates with regard to terrorism readiness and response can be met while still assuring the due process rights of citizens.

As important as this issue is, however, some observers see it as more or less a moot point. Thacher (2005), for example, argues that local police can play only a limited role in the war on terrorism because it is an international problem. Because of this, the best that local police can achieve is a so-called "community protection" stance which includes target hardening and protection of local assets as well as contributing to the fashioning of local and regional emergency responses (see Henry and King 2004). This would relegate municipal policing to at best the lower-level goal-attainment functions, which would pertain only to local governance and accountability issues as interpreted from mandates and directives from the federal level.

The unprecedented 9-11 terrorist attacks against the United States set into motion a flurry of government activities culminating of course in the "top down" directives of the Patriot Act and the establishment of the Department of Homeland Security. As these new mandates and operating procedures filtered down to local law enforcement levels, there was something of a feeling that the previous era of policing, community policing, must give way to new conceptualizations of the role of municipal policing in order to meet the demands of the changed operating environment. Yet, even with all the attention to this presumed changed condition by professional police organizations—represented especially tellingly in the object of this chapter, namely the Post 9-11 policing document— local police may be overplaying their hand in order to maintain what they may (rightly) perceive as tenuous and uncertain ties back to federal powerbrokers.

How this could be the case may best be understood by comparing the situation of British municipal policing to terrorism. The British Terrorism Act, which was passed in July 2000, reflected Britain's longstanding dealings with domestic and regional terrorist groups such as the Provisional Irish Republican Army (IRA). In response to bombings by these and other terrorist organizations the city of London constructed a so-called "ring of steel," which represented a bundle of high-level security measures including roadblocks, armed checkpoints, a closed circuit television (CCTV) security network, increased traffic restrictions, and the fortification of a number of buildings (Chriss 2007b, p. 152). More than a year later, when the 9-11 attacks were perpetrated against the United States, the security infrastructure of the ring of steel and the routine police operations already in place to support it were simply augmented in anticipation of the new global or international terrorist threat represented by such groups as al-Qaeda, Hamas, and Hezbollah, reflected in the amended British Terrorism Act of 2001. What this meant was that, at least in Great Britain, terror readiness and response was already a well-developed and –understood municipal policing function (Clutterbuck 2006).

On the other hand, because the United States had never experienced a long and sustained conflict with particular terrorist organizations—domestic or otherwise—there was never a systematic development of a security infrastructure like that of London's ring of steel. When the 9-11 attacks hit the United States, because there did not appear to be a systematically linked security infrastructure available to span large regions of the country, the governmental response was that something like this needed to be scrabbled together as quickly as possible.[10] As it turned out, local or municipal police organizations, especially those committed to the prevailing community policing model, were already engaged in the kind of intelligence-gathering operations (such as Compstat) which the federal government, under the auspices of the Patriot Act and Homeland Security, were now mandating as best or preferred practices (Innes 2006; Pelfrey 2005; Willis et al. 2007). The only difference now, of course, was that there needed to be a more systematic way of collecting information gathered from these multiple local sites and reporting it back to a central agency: the Department of Homeland Security.

Hence, the production of the Post 9-11 Policing document represents something of a self-fulfilling prophecy, a point consistent with institutional theory's emphasis on the mythologies and rituals of legitimacy with which all organizations are concerned. As we have seen in tracing the linkages between various subsystems of the social system, changes in one part of the system will produce changes in other parts of the system. When higher levels of the polity marshal their formidable resources to make sense of and respond to a situation as catastrophic as 9-11, the symbolic medium of interchange seated there and flowing throughout the system—power—will flow across networks and have ripple effects down to important frontline functionaries, who are in effect the "raw material" carrying out new mandates and strategies. This means that municipal police agencies will "fall in line" with expectations, and will make their own recommendations regarding how best to proceed within the context of the situation as defined from the vantage point of higher-level systems and subsystems.

Given the realities of functional linkages between subsystems and the propensity for higher-level systems to steer or direct the activities of those lower to them within the cybernetic hierarchy of control, the Post 9-11 policing document produced by the International Association of Chiefs of Police (2005) could hardly have been done any differently.

CONCLUSION: WHERE DO WE GO FROM HERE?

The issue of security, specifically as it involves the threat of international terrorism, has reintroduced in a profound way the political dimensions of local governance and policing. Modern policing began as an overtly political undertaking in the first era of political spoils, but over time there were efforts to place distance between politics and the everyday operation of local police forces. The massively destructive attack on the United States on September 11, 2001 was perpetrated by Islamic extremists operating with a distorted picture of the teachings of Allah, and so it is easy for Americans to place the blame squarely on a readily identifiable group of persons—Muslims or Middle Easterners—who, according to this thinking, should be set aside for special attention from security personnel. This of course flies in the face of the egalitarianizing impulses within modern democracies, where an essential precept is that all persons be provided access to full participation in society barring good reasons to do otherwise (such as possessing a felony record; strange, threatening, or odd behavior; and so forth). The new Obama administration is bending over backwards not to offend the sensibilities of Muslims who may be unfairly targeted, even going so far as to strike all references to the word "terrorism" in official documents and policy positions. In a 2009 interview with the German magazine *Der Spiegel*, Homeland Security director Janet Napolitano was asked why, in her first testimony before Congress as the new Homeland Security Secretary, she avoided use of the word "terrorism." Napolitano answered,

> I presume there is always a threat from terrorism. In my speech, although I did not use the word "terrorism," I referred to "man-caused" disasters. That is perhaps only a nuance, but it demonstrates that we want to move away from the politics of fear toward a policy of being prepared for all risks that can occur.[11]

Also, since the events of 9-11 there are continuing differences of opinion regarding whether terrorism—or so-called "man-caused disasters," whichever you prefer—should be understood as a military issue or a crime issue.[12] President George W. Bush consistently referred to terrorism as military actions, to the extent that most such attacks seek to change political policies of targeted governments, and the phrase "war on terrorism" was promulgated and until recently accepted as a reasonable description of government response to the threat of international terrorism. With the election of President Barack Obama, however, this sentiment has changed. Under the Obama administration there is a proclivity for treating terrorism as a set of activities which should be understood as crimes, and the perpetrators of which should be processed through the criminal justice system. Indeed, Attorney General Eric Holder recently announced that the mastermind of the 9-11 attacks, Khalid Shaikh Mohammed, as well as four other terrorists would be tried in federal court in New York. Critics of this decision argue that enemy combatants such as Mohammed should be tried in military tribunals, not criminal courts.[13]

Undergirding all of these political posturings is the very real and palpable sense that terrorism represents a grave threat to domestic security, and that training and resources should be provided to a variety of security forces at the federal, state, and local levels, including of course municipal police departments. The various counterterrorism measures currently in vogue, especially as they relate to preparedness among local police departments, must always be geared toward satisfying the functional exigencies that social systems always face, some of which were discussed above. Building upon and summarizing these points, Bayley and Weisburd (2009, pp. 87–88) identify ten key counterterrorism activities engaged in by municipal police departments. Just as we did above with regard to grouping the elements of the post 9-11 policing model by functions, police counterterrorism activities likewise can be grouped.

Reacting to events on the ground as they relate to terrorist acts best fits under the adaptation or A-function, and two of Bayley and Weisburd's (2009) strategies fit here, namely emergency assistance at terrorist incidents, and mitigation of terrorist damage. The goal-attainment or G-functions generally involve standard law enforcement activities directed toward the specific phenomenon of terrorism. Four strategies grouped here include covert detection, disruption of terrorist plots, risk analysis, and criminal investigation of terrorist incidents. The integrative or I-functions police could carry out in relation to terrorism include community mobilization for prevention and order maintenance when terrorism occurs. Finally, the latent pattern maintenance or L-functions include protection of important persons and infrastructure as well as target hardening.

By going through this exercise, the functions of police operations come to light as well, logically derivable from our application of Parsons' AGIL schema to the criminal justice system, the policing subsystem, and the special strategies police engage in with regard to the threat of terrorism specifically. The four basic field operations available to police are service (A), law enforcement or crime control (G), order maintenance (I), and pattern maintenance through the provision of security (L). Security is a broader and more general set of activities than law enforcement, although it may contain some law-enforcement–like elements (such as target hardening). Such clarifications of police functions with regard to field operations in general and strategies for dealing with terrorism specifically represent some of the payoffs of a careful and systematic application of Parsonian systems theory to policing.

NOTES

[1] This document is cited as International Association of Chiefs of Police (2005).

[2] Gowri (2003) argues that rather than a paradigm, community policing is more aptly characterized as an epicycle, or simply a variant of the original or underlying paradigm, which is municipal policing. This is mentioned only to the extent that the claim of a new paradigm by framers of the Post 9-11 document must be taken with a grain of salt, in that paradigm claims function rhetorically as well as cognitively to lend stability to human activities that demand policy guidelines for funding, research, and strategic planning.

[3] See, for example, the report published by the National Commission on Terrorist Attacks upon the United States (2004).

[4] These are discussed on pages 9 through 12 of the document.

[5] Municipal police departments have experienced rising costs concomitant to their increased responsibilities in local counterterrorism intelligence gathering and preparedness. Although some new federal grant funding has helped some agencies, the funds are targeted more for equipment purchasing and leasing of spaces and less for actual intelligence gathering and analysis activities (Riley et al. 2005, p. 36).

[6] For a more thorough discussion of Parsons' AGIL schema as it relates to issues of crime and deviance, see Chriss (2007a).

[7] The generalized (or symbolic) media of interchange arise with increasing societal modernization and structural differentiation, solving in large measure the problem of facilitating interaction and exchange between an increasingly disparate citizenry. The primordial generalized medium is blood, which in the organism carries nutrients to all parts of the body. If, like Parsons, one views society as an organism, it would make sense to extend the analogy of blood to all other elements and structures of the social system. Although seated in specified subsystems, the media nevertheless circulate throughout the system. Further, they can go through periods of inflation and deflation, and in this sense are neither a finite resource nor support the view of society as a zero-sum game. For a fuller elaboration of the symbolic media, see Parsons (1975).

[8] There have been previous efforts to apply a systems framework to the analysis of the criminal justice system, but most have not gotten into the details of the functional linkages within the criminal justice system as well as environment-system inputs and outputs between the criminal justice system and the society within which it is embedded. A relatively recent discussion of this issue by Bernard et al. (2005) claims that a general systems theory (GST) framework can be applied to the criminal justice system, yet the authors fail to fill in the details of how the political system links up with the criminal justice system or identify the generalized media of interchange (such as power) flowing throughout the system. Perhaps this lack of detail is due to their neglect of Parsons' AGIL schema, which is compatible with the "open" systems approach of GST which the authors favor. Unlike GST, Parsons has already gone to the trouble of conceptualizing the social system in its entirety, as well as specifying functional

subsystems of the system at the level of institutions (such as government) which allow for more highly refined tracing of linkages into the criminal justice system and down to its major subsystems.

[9] It is unclear where law in the abstract should be placed within any of the systems or subsystems of the social system. A first impulse would be to place law in the I subsystem of the action system alongside the societal community. This would be in keeping with Durkheim's idea that under modernity (organic solidarity) a special type of law, namely restitutive or civil law, arises and functions as an integrative mechanism in societies marked by increasing heterogeneity and diversity among its members. But there are many types of law, including criminal, civil, and administrative. It is neither simple nor straightforward to place law in any particular subsystem due to the multifaceted nature of law and the lawmaking process itself. Consistent with a functionalist paradigm, law is conceptualized as a type of reinstitutionalized custom (Bohannan 1973), hence law is an element of the broader ideational system known as culture. However, criminal law is also an element in the coercive power of the state, represented by the police and other agents of the criminal justice system, and hence law has a materialist dimension as well. Because of this complexity and hybridity, law resists facile placement in any particular societal subsystem.

[10] Although the United States did not have anything resembling Britain's ring of steel before 9-11, there were resources in place to deal with emergency or crisis situations. For example, in 1989 the FBI established the Strategic Information Operations Center (SIOC), whereby emergency information could be shared across federal, state, and local law enforcement jurisdictions. Nevertheless, the SIOC was seen more as a resource for integrating law enforcement on an ad hoc basis, spearheading regional and national strategies for multiagency cooperation in case of such emergencies. Obviously by the time of the 9-11 attacks, the SIOC was deemed inadequate, as the Federal Emergency Relief Administration (FEMA) along with a host of other agencies were folded into the newly formed Department of Homeland Security.

[11] This information was collected from the article "Obama-Speak: Homeland Security Secretary Replaces 'Terrorism' with the Term 'Man-Caused Disaster'," located at http://newsbusters.org/blogs/tim-graham/2009/03/19/obama-speak-homeland-security-secretary-replaces-terrorism-term-man-caus.

[12] This ambiguity also extends to scientific observers of terrorism. Some researchers refer to terrorism as an act of war, while others are more apt to treat it as a crime. An example of the latter is the perspective of LaFree and Dugan (2009, p. 43), who refer to terrorism as a "form of crime." A page later in their discussion of the primary sources of data on terrorism, the authors refer to it not as "terrorism" but as "illegal violence" (LaFree and Dugan 2009, p. 44). Perhaps the most sensible position, one that I have adopted, is that terrorism is *both* an act of war and a crime.

[13] For a summary, see "Accused 9/11 Mastermind to Face Civilian Trial in N.Y.," available at http://www.nytimes.com/2009/11/14/us/14terror.html?_r=1.

6

Elements of Police Discretion

Although we have referred to discretion at points throughout the book, here we must define it explicitly. I follow Gelsthorpe and Padfield (2003, p. 3) in defining discretion as

> ...the freedom, power, authority, decision or leeway of an official, organisation, or individual to decide, discern or determine to make a judgment, choice or decision, about alternative courses of action or inaction.

Put simply, discretion refers to the range of behavioral options available to a person in the course of his or her work. The stipulation that discretion refers to work-related activities is important. For the most part we will not be interested in explaining how discretion works and how much of it persons possess within the context of their everyday lives. Rather, we are more concerned with explaining the factors that either limit or increase professional discretion, that is, the types of prescribed actions persons may take in the course of their employment. And to narrow this investigation even further, this theory of discretion shall be formulated with regard to the kind of work that is done within the criminal justice system specifically.

According to criteria laid out in the chapter, among all criminal justice personnel the ones that possess the highest levels of professional discretion are police officers, and specifically those working out in the field (i.e., patrol and investigations). Within the police ranks plainclothes officers (such as undercover detectives or investigators) have greater discretion than uniformed patrol officers, primarily because of the higher visibility of the latter. Nevertheless, uniformed or nonuniformed sworn police officers have more discretion than judges and prosecutors within the criminal court system, and court personnel have in turn more discretion than key functionaries within the corrections system, the two highest positions there being the prison warden and members of parole boards. Indeed, without going into detail here, a schematic of the so-called discretion funnel is provided in Figure 6.1.[1]

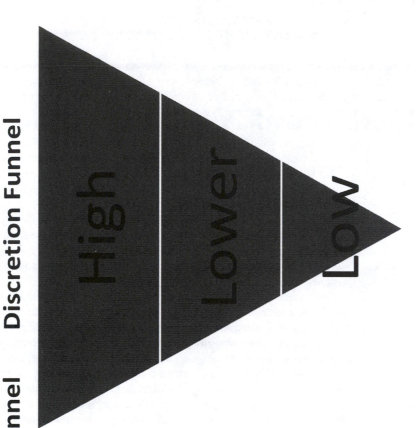

Figure 6.1. The Criminal Justice System DiscretionFunnel

FACTORS IN THE
PRODUCTION OF DISCRETION

As Nickels (2007) has summarized, the literature on police discretion has traditionally focused on two broad factors, namely organizational and operational. Organizational factors are the broader coordinating structures in place within which policing occurs. For example, virtually all local or municipal police departments in the United States share certain organizational characteristics, such as a central office (police headquarters), specialized units within the department (administrative, field operations, internal affairs, and technical services), and for larger police departments, subunits or precincts which, although physically separated from the main office, nevertheless operate under the jurisdiction of headquarters. Also, most police departments are formal organizations or bureaucracies, and follow the military model of organization (Leichtman 2008), emphasizing a pyramid-shaped organizational structure, impersonal criteria for evaluating job performance, a chain of command, and files for maintaining a continuous written record of the organization's activities.

Operational factors refer to the actual things police do in the carrying out of their official duties. Ideally, there is supposed to be a close correspondence—or an isomorphism—between the rules and structures of an organization (its framework or structure) on the one hand and the work being conducted by organizational actors (its process or agency) on the other. As we shall see, however, the isomorphism assumed to exist between structure and process in the ideal bureaucracy does not seem to hold (or at least hold as strongly) for the special case of the police organization or bureaucracy. To be sure, like most formal organizations, police departments place heavy emphasis on rules (for example, the standard operating procedures manual for police officers, and the codebook of legal statutes for their jurisdiction). There seems to be two distinct set of rules in play for police officers: one, the standard, officially recognized organizational rules; and two, the informal, tacit, and unofficially recognized set of rules arising out of the police subculture and information gathered outside of and in addition to initial recruit training (for example, within the context of interactions with field training officers).[2] Following Black (1976, 1980), Nickels (2007, p. 576) suggests that police officers enjoy five basic types of operational discretion:

- *Surveillance* **discretion**—The freedom to choose where to place oneself in the public realm and whom to monitor;
- *Response* **discretion**—The freedom or power to negotiate citizen requests for services;
- *Record* **discretion**—The ability to document or not document criminal or noncriminal events;

- *Seizure* **discretion**—The ability to search and seize private persons or properties;
- *Coercion* **discretion**—The ability to apply coercive force, or its threat, to extract compliance.

Three Additional Factors

Above and beyond the operational and organizational factors in the production of discretion discussed above, there are three additional factors which rarely have been discussed in the literature. These three factors are openness of horizons, personnel density, and visibility.

1. *Openness of Horizons.* Some persons work in an enclosed space, such as an office, a classroom, or a courtroom, during the entirety of a work shift. Usually, also, there is a fairly regular group of people, such as co-workers, customers, or specific groups receiving the services offered by the organizations (such as students in a classroom) who are present to observe the day-to-day work of the worker. The physical enclosures of such spaces greatly reduce the possibilities for diverse or unexpected actions. Conversely, other persons work with few or no space restrictions, and therefore operate in a relatively open territory. Police officers working a patrol beat possess open horizons, indeed, the most open of all criminal justice personnel. The mere fact of these open horizons allows the police officer extraordinary territorial discretion, in effect, wherever he is called to serve, in whatever capacity, he is obliged to bring to bear his expertise, training, and personal proclivities to the situation at hand. Although the personal proclivities or informal side of the behavioral repertoire of police officers is supposed to be controlled as a result of the bureaucratization of their work (in the guise of the standard operating procedures manual), the reality is that such formal regulation does a poor job of following the officer out into the field. The phenomenological realities of bodies roaming across a potentially vast territory in planned or unplanned contact with others, as is the case of the police officer on patrol, renders the legal or technical limitations on their behavioral discretion incomplete and oftentimes unattainable (Wender 2008).

2. *Personnel Density.* In some situations a person works either in a team or in the presence of many other co-workers doing various jobs. In modern society there is increased specialization in the division of labor, and this specialization means that others are close by doing their parts in the work organization. To reiterate, personnel density is high in the case of teamwork or task-specialization occurring within a relatively confined space such as a factory, an office, or a similar work space. In other types of work, persons work relatively autonomously with few if any fellow workers in close proximity. Police on patrol work in conditions of low personnel density, and low personnel density is associated with higher levels of professional discretion. Patrol officers often work alone or

with one other partner, and at any given time there are few additional official police operatives in these areas. Granted, police are observed by citizens moving through their patrol areas, but for the most part these observations are inconsequential and perfunctory. Conversely, although military personnel in the battlefield possess wide territorial discretion, they also are closely observed by fellow members of the unit, including a supervising platoon leader, and in such cases personnel density is high. To summarize, wherever personnel density is low, discretion is high. And patrol officers are characterized by extremely low levels of personnel density because they typically operate solo or with one partner.

Although the decision to arrest was covered in detail in Chapter 4, it is worth noting that the hypothesis concerning the relationship between personnel density and levels of discretion is supported in the specific case of arrest discretion. Groeneveld (2005) created an Arrest Discretion Control Scale, surveying high-level administrators of police departments about the extent to which department policies place explicit controls on various elements of the arrest process. This was Groeneveld's operationalization of police discretion. He also gathered data on the organizational characteristics of police departments included in the survey. Groeneveld (2005, p. 131) examined the relationship between supervisory span of control and levels of officers' arrest discretion. Span of control refers to the number of employees for which a supervisor is responsible. When the employee-to-supervisor ratio is high, the span of control is high. For example, a police supervisor who is responsible for five patrol officers has a lower span of control than a police supervisor who is responsible for nine patrol officers. Supervisors act as a check on and an overseer of the activities of patrol officers. As the span of control increases, that is, as the number of patrol officers under the supervision of an administrator increases, the ability of the department to control the arrest discretion of officers decreases as well. What this means, then, is that as span of control increases arrest discretion increases (or conversely, the ability to control officer discretion decreases).

To clarify the concept of personnel density, one should be cautious not to confuse it with police per capita, or the size of a police department. For example, Groeneveld (2005) found that as the size of a police department increases it holds weaker control over the arrest discretion of officers out in the field. Yet, this does not contradict the hypothesis of personnel density being positively associated with higher general officer discretion. This is because personnel density refers to the number of officers working in relatively close physical proximity to other officers. For example, members of a police SWAT unit would be expected to possess lower levels of discretion because of propinquity, or physical closeness (and also likely because a supervisor is close at hand as well, unlike the situation for patrol officers). As we have seen here and throughout the book, a consistent feature of police field operations, specifically with regard to uniformed patrol officers and undercover plainclothes detectives, is that they work alone or with a partner (see below), and this holds regardless of how large the department is or what the police per capita figures are for a particular city or jurisdiction.

3. *Visibility*. This may be stated as a proposition: as visibility increases discretion decreases. A person who occupies some work position is visible to the extent that other persons can watch the person at work and also recognize that the person is engaged in some type of legitimate work. A patrol officer is highly visible because of the requirement that he or she wear a uniform, yet being out on random preventive patrol, patrol officers encounter citizens in a somewhat random and haphazard manner (the random arrivals of the Poisson distribution to be discussed in Chapter 8). (Of course, the situation is somewhat different in the case of directed or targeted patrol, only to the extent that encounters with citizens are, ideally, planned and hence less haphazard.) Although higher visibility reduces somewhat the overall possible discretion of the patrol officer, because he or she measures so highly on the other two discretion factors—openness of horizons and personnel density—the patrol officer still retains the highest level of discretion in the criminal justice system save for the non-uniformed or plainclothes police detective. Because he or she scores extremely low in visibility, the plainclothes police detective has even more discretion than the patrol officer, and this is reflected in Figure 6.1.

INCREASED DISCRETION WITH ROLE DIVERSITY

Consistent with much of the discussion above, George Kelling (1999, p. 38) illustrates the unique conditions which give rise to high levels of discretion among police officers, including:

- The great majority of police officers work alone or with a partner;
- For the most part these officers make decisions outside of the direct oversight or purview of supervisors;
- Police are placed in numerous situations which require quick judgments or actions, and thereby must rely on internalized knowledge and skills picked up from their training, experiences, and personal view of the situation at hand.

Another thing to keep in mind is that since the dawning of community policing in the 1970s, police officers are being asked to do more things and to play more roles in their official capacity as police officers. This is aptly illustrated in the case of the police department in Kenosha, a modestly sized city of 100,000 in Wisconsin. Patrol duties include:

- Protecting life and property;
- Rendering aid to the injured;
- Preventing crime;
- Preserving the peace;
- Apprehending criminal violators;

- Recovering stolen property;
- Traffic accident investigation, traffic control and direction;
- Responding to and handling calls for service and providing service as required;
- Preliminary investigation of all crimes and incidents unless otherwise specified;
- Enforcement of statutes, ordinances, and traffic laws;
- Regulation of certain businesses or activities as required by law;
- Follow-up investigations when feasible.[3]

As this list illustrates, even in the narrow case of patrol work police are expected to engage in an extraordinary range of activities. Notice that within each of the twelve categories, there is almost an unlimited range of actions officers could take (or not take) to meet the requirements. Perhaps the most diffuse and open-ended of all of the patrol duties is "responding to and handling calls for service and providing service as required." Although the police communications center is supposed to dispatch officers to situations which meet the legal or technical definition of actionability, in reality officers are often dispatched even in close-call cases or when it is unclear what the situation out in the field actually is. This reflects the negotiability of service calls discussed by Nickels (2007) previously. Some frantic calls to 911 can be dismissed as a crank and not worthy of serious attention, such as when a disgruntled customer called the police to report that McDonalds had run out of chicken nuggets.[4] But many cases are not this clearly frivolous, and to play it safe police departments are likely to dispatch an officer and trust his or her professional judgment upon arrival at the scene.

DECISION POINTS IN POLICE DISCRETION

Samuel Walker (1993) has pointed out that police discretion does not occur at a particular point in time, but over a sometimes lengthy and complicated set of circumstances and exigencies. This real-world complexity must be taken into account in any attempt to conceptualize the vagaries of police discretion in particular, and discretion within the criminal justice system more generally. For example, as we have already seen in Chapter 4, the arrest decision is complex as multiple factors converge in producing arrests. Within any particular situation involving police and citizens, there are multiple points at which police decide on certain lines of action as well as refraining from other potential lines. This is simply a restatement of the fact that police officers possess both positive discretion and negative or "do nothing" discretion.

Walker (1993) illustrates a few of these decision points for a typical officer out on patrol. First, if the officer receives a call for help he or she can decide how quickly to arrive at the scene (response discretion). Although there may be an ideal set of guidelines for determining this, the reality is that officers often act "off the books" and use their own judgments in many cases. And when it becomes apparent that officers are indeed using their own discretion to decide upon the speed of response, the bureaucratic side of police operations will likely promulgate a new set of rules designed to further formalize the decision to pursue and the speed of pursuit, especially in the cases of so-called "hot pursuit" which may result in a high-speed automobile chase (Hoffmann and Mazerolle 2005). But continuing formalization, in effect the attempt to create a "connect-the-dots" policing, is problematic because, as mentioned previously, the rules police operate with and which inform police discretion are created within street-level police operations and reside within the commonsensical values of the police subculture (Mastrofski 2004).

Second, once at the scene officers can decide whether to take charge of the situation, including pursuing formal actions against a suspect, or to do little and leave quickly (Walker 1993, p. 24). Within the setting they can decide on a variety of presentations of self, such as being pleasant or discourteous. They can further decide to mediate the dispute themselves or refer the parties to a social service agency or some other third party.

Third, if a crime is alleged the officer at the scene has complete discretion over whether to file a report (record discretion). Even when a citizen complains that a crime has occurred, it is possible for the officer to decide that nothing has happened, thereby engaging in "unfounding" of a crime (Walker 1993, ibid.). And even if the officer decides that a crime has likely occurred, there are options as to whether an arrest should happen immediately or whether it should be delayed pending further investigation. Fourth, officers can decide not only on whether an investigation should occur involving a possible crime, but how *seriously* the investigation ought to be pursued. This issue came to light in the past particularly in the case of domestic disturbance calls, as many female citizens who were victims of such abuse charged that police simply were not taking them seriously. As a consequence, new policies were implemented in most police departments with regard to police responses to domestic violence, including mandatory arrest policies (see, e.g., Felson et al. 2002; Frantzen and San Miguel 2009).

Fifth, investigations of suspected crimes and criminals involve a series of decisions about searching, interrogating, and possible seizure or arrest (seizure discretion). Decisions to stop and question, to engage in a frisk, and at what point mere questioning turns into criminal interrogation (the latter of which requires the reading of a suspect's Miranda rights) are all consequential decisions that are under control of the discretion of particular police officers out in the field.

Sixth, officers decide how much force to apply in a situation (coercion discretion). Most officers are trained on the continuum of force, which is a set of guidelines by which the level of suspect resistance is matched with the level of force needed to subdue or control the suspect.[5] There are a variety of controversies involving police use of lethal force as well as less-than-lethal force (such as, for example, the employment of Tasers), including civil rights litigation over excessive use of force by the police against minority suspects (Skolnick and

Fyfe 1993). In light of the many complications visited upon police departments whenever fatal shootings of citizens occur, there has been a renewed emphasis placed on the use of less-than-lethal force as a policy mandate within patrol operations. Interestingly enough, although less than 1% of all cases involving the use of Tasers eventuates in a suspect's death, this small 1% of cases has raised enough of a firestorm whereby a growing number of departments no longer authorize their use (Smith et al. 2007; White and Ready 2007, 2010).

There are many more decision points than these, but the point is, the process by which police arrive at decisions in the course of their duties is complex and multilayered. I mentioned above that much of police discretion resists bureaucratic or legal codification, and that more importantly than formal control is the more informal "working rules" arising out of actual police work and the sedimentation of these common sense understandings within the police subculture. Indeed, in their research Stroshine et al. (2008) identify eleven categories of working rules which inform police discretionary decision making, and in the next section we will examine these rules.

ELEVEN WORKING RULES FOR POLICE

Stroshine et al. (2008), along with a group of trained observers, rode along with police officers on patrol in Miami-Dade County, Florida and Savannah, Georgia, paying close attention to officers' behavior upon encountering citizens. Officers were further asked to "think out loud" so that researchers accompanying them could get a feel for the thought processes and perspectives directing their behavior. Through these observations as well as discussions with the officers, the research team identified a set of rules officers formulated in the performance of their duties. The eleven substantive categories of rules that emerged were as follows.[6]

Importance of Time and Place

Officers on patrol are keen to notice things that do not "fit" given a particular time and place. This implies that officers are patrolling a familiar beat and are aware of settings, activities, and persons they are likely to observe or encounter. Examples given by the officers included a White person in a predominantly Black neighborhood, or persons in a warehouse district at night (Stroshine et al. 2008, p. 322). Officer suspicion is heightened when such activities are observed during the nighttime.

Importance of Appearance

The appearance of persons and things is an important element in the observational repertoire of police officers on patrol. Chief among the appearance variables are vehicles that seem out of place or that possess certain characteristics which are associated with untoward activities. For example, a car in traffic that does not start promptly when the light turns green is likely to be pulled over regardless of the characteristics of the driver. In this vein, cars are especially likely to be pulled over that have something wrong with them, whether a broken light, tinted windows, or loud exhausts.

Importance of Information

Officers rely on various sources of information as they carry out their duties. Some sources of information are informal, such as people in the neighborhood, while other sources are more formalized or bureaucratic, such as stolen vehicle lists. On some level, then, officers seek to maintain cordial relations with citizens on the beats they patrol so they will feel comfortable sharing information. As we saw last chapter, informal sources of information are particularly important in post 9-11 policing, as there is no better intelligence than everyday persons in their homes, at work, or on the streets watching for suspicious activities and feeling secure enough to approach law enforcement officials with such information.

Importance of Behavior

So far we have seen that police officers make note of time, place, appearance, and information in formulating rules for decision making in the discharge of their duties. These are generic categories which stand on their own as important elements in the discretionary decision-making calculus. But within this mix, ultimately police officers will take into account the actual behavior of real, flesh-and-blood human beings within these scenes, settings, and time frames. Indeed, because police are available whenever a call to dispatch is made and can invoke their formal powers of interrogation, detainment, or arrest upon arrival, it is truly the case that we may consider the wide range of such instances as "police occasions" (Bittner 1970; Sanders 1979). Police occasions are simply situations in which police are on the scene and interacting with persons in some meaningful way. This represents official police business, rather than, say, a police officer shooting the breeze with a friend while out on patrol.

Sanders (1979) suggests there are eight basic types of police occasions, the variability of these occasions owing largely to the types of behavior engaged in by both suspect or citizen and police personnel at the scene. In other words, behavior does not occur in a vacuum but can be made sense of only within a complex strip of social interaction involving time, place, appearance, available information, and the broader behavioral norms operating within that particular occasion. Following Goffman (1963), Sanders identifies four general categories of police occasions along the dimensions of structure, schedule, focus of attention, and contact rules. Each of these four dimensions can exist in a high or low state, and this produces the eight police occasions.

With regard to structure, police occasions can be either tight or loose. A police officer in a *tight* police occasion finds him- or herself in a setting that is highly structured and formalized, such as in a courtroom. On the other hand, a *loose* police occasion is one in which there is informality and a diversity of permissible activities, such as the open horizons of the anonymous public sphere. With regard to the dimension of scheduling, police occasions can be either scheduled or unscheduled. Sting operations or directed patrol would be an example of a *scheduled* police occasion, while chance meetings with persons on random preventive patrol or traffic patrol would be examples of *unscheduled* police occasions.

With regard to focus of attention, *focused* police occasions are gatherings in which people come together and sustain a single focus of attention, for example, at a play, movie, or ballgame, a town hall meeting, or couples in conversation. This does not imply that the police officer was part of the focused gathering initially. Instead, it is more likely that the officer arrived at or was called to the focused gathering because of some disturbance which occurred there. On the other hand, *unfocused* police occasions are those in which people are in each others' immediate presence but who do not sustain a single focus of attention, for example, people waiting for the bus or waiting in line. Finally, with regard to contact rules, *closed* police occasions are ones in which contact is permitted only among the acquainted, or where formal rules are in place for such meetings to occur (such as in a courtroom). *Open* police occasions are ones in which contact is permitted between the unacquainted, such is the case at parties, singles bars, or typical public places.

Sanders (1979) and a team of trained observers went out into the field and watched police officers arriving on the scene and injecting themselves in the flow of activities over a five-month period. In other words, they observed police occasions in the making, taking note of the characteristics of these occasions. They distilled the four basic dimensions of police occasions—structure, schedule, focus of attention, and contact rules—from these empirical observations. The percentage of time police spent within each condition with regard to each of the four occasion dimensions is as follows:

- Tightly structured—15.9%
- Loosely structure—84.1%
- Scheduled—15.2%
- Unscheduled—84.5%[7]
- Focused—19.7%
- Unfocused—80.3%

- Open—72.9%
- Closed—27.1%

Notice the pattern that emerges with regard to the behavioral dimension of policing and the nature of discretion implied therein. Police were overwhelmingly more likely to find themselves in situations that were open, unscheduled, loose, unfocused, and informal. This is exactly what Bittner (1970) suggests regarding the core role of the police officer, which is the availability to be called to a situation and exert force, and if need be, to resolve it. The fact that police are vested with the coercive power of the state, and have at the ready the use of coercive force if called for—although most of the time coercive or physical force is NOT applied—means that the police mandate is diffuse and virtually limitless because of the various ways "trouble" can be interpreted by people who are requesting their services. This means also that police are less often called on to intervene in places which are organized or structured for particular activities, and are more likely to be called by average persons dealing with open and fluid situations, whether in their homes, on the streets, at a business, or what have you. Because of this high degree of looseness, openness, and informality, police have to respond literally "on the fly," because the bureaucratic rules for taking care of "trouble" in the diffuse sense do not do a good job of following officers out into the field. The behavioral exigencies of the moment and the occasion are what drive police decision making, and this implies extraordinarily high levels of behavioral discretion on the part of officers, as opposed to bureaucratic or connect-the-dots solutions.

Fairness

Most police officers operate with an implicit sense of fairness or social justice in their dealings with citizens. They strive to live up to the biblical precept or the Golden Rule: "Do unto others as you would have them do unto you." Of course, this is often unattainable because of the asymmetrical nature of police–citizen interactions (Skogan 2006b). In interactions where one side holds enormous power in relation to others who holds relatively little, it is very easy for persons with little or no power to interpret the actions of the powerful person—in this case, the police—as untoward, egregious, or disreputable simply because of the enormous power imbalance instantiated in the occasion or setting. When such power differentials are also woven into the very fabric of the society within which police officers are operating, especially with regard to gender, race, and class disparities, it is easy to see that at the point of contact—the so-called police occasion—many will come away with the feeling that they have been treated unfairly, especially if they are themselves targets of police action (see Chapter 1).

Given the inherent inequalities that operate in the broader society and which likely will be magnified in any encounter between citizens and the police,

police attempt to act proactively by committing to a set of rules for conduct regardless of the particular characteristics of the persons encountered at the scene. As Stroshine et al. (2008, p. 325) noted in their research, "One officer mentioned deciding in advance what actions he will take with a person who is stopped, so that he could not be influenced by characteristics such as race."

Threshold

Officers have an informal, working sense of how much of a certain type of behavior they are willing to tolerate before they invoke their formal powers to act. This means that officers operate with implicit thresholds regarding all manner of activities they may be witness to out on patrol. For example, on traffic patrol officers do not enforce exact speed limits, but tolerate a certain amount of speeding over the limit given specific settings and circumstances. For example, low speed limits posted in school zones or neighborhood streets are enforced more strictly than highway speed limits. On the highway many state or municipal police patrols will not ticket drivers unless they are going 15 miles over the limit (Stroshine et al. 2008, p. 327). In California, for example, a serious speeding violation is considered going 15 or more miles over the posted speed limit.[8]

Interestingly enough, it is unclear what the relationship is between speed limits and the number of driver fatalities or accidents. The standard notion is that lower speed limits are safer, but is this true? In the state of Montana the National Maximum Speed Limit was repealed in 1995, and in its place was used so-called Reasonable and Prudent speed limits. The Montana State Patrol did attempt to enforce a de-facto threshold of an 80 to 90 mph limit for Reasonable and Prudent enforcement during this time. However, many drivers challenged receiving these speeding tickets, and in 1998 the Montana Supreme Court upheld their challenges and declared the Reasonable and Prudent speed limit to be unconstitutional because of its vagueness. As a result of the ruling, for the following five months and through much of 1999 Montana had no daytime speed limits on its rural highways.

The National Motorists Association (NMA) conducted a study and found that during this time of no speed limits the fatal accident rate declined to a record level. Additionally, seat belt usage rose 88%, which reflects the fact that people know that when they are going fast it makes sense to wear a seat belt. Interestingly enough, as well, average speeds on these no-speed-limit roads in Montana were actually lower than the reported speeds on Southern California's 65-mph speed limits posted along urban interstates. This indicates that people went as fast as they needed to go, but didn't use the absent speed limits as an excuse to drive faster than they normally would. It appears that in open and non-congested driving conditions, such as on the highways and rural byways of Montana, no speed limit makes more sense and produces better results in terms of reducing accidents, fatalities, and driving infractions than a posted speed limit.[9]

Police officers are also trained to withstand surly or rude behavior on the part of citizens, but they are free to invoke their formal powers to deal with especially uncooperative, boorish, or challenging behavior as their professional judgment allows. Notice there are no connect-the-dots rules for determining where a citizen crosses the line into unacceptable or intolerable behavior. This reflects the enormous discretion officers possess in all manner of encounters with citizens, a point that must always be kept in mind when thinking about the police role in society.

Pissing Off the Police

Perhaps this category should belong in the fairness or even threshold categories discussed above, but Stroshine et al. (2008) argue that "pissing off the police" (POP) is analytically distinct from the other two categories. This is because the category of fairness refers to rules by which police attempt to act fairly towards citizens. The POP category, on the other hand, refers to police expectations that citizens treat them fairly or appropriately. Police assume, perhaps rightly so, that they are as good a judge as anyone regarding the perception of other actors' normative appropriateness or propriety. As fellow human beings, even given their power advantage over average citizens, the police are entitled to be outraged and act upon it, within of course the bounds of their professional obligations and duties. For example, officers on traffic patrol often operate on the basis of a tacit rule by which a suspect's demeanor will play an important role in determining whether that suspect receives a warning or a ticket. As Seron et al. (2004, p. 703) suggest, the public recognizes that aggressive behavior on the part of citizens requires aggressive and deterrent responses on the part of police, just so long as they do not cross over the line into abusive behavior.

Hence, police officers have legal remedies to deal with suspects who are rude, challenging, or disrespectful. But as fallible human beings, police may also step over the line themselves and mete out various forms of street justice, namely informal or "off the books" solutions to problematic situations confronting them in the field (Klockars 2006). For example, police who finally catch up with a suspect after a long and grueling chase may feel that the suspect deserves to be "roughed up" for having the audacity to run from the police. This is clearly one of the maximal conditions of POP and may generate illegal street justice remedies on the part of police. It is such examples of police brutality or abuse that leads to calls to reign in police discretion.

Safety

Police formulate working rules involving safety. These are in addition to the technical safety rules which officers are legally obligated to follow (for example, handling of service revolver, engaging in high-speed automobile chases, and use of force according to the continuum of force training and protocols). For example, officers place high priority on calls involving children, and are more likely to intervene in situations involving them. There are also elements of the police subculture that warn officers to "lay low," "cover your ass," and get home safely at the end of the shift (Herbert 2006b; Skolnick 1966).

"One Act Evolves into Another"

In their everyday field operations police develop understandings of the predictability and consistency of persons or situations with whom (or which) they have had dealings in the past. This is the basic process of stereotyping with which all persons operate in their daily lives. Stereotypes are cognitive tools which provide information to persons regarding current or the next line of actions in relation to other persons. Police feel they can peg people pretty well in terms of their predictability, embodied in the sentiment "you can't teach an old dog new tricks." As one police officer reported to Stroshine et al. (2008, p. 331), "Previous experience—if he has dealt with the individual before and knows them by arrest or that they are a drug dealer and has probable cause, he [the officer] will pull them over."

Keeping Busy

Out on patrol police learn to create the appearance that they are busy. A good portion of time spent on patrol is rather uneventful, typically referred to as "down time." Police can of course make work for themselves, and one way this is accomplished is by seeking tickets and arrests (especially as we saw in Chapter 4). On slow days with few service calls, police can go to well-known places, for example, intersections where tickets are easy to write, or visit a person known to be engaged in nefarious activities or who hangs around with nefarious characters. Along these lines, checking expired tags is one of the preferred forms of busy work.

Work Shirking

Just as we saw in the case of seeking or avoiding arrests near the end of a shift, police can also seek to avoid more routine activities of their shift, including avoiding traffic stops because "they produce too much work" (Stroshine et al. 2008, p. 333). In general, work shirking amounts to officers trying to avoid contact with the public, and in most jurisdictions or beats there are known places where police can lay low and not attract much attention.

CAN OR SHOULD DISCRETION BE CONTROLLED?

If discretion refers to the many ways that police act "off the books" in the course of their duties, the question remains, how far and to what extent should police discretion be controlled? Actually, on one level the bureaucratic regulations already in place attempt to speak to this very issue, for there are proscriptions in place for all manner of activities undertaken by the police in their official capacity as representatives of some political jurisdiction. Additionally, over time more and more citizens have taken it upon themselves to hold the police more accountable for their actions, and one of the major movements within community policing has been the explicit push to get citizens more involved in police and community issues. One example of this is civilian review boards (sometimes referred to as citizen review boards), which are independent tribunals of citizens who meet regularly, hear cases of alleged police misconduct, and make recommendations either with regard to the sanctioning of a specific officer or policy recommendations for the police department as a whole. It is often the case that issues of police misconduct or abuse are framed as a problem of police discretion run wild and unchecked, hence, issues of police discretion which come to the attention of the public are usually understood as problems which call for the placing of further guidelines or restrictions on it (Palmiotto 2000).

Even given this relatively recent concern with police discretion and its control, many observers have doubts as to the efficacy or utility of further regulations of police work. Walker (1993, pp. 14–16) discusses four reservations with the control of discretion in the criminal justice system more generally. First, there is the cynical view that "nothing works," so any attempt to hold police accountable through greater administrative, legal, or technical oversight—whether through external means (e.g., Supreme Court rulings or civilian review boards) or internal means (e.g., police internal affairs or integrity testing [see Chapter 4])—are merely rhetorical flourishes which will have no real effect.

A second reservation is that even if reforms are implemented regarding the reduction of police discretion, police will find ways to give lip service to the new guidelines while changing their street-level activities very little if at all. For example, the Supreme Court decision in *Miranda v. Arizona* (1966) was aimed at fundamentally changing street-level police behavior to ensure that suspects are treated fairly, specifically with regard to assuring their Fifth Amendment (right against self-incrimination) and Sixth Amendment (right to an attorney) rights. Yet, the attempt to control the nature of police interrogations—thereby controlling a fundamental dimension of police discretion, namely, coercion discretion—via *Miranda* has not been successful primarily because the law cannot measure the force used in police interrogations. Further, even with the new requirement to inform suspects that they have a right to remain silent, about 80% of suspects still answer police questions (White 2001).

Third, new restrictions on police discretion may actually make the situation worse. In *Mapp v. Ohio* (1961) the Supreme Court ruled that evidence obtained by the police through unauthorized search and seizure is not admissible in a court of law. This is the so-called exclusionary rule, known by the motto "the fruit of the poisonous tree," hence, evidence gathered in a way deemed to violate the due process rights of suspects (particularly with regard to the Fourth Amendment right against illegal search and seizure) must be excluded from criminal trial. To get around this requirement, police have been known to claim that evidence (say drugs) gathered against a suspect was not produced as a result of a search, but was in plain sight, for example, because the suspect dropped the drugs on the ground while running from the police. This gives police officers unhealthy incentives to lie about the true nature of searches and interrogations, and more innocent persons could be caught in the net of legal control as a result.[10] There has also been a steady expansion of the Good Faith Exception, whereby evidence gathered illegally may still be used in court if the police officer acted in "good faith" in the presenting of a warrant (Davis 1997).

Fourth, perhaps it is the case that rules seeking to restrict discretion simply move it around, or displace it to some other actors in the criminal justice system. Walker (1993, pp. 15–16) discusses how limits on plea bargaining may shift the discretion "upstream" to the police or "downstream" to the judge, and there is some evidence to support that this is in fact happening. To what extent it is happening with regard to the targeting of police discretion specifically is a question that deserves further investigation.

Discretion and Hot Spots Policing

One particular area that is ripe for further analysis of the control of discretion in policing is the practice of police hot spotting. Hot spotting is the concentrating of "police surveillance and enforcement efforts at a particular location that is 'hot' with undesirable activity (e.g., drug dealing)" (Mastrofski 2004, p. 112). Mastrofski (2004) goes on to explain that hot spotting comes in either a low- or high-discretion version. In the low-discretion model of hot spotting, decisions about where to send patrol or beat officers are made by supervisors and other higher-ups in the police administration. The high-discretion version, on the other hand, allows patrol officers to decide where the hot spots are within their own beats. The highest form of discretion would represent a problem-oriented policing approach, where officers would be responsible not only for patrolling their beats, but also gathering information about trouble areas and fashioning interventions for dealing with the problem. Indeed, this is the SARA model of problem-oriented policing mentioned earlier in the book, namely, scanning (check to see what problems there are), analysis (consider possible ways of dealing with the problems identified), response (implement a plan for the specific problems targeted), and assessment (evaluate whether the intervention was successful; see Eck 2006).

Even in the low-discretion model of hot spotting, where the administration decides where the hot spots are rather than the beat officer, there nevertheless could be opportunities for officer discretion and proactivity. Specifically, under some versions of low-discretion hot spotting, it is not specifically mandated what sorts of activities officers engage in once they arrive at the hot spot. They are asked merely to keep logs tracking time spent at the hot-spot location. Hence, a higher level of discretion even in the low-discretion model would allow officers at the hot spot to choose tactics they deem most helpful for the problems at hand. Research could be conducted as to how well goals are being achieved given the various levels of discretion officers have at their disposal in different hot-spot models.

For example, say there has been a string of burglaries in a particular neighborhood. The police department has identified this neighborhood as a burglary hot spot. The department decides to send additional officers to patrol these beats, relying simply on officer presence to deter burglaries. The extra officers sent out on these beats are asked to do nothing special, but simply to engage in directed automobile patrol in the designated areas. In another version, extra officers are sent out to the hot-spot areas, and asked to spend thirty minutes of their shift every two hours on foot patrol along particular streets which have experienced burglaries. While out on foot patrol, officers of course are given full discretion to deal with incidents as they see fit. Finally, a third version would send additional officers to the hot spot and make home visits to conduct needs assessments with the residents of the area. Simultaneous with these directed activities, heavier foot patrols would be targeted at houses suffering repeat burglaries, as well as stationing more patrol officers along escape routes leading out from the neighborhood.[11]

The first condition could be operationalized as low officer discretion, the second medium officer discretion, and the third high discretion. Data would be gathered as to the effectiveness of cessation or deterrence activities during the period of the intervention (typically, looking at the burglary rates before, during, and after the intervention). Assessment of officer discretion in relation to hot-spotting outcomes could be conducted on all manner of criminal problems. One thing that must be kept in mind is that outcomes in hot spotting seem to improve with implementation of diverse responses (Eck 2006, p. 125), such as was described in the case of the third version of burglary hot spotting mentioned above. This does not pose a methodological dilemma, however, because diversity or range of interventions can simply be one of the variables included in the analysis.

Finally, it should be noted that unlike the Kansas City Preventive Patrol Experiment conducted in the early 1970s which found high levels of crime displacement as a result of saturation patrols through hot spotting, later research by Sherman and Weisburd (1995) and Weisburd and Braga (2006) found that preventive patrols and hot spotting can be effective without producing high levels of crime displacement. One of the breakthroughs, in terms of improved outcomes in hot spotting, was the discovery that intervention efforts should be concentrated on repeat victims or in areas where many repeat victims reside.[12] Because persons who suffer repeat crime victimizations tend to hold even more negative views toward the police than persons not serially victimized, urban police departments which are attempting to help persons in these communities must be especially sensitive to citizen concerns about not only crime but also increased police presence. A community-oriented or problem-oriented approach, emphasizing foot patrols where officers gain a modicum of trust from and familiarity with residents, would presumably set the stage for successful hot-spotting outcomes in these neighborhood, especially if citizen feedback indicated a need for such directed patrols.

NOTES

[1] My understanding of the nature of discretion among criminal justice personnel has been informed from a variety of sources, some of which are specified in this note. For literature on discretion in the criminal justice system in general, I have drawn on Hawkins (2003). For literature on discretion among corrections personnel, I have drawn upon Liebling (2000) and Liebling and Price (2003). For discretion among court personnel, I have drawn primarily from Gabbay (1973). And for discretion among policing personnel, I have drawn upon Arcuri (1977), Seron et al. (2004), and Wortley (2003). Additional items will of course be cited in the chapter.

[2] A word of caution is needed here. As Gouldner (1954) and many other scholars have pointed out, no matter how formally an organization is structured, there will always be informal elements operating within the organization. In other words, formality does not and cannot squeeze informality out entirely. Nevertheless, I would suggest police organizations are special to the extent that informal systems of rules may be as important, and often more important, than the official, formal rules (see, e.g., Ericson 2007).

[3] This is taken from the document "Kenosha Police Department Policy and Procedure Manual: Patrol," available at http://kenoshapolice.com/UserFiles/File/Policy%20and%20Procedure%20Manual/Chapter%2041%20%20Patrol/41.1%20Patrol.pdf.

[4] See "McDonald's Out of Nuggets; Woman Calls Police," available at http://www.wptv.com/content/tcoast/story/McDonalds-out-of-nuggets-woman-calls-police/AqFDuKVxkEKDMopvIc4LWQ.cspx.

[5] Although it is widely accepted that the problem with the police is that they tend to apply too much force given an opportunity to do so, newer research indicates this is not the case at all. Wolf et al. (2009) found that police officers are actually operating with a force deficit, and that levels of force exerted by them are consistently less than levels of suspect resistance. This finding should spark further research in this area.

[6] Stroshine et al. (2008) actually came up with twelve categories, but I have eliminated the "other" category for the purposes of this discussion.

[7] There was one missing case along the scheduling dimension, and this is why the percentages do not total 100 in this category.

[8] For information on this and other aspects of speeding in California, see
http://www.speedingticketcentral.com/California-speeding-ticket.html.
[9] For more on the NMA study of Montana's no-speed-limit experiment, see
http://www.motorists.org/pressreleases/home/montana-no-speed-limit-safety-
paradox.
[10] Walker cites Oaks (1970) regarding his discussion of problems with the exclusionary rule. Later research that is consistent with Oaks' findings include
Skogan and Meares (2004), and Pearse and Gudjonsson (1999). Skogan and
Meares (2004) conclude that the great majority of police officers engage in
"lawful policing," yet the few and egregious cases of police misconduct, often
involving the misuse of the extraordinary discretion afforded them, are troubling
and cannot easily be set aside as mere anomalies. It should also be noted that
Peter Moskos (2008), a sociologist, spent fourteen months as a police officer in
Baltimore before resuming his graduate studies at Harvard University. Moskos
experienced all the grit, grime, and turmoil of life in the ghettos of Baltimore,
yet for the most part he came away with the impression that although some cops
are corrupt, the police culture is not.
[11] This was actually a strategy utilized by the Cambridge, UK police department
in its hot-spot efforts against rising burglary rates in the city in the early to mid-
1990s. For a summary of the work of the Cambridge Domestic Burglary Task
Force, see Bennett (1995).
[12] Critics of hot-spot policing, such as Rosenbaum (2006), suggest that positive
outcomes of hot spotting are largely short term, that police sent into these areas
are more likely to be abusive to residents than regular beat cops, and that the
claimed reduction in crime displacement is questionable because of the complex
forms displacement can take (see Lab 2007, pp. 100–101).

7

The Concept of Proactivity: From Indirect Conation to Modern Municipal Policing

To be proactive is to act in ways that either keep unwanted things from occurring (negative proactivity) or promote or make more probable a desired future state of affairs (positive proactivity). As a concept proactivity is championed in a variety of social science and policy arenas, including management and organizational studies, trend analysis and social prediction, public health, small group research, and increasingly across the criminal justice and juvenile justice systems. But where and when did the concept of proactivity begin? This chapter provides an answer to that question, and in so doing ties together a string of intellectual undertakings—running from the 1880s through the 1960s (and beyond)—that heretofore have only been dimly perceived as sharing a lineage. Perhaps surprisingly, the classical innovator of proactivity within sociology is neither Simmel nor Weber nor even Durkheim. Instead, the classical innovator of the concept of proactivity within sociology is the early American sociologist Lester Frank Ward. Since Ward's time the concept of proactivity has continued to be refined and applied in more areas, including most prominently modern municipal policing.

PRELIMINARIES: THE BEGINNINGS OF PROACTIVITY

Although the concept of proactivity proper does not appear in the sociological literature until the 1950s, there were conceptual foundations laid before the turn of the century that paved the way for its later usage. Although he never explicitly used the term "proactive" or "proaction," early American sociologist Lester F. Ward nevertheless developed a typology of action built upon the distinction he made between direct conation (synonymous with "action" or "reaction") and indirect conation (synonymous with the more sophisticated cognitive work involved in what today is referred to as "proaction"). Because Ward's was the first typology of action to conceptualize, from a sociological perspective, what would later come to be called proaction, we will first summarize his system of thought.[1]

The next development along the sociological timeline bearing upon issues of proactivity appears with William F. Ogburn's early efforts at predicting social change and social trends. Beginning in the 1920s Ogburn developed the concept of "cultural lag," and by so doing was attempting to understand how elements of material culture (science and technology especially) impact ideational culture and everyday life (see, e.g., Ogburn 1933a). These studies were and have been broadly concerned with both the benefits, but also the deleterious impact, of science and technology on the family, business and industry, and everyday life. Indeed, modern risk analysis began as a response to the perceived or real hazards of science and technology.

Where initially unwanted events such as accidents, illness, and disease were the focal point of the later public health model of population surveillance and assessment, eventually this medical hazard or risk model was being applied to social phenomena such as deviance and crime. James Short (1984, p. 713) goes so far as to suggest that "The technical aspects of crime management and the management of risks to human health have much in common."

Some terminological issues deserve to be addressed early on. The term *active* is rather straightforward, and it means being engaged in some activity, described as a "doing of the moment," which emphasizes dynamics over statics (see, e.g., Ward 1883, 1895; Small 1895), or agency over structure (Hays 1994; Wharton 1991). Another term, *reactive*, refers to active behavior in response to an earlier action. Reaction is a form of action, but it is always understood in relation to a preceding action or stimulus.

Proactive has been defined somewhat differently by different persons depending on their specific emphasis, but two broad emphases can be specified. In the first, proactive behavior can mean action that takes place to head off unwanted or undesirable future actions. In this sense, proactivity has a negative connotation, in that it is synonymous with preventive actions or behaviors. This negative or preventive connotation of proactivity is often employed in the arenas of public health and, more recently, in criminal justice. The other sense of proactivity has a more positive connotation, in that rather than attempting to negate or forestall a line of unwanted actions or events, the emphasis is on promoting a series of actions which are assumed will have some positive result in the foreseeable future. Although this connotation of proactivity is found in many literatures, it is especially emphasized in management and organizational studies, but also in newer policing approaches such as community policing, problem-oriented policing, and information-led policing.

It should also be emphasized that, rather than a project of theory development or construction, this chapter has the more modest goal of conceptual clarification or history (see, e.g., Farr 2004; Hutcheon 1972; Sprey 1966). The most directly relevant model for this type of study within sociology is Gouldner's (1960) analysis of the concept of reciprocity (Chriss 1999a). Gouldner (1960, p. 162) specified three aims of his paper:

- To indicate the manner in which the concept of reciprocity is tacitly invoked but formally neglected within functionalist theory;
- To clarify the concept and illustrate its diverse uses and applications within sociology; and
- To suggest ways the clarified concept may help to inform central problems of sociological theory, specifically those of stability and instability within social systems.

I follow Gouldner in my specification of the aims of this chapter, which are as follows:

- To indicate the manner in which the concept of proactivity first appeared in sociology, and how it has developed historically both within sociology, criminology, and neighboring disciplines;
- To clarify the concept (for example, the distinction between negative and positive proactivity) and illustrate its diverse uses and applications within sociology, criminology, and neighboring disciplines; and
- To suggest ways the clarified concept may help inform central problems in sociology and criminology, specifically with regard to policing and police operations.

TRUE BEGINNINGS: LESTER F. WARD AND CONATION

Lester F. Ward was a prominent early American sociologist who, for reasons too involved to get into here (but see Chriss 2006), is hardly discussed by sociologists today. Stretching from the publication in 1883 of *Dynamic Sociology* in two volumes to his *Applied Sociology* in 1906, Ward presented a sweeping cosmological vision which promised to reconcile the natural sciences with sociology and other social sciences. Ward's system is naturalistic and positivistic, to the extent that he assumes that social forces are analogous to physical forces, and that all matter—including organic matter and the higher faculties of the human mind—is derived from the cosmos.[2] But rather than being a pure monist, which would have been more in line with the Spencerian evolutionism and naturalism which was in ascendancy during his time, Ward was as much a dualist (Chriss 2008).

How could this be? Ward (1883) argues that there are two causal forces in the universe, which are genetic and teleological. Genetic causation has to do with the movement and change of inorganic bodies as well as organic bodies below the level of human existence. It is assumed that laws of nature work blindly upon such inorganic and organic objects. But when considering the phenomenon of human existence, the original or primordial genetic causation is modified and gives way to teleological causation. As Ward (1883, v. 1, p. 28) states,

To this especial conception, therefore, of man, in his social capacity, seeking to improve society by the exercise of an intelligent foresight, in seizing upon the laws of nature and directing them to the ends which his reason, combined with his acquaintance with these laws, teaches him to be those certain to secure the advantages of society—to this notion let us apply the term *teleology.*

Ward argues that organic matter must have sprung from inorganic matter, and that this new life force or vitalism (protoplasm) somehow arose from a complex combination of chemicals and chemical reactions (elective affinities) which individually were already in place in the original state of nature. The primary social force guiding human existence is feelings or desires, and it is here that Ward makes use of Schopenhauer's notion of the *will.* The lower animals and primitive man were guided by raw passion, a form of will which was largely irrational or, at the very least, which rarely took into account the long-term consequences of action.

In the philosophical parlance running from Locke and Spinoza to Sir William Hamilton and on to Ward, this was known as *conation,* namely, the efforts organisms put forth in seeking the satisfaction of their desires (Ward 1883, v. 2, p. 93). Living organisms below the level of Homo sapiens are, for the most part, trapped in a condition of *direct conation,* meaning that they directly react to stimuli they receive from the environment and other organisms. Granted, some animals below the level of human being—such as foxes—use cunning, stratagem, and reason to obtain desired ends, but these are exceptions rather than the rule. In this sense, direct conation is consistent with behaviorism or the stimulus-response (or S-R) theory of behavior, namely, that organisms will seek activities that are associated with pleasurable stimuli and avoid activities that are associated with painful stimuli.

It was not until the later development of the intellect that *indirect conation* came into view, whereby human beings now focus on the means available for satisfying desires in the (perhaps distant) future rather than on the instant gratification of ends themselves. As Ward stated (1883, v. 2, p. 130),

> The employment of indirect means of gratification commences with the beginning of the rational faculty, and grows in exact proportion to its growth. The two are one and the same. The higher development of this power is marked by the adoption of indirect means of gratification on a wider and increasingly wider scale.

Hence, in the lower animals desires are "present impulses" which impel them into action in direct fashion, while humans, the possessors of intellect, are able to judge and even predict the consequences of their actions. Progress has consisted in the continual expansion and securing of human satisfactions through indirect conation. An increasingly complex array of human actions has arisen from the methods of indirect connation which have been pursued and multiplied over time. It is here that Ward (1883, v. 2, pp. 312–376) presents his classification of human actions, beginning with the two primary departments into which all actions are separated, namely involuntary and voluntary actions.

Because they are implicated in indirect conation much more so than in direct conation, the category of *voluntary actions* will be the focus here. In direct conation, actions are dependent upon conditions, that is, there tends to exist a rote reaction or response to some stimulus. But often in indirect conation, one finds a range of voluntary actions whereby persons seek to disguise the fact that actions flow from antecedent causes. One strategy employed here includes *eccentric* actions, namely, actions performed by an individual which are unexpected or not readily anticipated. Another widely used strategy is *deception*, namely, the overt attempt to mask the intentions of one's actions. (Notice, for example, that one of the major categories of proactive policing is undercover or vice work, where deception is used routinely in "stings" and similar operations.)

A large subcategory of voluntary actions consists of *deliberative* or ideo-motor actions. As opposed to merely impulsive or sensori-motor actions, deliberative actions involve the cognitive functioning of the human brain. Influenced by Kant and Spencer, Ward is a sensationalist when it comes to explaining consciousness. The phenomena of mind belong to two distinct classes, namely, those of feelings and those of intellect. For Ward, (1893, p. 125) the department of feeling is *subjective psychology*, while that of the intellect is *objective psychology*. Impressions of objects on nerves produce sensations, some of which humans are consciously aware, others of which they are not. Intensive sensations may be pleasurable or painful (the classic pleasure–pain calculus of utilitarianism), while indifferent sensations may be conscious or unconscious.

While subjective psychology relates to the intensive sensations, objective psychology results from indifferent sensations. Encountering everyday objects, whether persons, animals, or inanimate objects, often produces indifferent sensations to the extent that they evoke neither pleasure nor pain, but simply "are." These indifferent sensations are percepts, meaning that information is stored in the brain regarding the nature of these things encountered by human beings. Receiving notions about things are acts of perception, which become permanently registered in the brain, with of course the possibility of modification as experiences with these and similar objects dictate. These perceptions are combined, grouped, compared, and classified over the course of our lives, first giving rise to judgments, then to various forms of thinking and reasoning characteristic of advanced stages of human existence. This process constitutes objective psychology, or the phenomena of the intellect (Ward 1893, p. 126).

In sum, the ends of indirect conation are assured through the rational faculty of the intellect seated in the objective mind, and actions that work to secure such ends are described as deliberative and dynamic. As Ward (1883, v.2, p. 378) explains,

> Dynamical actions are distinguished from statical actions in proceeding
> according to the indirect, or intellectual, method of conation instead of

the direct, or physical, method. All actions consist in efforts to attain desired ends. In all, the end is present to the mind before the action is attempted. In statical actions the movements of the agent are made in straight lines toward the end. In dynamical actions they are not so made, but may proceed in any other direction. In statical actions the end is sought *immediately*. Nothing intervenes between the act and the end, between the agent and the object. In dynamical action ends are sought *mediately*. There intervenes between the action and the end a third something which is called a *means*.

Ward goes on to argue that the indirect method of conation possesses vast and incalculable advantages over the direct method, and it is the indirect method that accounts for human social progress. For example, a man may seek to directly alleviate his hunger by killing a small animal, thus preserving a single life. As knowledge of nature and society and the understanding of how to apply the principles of this knowledge increase, collective ends are secured that allow for social progress of the collectivity, not simply preservation of the individual. Inventions represent the most important class of actions associated with the indirect method of conation. For example, the invention of the plow dramatically increased the human ability to produce food, thus allowing the human species to multiply and to secure dominion over the animal kingdom and the rest of nature (Ward 1883, v. 2, p. 383).

In developing the notion of indirect conation, whereby dynamic and indirect forms of action may be strung together across space and time in complex sequences to achieve desired ends, Ward was also describing what decades later would be referred to as proaction or proactivity. Before the term actually surfaces, however, another link in the conceptual chain appears in the work of William F. Ogburn, whose work we next turn to.

OGBURN AND THE PROJECT OF SOCIAL PREDICTION

As we have seen, the conceptual groundwork for what later would be termed proactivity was laid first by Ward beginning in the early 1880s.[3] It would take a few more decades for William F. Ogburn—a student of Franklin H. Giddings at Columbia University—to apply the method of indirect conation to the project of predicting social change and social trends. Ogburn's (1922) work on "cultural lag" in the 1920s was ostensibly an attempt to understand how elements of material culture (science and technology) impact ideational culture and everyday life. Indeed, later futurology studies by Alvin Toffler (the author of *Future Shock*) and others were influenced by Ogburn.

Ogburn argued that continuing and profound changes in modern society brought about by scientific and technological advances—such as automation in the workplace, the mass production of the automobile, and new communications technologies—were leading to disruptions and strains across society. Ideas change quickly in comparison to slow, gradual biological evolution. In essence culture cut the ties between biology (Spencer's superorganism) and sociology

(Ogburn 1937). In conditions of relatively rapid change, parts of the whole may be out of synch. Some parts change rapidly, while others more slowly. Inventions represent diffusion of innovation and can instigate rapid change, while the social structures already in place change not nearly as rapidly (if at all). This is Ogburn's cultural lag thesis.

The changes in the family in particular, and in society more generally, were perceived as so monumental and alarming that in 1929 President Herbert Hoover assembled a group of eminent social, behavioral, and natural scientists to conduct a national survey of social trends in the United States. The President's Research Committee on Social Trends, headed by Ogburn as research director (Bannister 1987, p. 179), published their report in 1933 in a volume titled *Recent Social Trends in the United States*. In his chapter on "The Family and Its Functions," Ogburn (1929, 1933b; see also Burgess and Locke 1945) showed how the family as an institution was slowly and inexorably losing many of its functions. One of the earliest and most profound changes was the loss (or at least the diminution) of the family's economic functions. With the continual expansion of industrial capitalism, and the concomitant shift from a largely rural to a largely urban society, the family shifted from being a production unit (especially, for example, in the case of the small family farm) to a consumption unit. The family was losing other functions as well, such as its protective role (which governmental law enforcement largely had taken over), its educational functions, and its religious functions (Ogburn 1933b, p. 662).[4]

Influenced by Ogburn, the project of social prediction accelerated during the 1940s. For example, Walter Reckless (1941) argued that sociologists could conduct actuarial studies of social problems, whereby the risk of various categories of persons implicated in such problems could be ascertained. This would provide sociologists a purchase on predicting outcomes, a model which had yet to be fully realized (circa 1941) following from Ogburn and other Chicago School studies from the 1920s and 1930s. Although these studies were largely concerned with predicting criminal behavior, recidivism, and youth problems resulting from family decline or dysfunction, the approach could be extended to predicting virtually all social problems. Actuarial prediction would be by cases—who, not how many. Reckless noted that such data should already be available from social service reporting agencies in the areas of child welfare, probation, and delinquency.

One of the things Ogburn had stressed in his work on cultural lag is that every technological advance creates new social problems. It is therefore imperative to improve prediction regarding the potentially deleterious impact of various innovations, since these are only expected to proliferate and accelerate in our technologically-advancing world. Talcott Parsons (1946), taking the implications of Ogburn's work seriously, stressed that the then newly formed National Science Foundation (NSF) ought to fund the social sciences as a top priority. From Parsons' perspective, given the social ramifications on an increasingly technologized world, this only made sense. Parsons was one of the most vigorous proponents of the welfare state, and he did as much as anyone to ensure federal funding—through the NSF as well as other sources—for sociological research.

Also, in these rapidly changing times there would likely continue to be more disagreements over the interpretation of family roles and values than ever before. Following from Ogburn—by way of Spencer, Ward, and Giddings—heterogeneity leads to cultural change which leads in turn to family conflict. The changes in family functions are symptomatic of broader changes and cultural clashes affecting the social system more broadly. To keep families intact in the face of such sweeping change, F. Ivan Nye (1955) argued that sociologists must act proactively to head off further erosions of the stability of the family. Among Nye's suggestions was taking a family "values inventory," to ascertain exactly where and on what topics family roles are most in conflict. The most immediate goal of such proactive research is better prediction of compatibility between potentially marrying couples so as to stem the tide of rising divorce rates.

PROACTIVITY IN THE 1950s AND 1960s: SMALL GROUP AND COMMUNICATONS RESEARCH

At about the same time that marital and family therapy—as well as other social services—were expanding during the 1950s and 1960s, explicit mentions of proactivity began appearing in the communications and small group research literature. Much of this impetus grew out of Robert F. Bales's studies of small group interaction (most notably Bales 1950). Nearly simultaneous with Bales, Henry A. Murray (1951) provided a definitional distinction between proactive and reactive behaviors.

Behavior directed towards distal goals—receiving a Ph.D., composing a symphony, educating a son—requires planning, directing, and foresight. It is serial behavior. Rather than confronting an external stimulus directly (as in S-R theory), it is stimuli from within being created and responded to in serial fashion. This is proaction. *This is also a nearly exact recapitulation of Ward's notion of indirect conation, of which Murray, Bales, and virtually all other sociologists were unaware.* It is not homeostatic, that is, merely returning the organism to a previous state. Instead, if successful proaction results in something additional: better construction, money in the bank, greater social cohesion. Directing proactions toward distal goals inhibits impulses toward immediate gratification, hence it is an aspect of self-control. Murray (1951, pp. 439–440) further argued that proactions by leaders seeking goals, with followers reacting in predictable ways, lead to more predictability and control throughout the system more generally.

In his 1953 chapter in the volume *Working Papers in the Theory of Action* (co-authored with Talcott Parsons and Edward Shils), Bales returned as well to the issue of control. In small group settings influencing the action of each other is best facilitated through proaction, or serial actions of one person oriented toward goals. In proaction, the actions taken by one person act as the stimulus for the next serial response by the same person.[5] Instead of reactivity this is proactivity, and a chain of connected actions build up concerted plans of action which are an improvement over ad hoc or random reactions on the part of a multiplicity of actors. Proaction is serial activity of one person that produces (ideally) preferred reactions from others. In

Bales's (1953, p. 130) studies higher ranking "men" (all his subjects at Harvard were men) tended to be more proactive, while those lower ranked tended to act more reactively. "Leaders"—instrumental but also emotional—initiated actions most often, and were judged to have the best ideas, which in turn were more likely to be accepted and implemented by group members.

More small group research, influenced by the notion of proactivity, which was developed in Bales' work, appeared during the 1960s. For example, George Psathas (1960) applied and extended Bales' phase movement system to a study of problem solving in small groups. Psathas observed that members of experimental small groups attempt to solve problems of orientation ("what is it?") before attempting to solve problems of evaluation ("how do we feel about it?"), while even later attempting to solve problems of control ("what shall we do about it?"; Psathas 1960, p. 177). If balance or equilibrium in groups is to be achieved, actions and reactions must be balanced. Consistent with both Bales and Murray, Psathas viewed proaction as a series of acts generated by the same individual, while reaction is an act following the act of another person.

The notion of proactivity in small group research was similarly employed by James Davis in a 1961 paper. Davis (1961) found that within small discussion groups someone would invariably take on a proactive task role which he referred to as a "fuel role." Fuel roles are proactive task roles, whereby persons provide fuel for discussion by introducing ideas and opinions for the rest of the group to consider. Such persons—so-called "leaders"—are judged by others to be effective and valuable members of the team.

MESO- AND MACRO-LEVELS

During the 1960s and 70s the concept of proactivity began being applied at the meso-level (e.g., organizations) and the macro-level (e.g., institutions or social systems). In management and organization studies, for example, the idea of "proactive management" or the "proactive organization" (see Crant 2000) appears, emphasizing a vision for the future which facilitates staying one step ahead of competition in the turbulent world of markets and organizational competition. Particularly emblematic of this movement of thought is Hirsch's (1972) paper on the proactive organization and how a special social type—the contact man—arises within the arts and entertainment industry specifically to meet the functional needs of the organization. Although this argument cannot be elaborated here, in the next chapter we will explain how Hirsch's view of the "contact man" is consistent with how police are conceptualized under community policing and beyond, namely, as proactive, boundary-spanning multitaskers.

Another interesting use of proactivity couched at the macro-level, as opposed to the micro-level of small group or individual behavior, is Charles Tilley's (1976) study of collective action in Western Europe taking place between 1500 and 1975. According to Tilley, collective action can take one of three broad forms: competitive, proactive, and reactive. Competitive actions involve laying claims to resources that other groups feel they are either entitled to or legitimately control. These other groups are then viewed as rivals or competitors. Reactive social action may follow from competition, but not always. Reactivity in this sense often appears as group efforts to reassert the validity of claims when other groups violate or challenge them (Tilley 1976, p. 367), such as when dispossessed persons attempt to reclaim land from a government that they believe was rightfully theirs to begin with.

On the other hand, proactive claims reflect new sorts of claims which previously have not been exercised. Again, innovation is emphasized here, as in striking for higher wages (Tilley 1976, p. 368). Other proactive collective forms include the demonstration, the petition drive, and sponsored public meetings. These become observable only when mass electoral politics is institutionalized in a society. In earliest times competitive actions dominated, then later reactive, then even later beginning in the nineteenth century, proactive forms emerged and began to predominate over the other forms.

PROACTIVITY AND PUBLIC HEALTH

One of the clearest and most forceful articulations of proactive policy is embodied in the broad public health model of social problems. In its most general form, the public health approach includes "both the art and the science of preventing disease, prolonging life, and promoting health" (Weisheit and Klofas 1998, p. 198). Since the 1980s law enforcement has been moving toward a more explicit emphasis on proactivity, and the models for community-oriented policing (COP) and problem-oriented policing (POP) appear to replicate or mimic the typology of social interventions previously developed within the field of public health, as intimated by Short (1984) above.

From the public health perspective, both the earlier models of punishment and rehabilitation (or treatment) were reactive in that they dealt with criminals or clients only after their offending or problematic behaviors came to light or were "diagnosed." Although public health proponents acknowledge that interventions aimed at rehabilitating defendants/clients who have already offended is an improvement over the criminal justice emphasis on punishment for the sake of deterrence, retribution, or justice, the treatment model does not go far enough. Rather than intervention, the public health model's primary objective is *prevention*, which is, ensuring that the disease never arises in the first place (see, e.g., Guetzloe [1992] and McMahon [2000]).

This idea may be illustrated by examining the tripartite classification of prevention strategies typical of public health (see Prothrow-Stith 1993). These three stages or strategies of prevention are summarized below.

- **Tertiary prevention**—Encompasses all those strategies designed to keep persons who are already ill from becoming sicker. This is the classic "reactive" approach to social and health problems.
- **Secondary prevention**—Involves the early identification of those who already have symptoms of some disease. At-risk profiles, generated

from heightened surveillance of the target population, help to determine who good candidates for early intervention are. Secondary prevention represents a mix of reactive and proactive approaches.

- **Primary prevention**—Focuses on stopping some problem behavior before it starts, the overall goal of which is to reduce health problems in the general population. Strategies may include educational and public information campaigns, changing the environment (or organization, or institution), immunizing potential hosts or victims, etc. These approaches are characterized as "proactive."

In a variety of literatures (business, medicine, public health, social and behavioral sciences, social and criminal justice policy) the assumption is being made more and more that reactivity is "bad" while "proactivity" is good, or at least to be favored over reactivity. Further, this new impulse towards risk profiling seeks to act "proactively," locating persons (or groups of persons) who are merely "at risk" for perpetrating some unwanted behavior, even if they have not broken the law. Although a number of scholars argue that criminal justice ought to strive even more diligently to base its operations upon the model of public health (see, e.g., Burris 2006; Lab 2007; Rosenfeld and Decker 1993), there is certainly at least one negative consequence of this form of proactivity. As the public health model is applied to more areas of operation the problem of net widening will be exacerbated, as more and more persons are pulled into the orbit of the formal system (whether the criminal justice system, the juvenile justice system, the public health or behavioral health systems for purposes of observing or surveilling populations, or even business or organizational oversight, for example, "employee assistance programs"). According to the logic of medicine and public health, if mistakes are made, it is much more preferable to diagnose a well person as sick than to diagnose a sick person as well. This is the classic Type II error, a systematic bias within medicine, risk analysis, and by extension criminal justice, which produces large numbers of false positives (see Chriss 2007b). This has especially important implications for the operation of the criminal justice system in general and the police subsystem in particular.

PROACTIVE POLICING: A BEGINNING

As the public health model was gaining more and more momentum during the 1970s and into the 1980s, around this same time, somewhat before the dawning of community policing in the 1980s, the concept of police proactivity came to the fore (see, e.g., Sun 2003). The literature seemed to indicate something was "in the air" with regards to the application of this model to policing and the criminal justice system.

The first article specifically on crime that mentions proactivity was published in 1966 in the *American Journal of Sociology*. The authors, David Bordua and Albert J. Reiss, Jr., noted that in the movement to professionalize municipal policing, the local hierarchical command structure (the classic quasi-military organizational structure of the typical police department) was being replaced by a system of decentralized command whereby, for example, police officers out in the field were responsible for providing information to, and inter-preting information being sent out by, a communications or dispatch center. Ra-ther than a command function per se, newer generations of municipal policing perform more of an adjudicatory function, having to make decisions out in the field based upon "best practices" configured by information flows to and from the communications system. Traditional local and hierarchical command-and-control systems best fit a reactive strategy of responding to citizen calls for assistance on a more or less ad hoc, case-by-case basis. On the other hand, a "professionalized" decision-making model of policing lends itself more to a proactive strategy. As Bordua and Reiss (1966, p. 72) explain, "Vice requires an essentially proactive strategy of policing in the modern metropolis, whereas the citizens' command for service demands an essentially reactive strategy and tactics."

This early treatment of proactivity as it applies to municipal policing was ambivalent about the actual extent of discretion enjoyed by uniformed officers out in the field. With upgrading of training and educational requirements for their of-ficers on the way to the development of community policing, a decentralized, in-formation-led style of policing would imply that officers could be trusted with more discretion since they are released from the centralized command-and-control restrictions typical of the older model of policing. Yet, professionalization per se could also mean that officers are now "snappy bureaucrats" (Klockars 1980) who are held in check by a growing list of organizational mandates (embodied in the so-called "standard operating procedures" manual). It was this possibility that led Bordua and Reiss (1966, p. 72) to proclaim that "police organizations become 'professionalized,' not their members."

I would suggest, however, that Bordua and Reiss formulated their in-sights about police professionalization at the tail end of an "early" professionali-zation era that ran from the 1920s until the late 1960s. By the 1970s and espe-cially by the early 1980s a more advanced era of "professionalization" emerged under community- and problem-oriented policing (see Chriss 2007b, pp. 95–98). This was reflected, for example, in a paper Reiss co-authored with Donald Black (a student of Reiss's), which was published in *American Sociological Review* in 1970. Here the authors (Black and Reiss 1970, p. 66) established two basic types of police mobilization. One is *citizen-initiated*, which reflects the traditional reactive approach to policing whereby police are available to respond to citizen reports and calls for assistance. The other is *police-initiated*, a form of proactive mobilization in which police take the initiative to investigate situations or make arrests.

Black (1970) expanded on this a few months later in the same journal, explaining that proactive police operations predominate in conditions where there is no clear or specific complainant. This means that, at least initially, proactive policing is contained within specialized police units such as the vice or morals division, the narcotics squad, or the traffic division. Because most crimes occur at specific times and places which typically cannot be predicted, police must rely on citizen reports (namely, reactive mobilization). This means that much normal crime goes undetected, and clearance rates (depending on the nature of the crime) are relatively low. However, with police-initiated mobilization, there is virtual simultaneity between detection of the violation and the person committing it. As Black (1970, p. 735) explains, "In effect, the proactive clearance rate is 100%." A positive side effect of this, of course, is that proactive policing is associated with better outcomes, at least in terms of improved clearance rates. This in turn makes it easy for police organizations to identify proactive operations as representing the cutting edge of improvements in strategies and tactics, but also in the quality of personnel carrying out such operations.

By the late 1970s the distinction between proactive and reactive policing was well established (see, e.g., Teasley 1978). As will be discussed more fully below, in community policing one aspect of proactive policing involves the continual upgrading of aggressive law enforcement practices—addressing so-called "quality of life" issues (see Sun 2003)—including saturation patrols, crackdowns, field interrogations, and sting operations. Beyond just the "feel good" role of police in the community to shore up police–community relations (the service orientation where police act as much or more like social workers) there is also a very aggressive and punitive side to proactivity (stopping crimes presumably before they happen; seeking "root causes" of crime; see, e.g., Manning 1997; McConville and Mirsky 1995). This is merely indicative of the two emphases that proactivity can take on as described earlier in the chapter, namely, promoting positive or wanted results on the one hand, or forestalling negative or unwanted results on the other. A brief sampling of the literature on police proactivity, beyond the earliest works of Black and Reiss already mentioned, will help to illustrate this distinction further.

NEGATIVE AND POSITIVE POLICE PROACTIVITY

One way this appears is in the idea that police may be described as learning organizations. According to Brown and Brudney (2003), police organizations are now viewing their line staff—patrol officers—as knowledge workers who can act proactively to solve problems and thereby reduce crime and disorder in the communities they serve. Information technologies are touted as an important path toward fulfilling this idea of police as knowledge workers. A requirement, then, is to identify the ways in which end users (the police) might possibly identify and utilize knowledge and information technologies available to them to engage in this sort of problem solving. This is especially important because in turbulent environments (the public spaces that police enter in their routine patrols) it is vital to link up end users with the appropriate skills and knowledge base (see de Lint 2003). Yet in focus group studies conducted by the authors, the police identified the most useful information to be data already collected from the past, not projections for anticipating or predicting future courses of action. This may very well represent the real-world limitations of proactivity in policing, as well as the gap in conceptualizing proactivity (from the scholarly side) and attempting to implement proactivity as a policy initiative, "best practice," or demand structure for police organizations.

In an interesting study, Ankony and Kelley (1999) found that as officers' level of community alienation increases, their willingness to engage in proactive enforcement decreases. The authors define proactive enforcement as the active commitment of officers to crime prevention, community problem solving, and heightened police–community reciprocity and partnership (p. 121).

This tendency toward alienation among police with regard to proactive enforcement, however, has much to do with the nature of the community being served (see, e.g., Nolan et al. 2005). When citizen attitudes toward the police are generally favorable (such as in rural areas or small towns), citizens will tend to rate as more important and legitimate certain proactive police enforcement strategies such as conducting drug sweeps and investigation of gang activity (Benedict et al. 1999; Webb and Katz 1997, p. 19). When tensions between police and citizens are high, such as in urban areas with a concentration of poor, minority citizens, proactive policing strategies will tend to be viewed in a highly negative light (see, e.g., Brunson 2007; Brunson and Miller 2006; Mastrofski 2006).

Jackson and Wade (2005) argue that social capital—the quality and extent of informal ties between members of a community—impacts police behavior as well as police perceptions of their level of responsibility for the communities they serve. If community social capital is high, police presume residents can solve problems in their community more informally. In communities with low social capital, police may perceive that they must take it upon themselves to prevent crime, thus being more committed to proactive policing. In sum, when police sense of responsibility for the community is high, there will tend also to be a higher level of commitment to proactive, aggressive policing.

Demands for police to "get tough" on crime means police are placed into a preventive role as well as a reactive role. Examples of this sort of proactive policing aimed at forestalling unwanted behaviors include "more stop-and-frisk contacts, requesting proof of identification more frequently, conducting more drug sweeps, and dispersing citizens who gather to protest public policies of various sorts" (Jackson and Wade 2005, p. 51). Findings indicate that to the extent that police perceive that the community they serve has low social capital, they will use their own resources to solve and prevent crime, since they can't count on citizens to do their fair share of informal control. Police resources in this case are the powers of arrest, reflecting their law enforcement (coercive) powers more generally as stipulated by Bittner (1970). Police who view their geographical territory as characterized by low social capital will feel a sense of personal responsibility to do something, much more so than in higher social capital communities (this finding is also supported by Skogan [2006a]). The amount of crime in the community is still the best predicator of police proactive behavior. Here, police proactivity is viewed negatively, in terms of negative views by largely low-income citizens who view police tactics as overly punitive, invasive, and authoritarian (Weitzer 2000).

This negative aspect of proactive policing is also illustrated in Novak et al.'s (2003) study of aggressive policing. Proactivity combined with higher discretion for street-level officers makes it somewhat more difficult to monitor their activities. Yet, holding out the possibility of civil litigation against officers as a check may reduce police officers' proactivity, which most citizens value under community- and problem-oriented policing. In the police subculture officers learn to be not overly aggressive, to lay low and "cover their ass" (Van Maanen 1974). Liability issues, however, influenced police actions less than anticipated. This is because there is only a modest relationship between attitudes and actions. Liability issues are more likely to influence officers' attitudes, and to a lesser extent their actions.

On the positive side of proactivity, Meliala (2001) has analyzed the extent to which policing under the community-oriented or problem-oriented models could be characterized as sensitive to the needs of the citizens whom they are sworn to serve and protect. In order for police to work collaboratively with citizens to solve community problems, screening and recruitment procedures within police organizations must emphasize the police skills of human relations, including sensitivity toward the public and its needs. Sensitivity is the ability to understand people and social groups in general (Meliala 2001, p. 100). Although sensitivity appears in line with new community-policing mandates, it does not require organizational change, such as what was suggested under broken windows and reorientation of police back to foot patrol. Sensitivity seeks to find a middle ground between the binary opposites of conventional and community-oriented policing.

Sensitive policing is also consistent with the current emphasis on multiculturalism, acknowledging the uniqueness of membership in particular groups, but also the universal features group members share with all other persons. Implementing sensitive policing must simultaneously address the individual level, the group level (e.g., the police subculture), and the organizational level (the structure and policies of the police department). In reality, however, this is difficult to implement because policing is characterized by multiple tasks and purposes existing side-by-side, sometimes in conflict. For example, sometimes sensitivity has to give way to raw use of force (the law enforcement role). How and when sensitivity may inform other role tasks is an empirical issue which requires further analysis.

One other way that police proactivity may be perceived in a positive light is the kind of security work that police are being called on to perform since the 9-11 terrorist attacks. Similar to Loader's (2006) notion of "ambient policing," Innes (2006) refers to this particular strategy or preoccupation as "reassurance policing," whereby police make themselves highly visible, through strategically locating themselves in the community and conducting media campaigns, to let the citizenry know that they, the local or municipal police forces, are doing all they can to protect the community against terrorist threats. Of course, not all segments of the population are reassured with this heightened call for police security. The negative aspects of aggressive policing evident in urban communities especially with regard to racial profiling shifts to the problem of religious profiling of persons of Middle Eastern descent and/or the Muslim faith under what some are now referring to as post 9-11 policing.[6]

SUMMARY AND CONCLUSION

With careful attention to selected literatures within sociology and related social and policy sciences over the past 130 years, an unmistakable trend in human action and social organization becomes apparent. This is the inexorable movement away from "mere" reaction and toward more highly valued forms of proaction. Keeping in mind several of the caveats mentioned above, this trend lends itself to an ideal typical categorization over six specific time periods.

The first period, launched in the 1880s, represents Lester Ward's distillation of broader philosophical and evolutionary currents of thought in the service of establishing sociology as a scientific discipline. Ward's work was couched at a grand, some would say cosmological, level of analysis, and there were few hints given at this time as to its empirical application or utility (although Ward did attempt to do just this with the publication of his 1906 book *Applied Sociology*). Ward's great innovation was a theory of action which specified the movement from direct conation (reactivity) to indirect conation (proactivity) all of which was made possible through the evolutionary upgrading of the human intellect, which now acts as the directive or cybernetic agent for the great engine of all life, namely the passions.

The second period, beginning in the 1920s, was led most notably by William Ogburn's program of social prediction, especially with regard to the impact of technological innovations on human society.

The third period arose about a generation later, in the 1940s. This represents the refinement of a social problems agenda, whereby social prediction is expanded into the realm of human relations as opposed to the previous era's exclusive focus on the deleterious impact of technology on society and the types of cultural lag which may result. Here especially, more sophisticated delinquency prevention programs appear based upon the systematic collection of data from social service agencies as well as standalone projects, many of which were conducted by researchers at the University of Chicago. There is also an explicit attempt to shore up what is perceived to be a decline in informal control, especially as this involves the family institution.

The fourth period begins in the 1950s. Because the family was the focus of much of the attention of researchers in the previous decade, a conceptual orientation toward small groups was already in place, although now it was being applied not necessarily or exclusively to primary groups but also to secondary groups. One of the overriding issues of this era was conducting systematic studies of the emergence of leaders in small groups, represented most forcefully in Bales's small group research. This is also the period in which the concept of proactivity proper, as applied to sociological rather than to psychological concerns, appears.

The fifth period covers the 1960s and 1970s, represented by a shift to meso- and macro-levels of analysis. The trend toward proactivity that was theorized in earlier eras, often with little or no empirical content, was now being applied to particular world historical configurations (such as in Tilley's work), but also to professional undertakings such as public health, management, and organizational analysis. It is here also that clear distinctions emerge between negative and positive proactivity, such as in the public health agendas of pre-venting disease (which appeared first) and promoting health.[7]

Finally, the sixth era began in the 1980s, represented by the massive movement toward proactivity in policing. Although incipient elements of crime prevention were evident all the way back to the beginning of munici-pal policing in the 1830s—in the guise of random preventive patrols, for example—overwhelmingly policing up to this most recent period had been reactive, relying for the most part on citizen calls for help. This meant that for policing any proactivity that did appear was overwhelmingly that of neg-ative proactivity (crime prevention). But under community policing and va-riants such as problem-oriented policing, greater emphasis is being placed upon police collaboration with citizens and other stakeholders and organiza-tions in the community ostensibly to attack "root causes" of crime and de-viance. Indeed, police are not only acting like social workers; more recently under the auspices of positive proactivity, where promotion of the good be-comes an even more explicit focus than the prevention of the bad, they are also acting like sociologists, in effect making the case that policing is an applied social science which requires and even demands advanced training and education of its line staff.

The trend toward a continuing upgrading and refinement of proactive policing will likely continue, especially with the emergence on the positive side of such variants as information-led policing and data analysis orientations (such as CompStat); on the negative side with such innovations as post 9-11 policing; and of mixed approaches such as pulling levers and third-party policing (for discus-sions of the latter two, see Kennedy [2006] and Mazerolle and Ransley [2006]).

NOTES

[1] Although Weber's typology of social action is much better known, it came much later in time than Ward's earliest writings on the subject. Also, some would ask, "Why not Marx, Freud, or other better-known classical thinkers?" The response is that, I am concerned with tracing out the development of proac-tivity among specifically sociological thinkers, that is, thinkers who self-consciously worked as sociologists and were attempting to contribute to sociology as a specific disciplinary enterprise. Although most of Marx's writ-ings preceded Ward, Marx was not a sociologist and never developed his ideas as a self-conscious effort to contribute to the development of sociology. Like-wise for Freud, who was a psychiatrist not a sociologist. In addition, most of Freud's pertinent writings came after 1883, the year in which Ward published *Dynamic Sociology*. There are justifications for choosing Ward over all other possible sociologists or thinkers whom some may argue are or were relevant to the sociological enterprise, but this would be an exhaustive undertaking which would simply take us too far afield.

[2] Ward (1883) was the first sociologist to develop a theory of the social forces. Although Ward died in 1913, his influence was still being felt by the time of the establishment of the *Journal of Social Forces* in 1922. Early American sociologist Franklin Giddings (1922) wrote the inaugural article for the journal, and although he agreed with editor Howard Odum (1922) that a new era of specialization was dawning within sociology, he nevertheless acknowledged Ward's pioneering, albeit cosmological and grand, work on the social forces, writing: "To cite an item that recurs in more than one of them, many list-makers following Ward, name appetites and desires among primordial social forces" (Giddings 1922, p. 1).

[3] Although it cannot be discussed here further, the concept "proactive inhibition" appeared in the psychological literature beginning in the 1930s (see, e.g., Maslow 1934). Proactive inhibition is the idea that under specifiable conditions old information inhibits the remembering of new information. This concept may be traced to the work of German learning psychologist Georg E. Müller as far back as 1893 (see Haupt 2001). Among sociologists, however, the concept had little impact.

[4] Although he was a doctoral student of Giddings at Columbia, Ogburn was also influenced by William Graham Sumner, whose presidential address before the American Sociological Society in 1908 (published in *American Journal of Sociology* the next year) was on the topic of the family and social change. Sumner (1909, p. 591) was one of the earliest to articulate the family decline thesis, stating "Part of the old function of the family seems to have passed to the primary school, but the school has not fully and intelligently taken up the functions thrown upon it."

[5] This is similar to the notion of the internal dialogue between the "I" and the "Me" giving rise to the "self" according to Mead (1934). Because Mead was influenced most directly by Dewey, one might be tempted here to suggest that this incipient idea of proaction is traceable back to Dewey's 1896 paper which repudiated the behaviorist notion of the "reflex arc," that is, the standard S-R theory of behavior. Instead, Dewey emphasized human cognition, whereby stimuli are *interpreted* before actions, reactions, or even proactions occur. Hence, instead of stimulus–response (S-R) a fuller explanation would have to take the form of stimulus–organism-response (S-O-R; see Chriss 2005). Yet, Ward's concept of indirect conation, which appeared at least as early as 1883, beat Dewey to the punch by more than a decade. It is also noteworthy that neither Murray nor Bales cites Mead, Dewey, or Ward for that matter.

[6] See, for example, the document titled "Post 9-11 Policing: The Crime Control–Homeland Security Paradigm," prepared by the International Association of Chiefs of Police in collaboration with the U.S. Department of Justice (available at http://www.theiacp.org/pubinfo/FinalPost911Policing.pdf). And for more on post 9-11 policing, see Chapter 5.

[7] This same movement from negative to positive proactivity is evident in the shift in emphasis in clinical psychology and social work from a concern with clients' problems to clients' strengths. For recent discussions of this strengths paradigm, see Gerstein (2006) and Yip (2006).

8

Police as Contact Men and Women

In the arts and entertainment industries, special role types called "contact men"—agents, talent scouts, and public relations professionals to name a few—are said to have a knack of reading and acquiring talented performing artists and signing them to contracts for the organization. These role types are effective in filtering new products from creative personnel and placing them in the hands of a mass audience by way of the managerial system of the organization. This concept has never been seen as relevant to police operations, but in this chapter I contend it is. Especially under community policing, police officers act as contact persons, sifting through the raw creative (or destructive) potential of the mass of humanity with whom they come into contact, in the production of social order. In this chapter I explain how and under what circumstances modern municipal police officers act like contact persons.

THE HORIZONS OF PATROL WORK

The typical municipal police department is a formal organization consisting of a number of specialized units, including professional standards, internal affairs, technical services, management services, dispatch, investigations, and patrol. Although administrative positions such as those of chief of police, executive officer, and sergeant or heads of the various units listed above are usually "desk jobs," police personnel in line staff positions—especially those of investigations and patrol—spend a great deal of their time out in the field. This means that the typical patrol officer spends the bulk of his or her time away from the confines of an actual physical structure—the police department—and by necessity must interact with a wide assortment of characters out on the streets while conducting random or directed patrols.

As we saw in Chapter 6, the reality of the open horizons of the patrol officer's work means that, compared with other occupations, professions, or crafts, police officers must be allowed tremendous discretion to size up situations literally "on the fly" so that they may do their work effectively (Smith et al. 2005; Terrill and Paoline 2007). Indeed, this high level of discretion, combined with a territorial division of labor within community-policing work groups, means that officers take a "negotiated order" orientation toward those they encounter on their beats (Klinger 1997). This creates great variability in police behavior, consistent with the potentially wide array of behaviors and persons police encounter on the streets, a flexibility which points to the need for police to play the role of contact men and women (to be explained shortly).

An idealized notion of what police officers actually do while out on patrol is that they are crime fighters, protecting the public from all sorts of dangerous or unscrupulous persons. Yet, the reality is that crime fighting per se constitutes a relatively small portion of the officer's patrol activities. Even acknowledging that "down time" typified much of their work, police officers must still be on high levels of alert because of the unpredictable nature of their encounters with fellow human beings. This means that police out on patrol, even as they work a beat with specifiable boundaries (see Skogan 2006a, p. 60), are still nevertheless subject to perturbations in the form of the random arrival of all sorts of individuals and/or groups.

Out of this relatively random environment of humanity, and through the course of their daily work, patrol officers have developed a working knowledge—consistent with the "negotiated order" orientation of Klinger (1997)—of three basic classes of human beings that they are likely to encounter (Van Maanen 1978). The vast majority of encounters are with so-called *know-nothings*, namely typical citizens who are not necessarily criminal suspects. Patrol officers refer to them as know-nothings because they really have no idea what policing is really like, but must be tolerated as a matter of routine police work.

A second type of character encountered on patrol, and thankfully relatively few in number, are criminals or *suspicious persons*, namely those whom the police have reason to believe may have committed a serious offense. These are the prototypical "bad guys" police officers point to as providing the logic for their "true" roles as crime fighters.

Finally, *assholes* are people who may be subject to extralegal activities by the police falling under the rubric of "street justice." A person who gives an officer a hard time for being cited for rolling through a stop sign might receive a mild form of street justice from the citing officer. For example, the officer could add another citation to the ticket, such as not wearing a seat belt. On the other hand, a person running from the police could receive a much harsher form of street justice, namely being beaten up when the officers finally catch up to him.

The crucial thing to take away from this is that, especially with regard to patrol work, police are in the people business. Out on the streets, police officers always have the potential of coming into contact with citizens, whether or not actual physical contact is made. Although in some ways police have always done this sort of work, the nature of their contacts with citizens has changed over time. We are especially concerned with explaining the special types of roles and work that police officers perform today, which I describe as the contact man or woman.[1] How the contemporary role of contact person within policing emerged can be understood by first taking into account the slow and inexorable development of modern municipal policing in America which began in the 1840s.

THE EMERGENCE OF PROFESSIONAL POLICING IN AMERICA

After Robert Peel established the first municipal police force in London in 1829, the United States soon followed the lead of the British, with Boston being the first city to establish a professional police force in 1838, although it was not until 1854 that the department took on many of the characteristics of Peel's "new police." The New York City Police Department was established in 1844, followed later by Philadelphia in 1856, Chicago in 1861, Detroit in 1863, and Cleveland in 1866. By 1880 most of the larger American cities had done likewise.

To summarize from Chapter 2, the three eras of policing, according to Kelling and Moore (1988) with some modifications (see Chriss 2007b; Oliver 2000) are political spoils (1830s to 1920s), reform and early professionalization (1920s to 1960s), and community policing (1970s and beyond). As we saw in Chapter 5, some also talk of a fourth era of post 9-11 policing (see, e.g., Brodeur 2007a; International Association of Chiefs of Police 2005; Marks and Sun 2007). The earliest political spoils era saw the police heavily influenced by the local political machine as well as ward bosses. Even though the police provided an array of services, through this earliest era it was assumed that policing was a blue-collar occupation, learned through apprenticeship much like a trade or craft, which for that reason did not require much if any formal education. But because of the strong political influence as well as close contact with citizens, early municipal policing was shot through with corruption and patronage abuses.

During the second era of reform and early professionalization, there were attempts to be more selective in the recruitment and hiring of police officers, as well as placing more distance between patrol officers and citizens, as well as between officers and city hall. This necessitated that police departments become more bureaucratized and more overtly organized along quasi-military lines. By the 1930s with the mass production of the automobile, police traded foot patrol for automobile patrol, thereby placing even more distance between themselves and citizens. It was also during this era that police shifted from generalists occupying multiple roles (e.g., running soup kitchens, finding living quarters for newly arriving immigrants, taking care of youthful runaways, as well as order maintenance and law enforcement), to specialists in crime control.

The third era of community policing emerged hard on the heels of the social perturbations of the 1960s, as social movements such as civil rights, gay rights, women's rights, antiwar protest, campus unrest, and the emergence of the psychedelic era and new experiments in lifestyles (e.g., the rapid increase in cohabitation), often brought the police into high-profile conflicts with movement actors as well as other citizens. (See Table 8.1.) A widespread sentiment emerged that the previous era's emphasis on "professional" policing meant that the police were badly out of step in understanding the needs of increasingly diverse urban populations. Out of this came calls to increase the educational requirements of police officers, but also to recruit more women and persons of color so that police forces would match more closely the characteristics of the populations they served.

Table 8.1. The Three Eras of Policing and Changes in Community and Police Roles (adapted from Chriss 2007b, p. 190)

	POLICING ERAS		
	Political Spoils	Reform and Early Professionalization	Community Policing
Police as:	**Generalists,** attending to broad needs of citizens and political leadership	**Specialists,** primarily in crime control	**Generalists,** boundary-spanning multitaskers serving a diverse citizenry
Nature of community:	**Homogeneity** but appearance of incipient levels of heterogeneity and increasing social disorder	Increasing **heterogeneity** and crime rates achieving historic highs beginning in 1960s	**Heterogeneity** and diversity of community at historically high levels; crime rates decline while incarceration rates increase
Prevailing conditions:	Structural transformation in the division of labor: the transition from self-help to sworn police force means police are beholden to political machinery and local ward leaders	Attempts to professionalize and reform police in light of previous era's corruption (close citizen contact) and political patronage abuses	The return of police generalization, but this time in the context of community diversity and shrinking municipal budgets, where local governance seeks to extract greatest "bang for the buck" from safety forces
Direction of control emphasis:	Informal to formal	Increasingly formal	Formal to informal (or rather, attempts to combine various forms of control under the condition of police-community reciprocity)

By the 1970s and into the 1980s, police were also somewhat on the defensive, and sought to reach out to the communities they served, seeking to repair strained relations and to place themselves in more visibly positive roles. Hence, an array of community-policing programs were launched, included D.A.R.E., G.R.E.A.T., neighborhood watch programs, citizen safety training, establishment of police mini-stations, gun buyback programs, and so forth (see Skogan 2006a). This also meant that police returned to the generalist role they occupied during the political spoils era, except now it was being practiced within a condition of community heterogeneity rather than the first era's homogeneity. A special emphasis is placed on people or "soft" skills, presumably equipping officers better to handle both a wide array of interpersonal situations (e.g., domestic violence calls) but also an increasing number of technological innovations. Hence, in this third era police are expected to be multitaskers fulfilling numerous roles in the communities they serve (Anderson et al. 2005). In community policing and related orientations such as problem-oriented policing and information-led policing, the police are acting like psychologists, counselors, social workers, teachers, and social scientists as much as they are crime fighters. The multitasking requirements of the community-policing era become acute with continual upgrading of police technologies, both with regard to "hard" and "soft" skills.

POLICE AND TECHNOLOGY

Sam Nunn (2001c) has argued that technologies utilized by police agencies fall into seven categories. The backbone of criminal justice technologies, according to Nunn, encompass three categories of biometrics (the use of biological parameters to control people and places); monitoring (direct or indirect observation); and imaging (analogue or digital pictures, examples of which include passive millimeter imaging [PMI] and forward looking infrared radar [FLIR]; see Nunn 2001a, 2001b, 2003). Other categories of technology that encompass the internal environment of law enforcement (whether used internally or shared with other agencies) include communications (audio or video communications among or between agents or agencies); decision support (software or programmatic orientations geared to assisting human decision making, examples of which include the Computerized Statistics [CompStat] organizational design developed by the New York City Police Department; the Spectrum Justice System [SJS]; and the Crime Similarity System [CSS])[2]; and record keeping (maintenance of analogue or digital databases; see Chan 2001).

A seventh category according to Nunn is weapons technology. Although all seven of these categories of technology could be relevant to a summary and analysis of police use of information technology—since technology itself is always a form of information—technologies connected with the internal environment of law enforcement agencies (namely, communications, decision support, and record keeping) will be the focus here.

We want to understand how modern technological innovations have changed the role of police officers in comparison to earlier eras, and how this facilitates the emergence of the contact person role. Concomitant to the infusion of more technological demands on the patrol officer, there are also more expectations that he or she will be required to interact with an increasingly diverse array of citizens. This is a prominent part of the mission of community-oriented policing, where police are supposed to have more frequent and nonproblematic contact with citizens they serve in terms of community outreach, strategic planning, and collaboration with stakeholders in the community. In other words, simultaneous emphases are placed on both hard skills training—the physical equipment of policing, including technologies, and the skills needed to use them effectively—and soft skills training, especially in the form of multicultural sensitivity and the ability to service the needs of a diverse citizenry.

First, with regard to hard skills, since the wide adoption of the automobile for police patrols and traffic enforcement beginning in the 1930s, there has been acceleration in the demands placed on patrol officers with regard to (especially) information technologies. Even as recently as thirty years ago, the only less-than-lethal technologies issued to officers were a blackjack and/or straight baton. Now the gun belt (or utility belt) can hold an assortment of items including: baton holder, key holder, glove holder, handcuff holder, various belt keepers, Tasers, mini-flashlight holder, Mace holder, pistol holder, extra magazines, ASP collapsible baton, and various wireless gadgets including cell phone, BlackBerry, and pocket PC. As for technology, about all that a police officer was expected to have on his or her person was a portable radio for maintaining contact with dispatch. In the car were car radios and various other devices (radar for example). The job tasks of patrol officers has generally been the same since the 1930s, namely, report, drive, look, talk, check records, and manage and exchange information. But many technologies since then have been added, and there is an expectation that one should be able to multitask, or switch from task to task relatively effortlessly. These newer technologies and activities include mobile digital computers (MDCs), field reporting, radio, cell phone, text messaging, digital video camera, fingerprint reader, drivers license reader, records management, electronic donut shops, and even augmented reality technology (Anderson et al. 2005). On the soft skills or people side, the idea of police officer as contact person comes to full fruition as well. This will be explored further in the next section.

BOUNDARY-SPANNING STRUCTURES AND ACTIVITIES IN THE POLICE ORGANIZATION

One of the first applications of this idea to police organizations was a master's thesis titled "Boundary Spanning Processes in Complex Organizations," written by Donald E. Comstock in 1971. This was also one of the first tests of institutional theory, and the specific focus for Comstock's study was the police communications or dispatch system. Comstock was influenced by Thomas Drabek's (1965) dissertation titled "Laboratory Simulation of a Police Communication System under Stress." Institutional theory (see Crank 2003; Klinger 2004) is concerned with how broader institutional environments affect the internal workings and goal-strivings of organizations within that broader institutional environment. In other words, all organizations operate within an external environment consisting of other organizations (both similar and dissimilar), individuals, social groups, and physical environments which provide information and feedback about the nature of activities that must mesh with the needs of the surrounding environment. In order to facilitate this exchange of information between organizations and their environments, many organizations have evolved specialized, boundary-spanning units or features which facilitate transactions of information, services, or other provisions between the organization and its external (or institutional) environment.[3]

For purposes of police departments, the communications center seems best to fit the idea of a boundary-spanning unit since it is the central conduit relaying information to officers out in the field conducting their patrols. The radio room, in effect, "controls transactions across organizational boundaries" (Comstock 1971, p. 5). This is all well and good, and it is true that the communications center lies on the outer edge of the police organization, and abuts the organization-environment boundary. Yet, overwhelmingly the work of dispatch personnel is lodged within the physical confines of the police organization itself. The organizational function of the communication room is to facilitate information transactions between the organization and the external environment, but these personnel do not engage in true boundary-spanning activities. This is because they are physically stuck in the organization itself.

The distinction that is being made is that, although the communication center is a boundary-spanning unit for the police organization, the workers in the unit are not themselves boundary-spanning agents. The actual work of boundary spanning is left to an even more specialized group of employees—patrol officers—whose job it is to hit the streets and deal with the empirical realities that await them there. Their actions may indeed be guided or steered by information received from communications, but ultimately their horizons are open and essentially unlimited due in great measure to the unclear police mandate which has characterized policing (to varying degrees) throughout the three eras as previously discussed (see Manning 1978). Patrol officers under community policing are expected to engage not only in crime control, service, and order maintenance—they must also place themselves in increasingly less formal and even intimate settings, such as dealing with domestic disturbance calls, leading neighborhood watch meetings, teaching classes in schools, speaking to community clubs and organizations, engaging in media relations, and facilitating contacts between diverse stakeholders in the community. This leads to the full flowering of the police contact person role.

HIRSCH'S IDEA OF THE "CONTACT MAN"

The third-era model of policing which conceptualizes police officers as proactive, multitasking boundary spanners fits well Paul Hirsch's (1972) description of the "contact man." Hirsch's original formulation dealt with boundary-spanning activities of contact persons within the arts and entertainment industry, but I am arguing that it can be applied equally well to the case of police organizations. In the turbulent environment of the arts and entertainment industry, where the game is to connect potentially massive audiences with cultural creators (artists, musicians, writers, actors, and even athletes), Hirsch argued a new social type—the contact man—is needed. Cultural organizations face high uncertainty whenever they ship out products—a musical performance, a film, a book—to an audience. The industry has to swallow the costs of the production of the items—the books, films, or CDs—and hope sufficient sales on at least some of the titles offset the costs associated with all of them. There is an oversupply of cultural creators—artists, musicians, and actors—hence cultural organizations must delegate much of the work of weeding out the bad or merely good from the great to so-called contact men. This is a proactive strategy, to the extent that there is reliance on contact men as boundary-spanning multitaskers who get out, make contact with potential clients, and arrange to sign them to the organization. As Hirsch (1972, p. 650) explains,

> Contact men linking the cultural organization to the artist community contracts for creative raw material on behalf of the organization and supervise its production. Much of their work is performed in the field.

Agents, talent scouts, promoters, press coordinators, PR (public relations), and A&R (artists and repertoire) personnel are the designations of some of these contact men. In order to reach as many potential clients as possible, they need to "hit the streets," and this means having lunches. James Silberman, at one time the editor-in-chief of Random House, said "Over the years, I've watched people in the book business stop having lunch, and they stop getting books" (Hirsch 1972, p. 650). Contact persons must be allowed great discretion, to allow their special skills in human relations—in this case, judging talent, but also judging the best available fit between the raw resources (the artistry of potential clients) and the needs of the culture organization. Organizations must allow their contact men to use their skills of personal influence in ways best suited to garnering top talent.

As mentioned above, culture organizations have three proactive strategies by which to do their work. These three strategies are compatible with the demand structure of community policing and its emphasis on proactivity. Consistent with institutional theory (see Crank 2003), Hirsch follows Thompson (1967) in examining how goals of an organization are constrained by society. It is assumed that any organization acts rationally and adapts to constraints imposed by its technology and task environment (Hirsch 1972, p. 643). In order to minimize uncertainty, culture organizations utilize three proactive strategies to connect cultural producers to wider audiences through products created by the organization. Cultural organizations are "managerial subsystems" of the broader industry system, in that they select a sample of cultural products for organizational sponsorship and promotion (Hirsch 1972, p. 644). In addition to the contact man, the other two proactive strategies are (a) overproduction and differential promotion of new items, and (b) cooptation of mass media gatekeepers.

(a) Differential promotion of new items, and overproduction of all items (for the sake of turning a big profit on some big winners). In a condition of demand uncertainty and low capital investment (it does not cost that much to produce books and records; films are more costly), it makes sense to produce lots of products and get expansive market coverage. They mobilize promotional resources for "blockbusters" which leads to differential promotion. Most of the other items are allocated small promotional budgets and are expected to "fail" (Hirsch 1972, p. 654).

(b) Cooptation of industry regulators. Mass media gatekeepers—such as record stations for the music industry—are solicited by contact persons on a regular basis to win their allegiance to their products, or at least to give them a heads-up about current and forthcoming releases. Currying favor with mass media gatekeepers is an essential element in getting the word out about their products to a mass audience.

THE CONTACT MAN WITHIN MODERN POLICE ORGANIZATIONS

Although the empirical details are different, the underlying strategies of modern municipal police organizations are similar to the strategies of entrepreneurial organizations. Both cultural entrepreneurial organizations and police work in turbulent environments, and both rely on special role types known as contact persons to connect producers to mass audiences in particular ways. Also, like the contact man, both types of organizations are concerned with differential promotion as well as the cooptation of media gatekeepers. These details as they pertain to the operation of municipal policing will be briefly discussed.

In the era of community policing, police are being conceptualized more as boundary-spanning multitaskers who must connect with multiple stakeholders in the community. They are taking on the task of restoring communities and pushing initiatives with regard to police-community partnerships. This means that police wear many hats, and return them once again to the role of generalists played in the first, political spoils era of policing. However, the community is now diverse, which means that the police role represents an expanded generalism to meet the demands of an increasingly disparate citizenry (refer again to Table 8.1).

As contact men, police must be able to recognize and deal with not on-ly the average citizen—whether "know-nothings" or "assholes" according to Van Maanen's (1978) classification of citizen social types—they must also connect with and attempt to control various suspicious persons or "symbolic assailants" (Skolnick 1966). An analogy to game theory and network analysis is appropriate here. Social order may be seen as a problem of collective action, and the classic dilemma is how to motivate enough people to contribute to the production of this public good. In the "game" of society, centralized sanctions—those of the criminal justice system including police, courts, and corrections—must be available to apply against "free riders," namely those who do not con-tribute to the public good of social order, either through their overt violation of the social order (meat eaters) or through their failure to sanction other violators (grass eaters; see Chriss 2007b, p. 39). But the police must also cajole citizens who are not suspected of being either grass eaters or meat eaters, using their training in soft skills to present themselves as positive role models in the com-munity who can be trusted to use their discretion wisely to further the cause of community order and restoration.

This is also why the police are concerned with shoring up their image to the broader community. Once antagonistic toward the media, most police departments now have their own media relations departments and work with media organizations to get the word out about the goodness and even sanctity of the police mission. This is the project of legal socialization, and police are used as contact persons in a positive way to connect up with citizens as living, breath-ing examples of a new kind of educated and sensitive police force (Meliala 2001).

This is also consistent with differential promotion of new items as well as overproduction of all items. For example, police are doing more of their own number crunching, through such programs as CompStat and situational crime prevention through hot spotting. The overproduction of news concerning "fear of crime" is important to police organizations to legitimize their work in an era of dwindling municipal funding for their services (Skogan 2006a, pp. 255–268). The differential promotion of new items comes by way of various community-policing programs and initiatives, be it weed and seed, gun buybacks, classroom programs such as D.A.R.E. and G.R.E.A.T., personal safety programs directed toward the elderly or the young, and so forth. Those programs that are not suc-cessful (measured, for example, by citizen use of such programs or cost per citi-zen participation) are quickly abandoned or funding reduced, although they of-ten remain "on the books" simply to provide market coverage and to maintain the outward appearance of commitment to the tenets of community policing.[4] In fact, in some important respects, although it begins within the context of com-munity policing, conceptualizing police as contact persons takes them beyond community policing and into a new organizational design where the emphasis is placed not on power (standard or traditional policing) or influence (community policing), but on communication, value commitments, pattern maintenance, and the savvy use of media to manipulate the image of the police as "respectful," "professional," boundary-spanning multitaskers who act as fiduciary agents on behalf of the community, rather than simply enforcing the criminal law, maintaining order, or providing services (Bailey and Dammert 2006). These distinctions come into view and "make sense" if we keep in mind the four basic types of organizations as formulated by Talcott Parsons and as summarized in Chapter 1. This issue will be returned to at the end of the chapter.

COMMUNITIES AND NETWORKS

The rhetoric of "community" within community policing is rather transparent. There is this idea that in the "good old days" of mechanical solidarity (Durkheim 1984 [1893]), everyone knew everyone else, shared the same values, beliefs, and life experiences, and hence trusted one another to abide by and enforce norms of propriety. This was the condition of self-help or informal control writ large (Chriss 2007b). This was also the idea of the tight-knit community where collective efficacy and social capital were in abundance.

From the 1940s onward, but accelerating especially after the 1950s, the idea was that communities as we once knew them were being rent apart by population growth, increasing diversity, mobility, increasing crime rates, and growing segregation and isolation of the poorest of the poor within the urban inner city. After the tumult of the 1960s, many implicated the police, who after all must act as defenders of the status quo, in the decline and fragmentation of the community. After the 1970s and especially beginning in the 1980s with the policy implementation of "broken windows" and community policing, there was a widespread belief that the police could be mobilized to forge desired social changes. They could, so the sentiment went, become community builders, in collaboration with important stakeholders in the community. The race was on to repair strained relations on both sides (police and citizens), and concomitant to this there was hope that police agencies could set up more elaborate screening systems to select recruits who were more educated, more humanistic, and more compassionate than was the case in previous eras.

However, it might also be the case that "community" has always been fictive and idealized, a modernist notion invented by small town folk who were desperate to hang on to small town folkways of solidarity, homogeneity, predictability, and mutual trust (Buerger 1994). Analytically, however, it may be useful to think about what police do, even within the context of an overt commitment to something called community policing, as occurring within networks not necessarily communities. Both of these ideas emphasize control: communities attempt to maximize social control of individuality, while networks maximize individual control on sociality (that is, self-control or self-directivity; see Dal Fiore 2007, p. 860). Communities emphasize homogeneity and conservation within strong group solidarity, while networks emphasize heterogeneity, differentiation, and individuality, such as tastes and market niches (nodes within a broader structure).

In old-style "communities," because of the condition of cultural homo-geneity, a member of that community would be apt to come into contact with other persons similar to him or her, and hence there would be less of a need to have objective agents of formal control out in public policing the streets to deal with these "others" or "strangers." By contrast, in the urban social network, con-sisting of multiple and diverse subnetworks (or subcultures), the security concerns of these disparate groups would become palpable and likely be trans-lated into policy demands for municipal policing (Loader and Walker 2006). And in this condition of cultural heterogeneity, police on patrol would as a mat-ter of routine come into contact with a diverse array of citizens and noncitizens, and hence would also be pressed into the role, more so than ever before, of con-tact person sifting through this raw humanity. In this case, we are talking about nodes in network configurations, rather than the cozy systems of community characterized by mechanical solidarity (Durkheim 1984 [1893]).

Because of the unclear police mandate (Manning 1978), and because they are, unlike average citizens, vested with the coercive power of the state, modern municipal police are defining more areas of social life and more types of social activities as falling under their legitimate purview. With the randomness of individuals moving freely about in space and time (a more or less Poisson random arrivals problem), police are juggling their many technical and technol-ogical requirements in the areas of operations (particularly as this relates to the narrower crime control mandate) and also their soft skills training needed to interact with an increasingly diverse array of citizens. This vast assemblage of human and technological raw material can only be made sense of, or can only be managed, through a twin appropriation of the symbolic medium of power flow-ing from the polity, coupled with influence (as a symbolic medium) flowing from the societal community (Parsons 2007). In this scenario, within the social system which is now conceived as a vast social network, police are the premier gatekeepers (Corra and Willer 2002) and access brokers (De Lint 2003) deciding who belongs where and under what circumstances according to cultural man-dates both formalized (law) and informal (community standards, group senti-ment, etc.).

The product or public good—social order—is pursued via the boun-dary-spanning work of the contact man, namely the police, as described above. On first blush this may appear to mark a dystopian turn toward authoritarian social control, but I believe it need not necessarily be interpreted this way. In-stead, police are pressed into the roles of contact men and women based upon the unique array of factors within the communities or networks (however one prefers to understand them), as well as in the institutional environments within which they operate. This unclear police mandate, rather than being seen as a negative, instead acts as an empty vessel into which can be poured the particular configuration of needs and desires of the assemblage of persons (communities, networks, etc.) potentially or actually being served by the police in a jurisdic-tion.

POLICE AS CONTACT PERSONS WITHIN THE COMMUNITY

A community conceptualized as a network structure points to four functional requisites that must be fulfilled for such organizations of humanity to maintain themselves as a going concern (to be discussed below). In the early modern era, these functions were filled first by citizens within the context of their everyday lifeworlds (that is, the condition of self-help or informal control). By the time of the arrival of the first era of policing (1830s), police began fulfilling some of these functions, but only incompletely and sporadically.

Policing appears on the scene only with the advent of modernity, especially with industrialization which gave birth to what Eric Monkkonen (1988) has called the "service city." Some of the most important services provided within municipal service communities or cities are, of course, the safety forces, specifically police and fire. By the second era (reform and early professionalization) and especially continuing on through the third era of community policing, service provision has become an even more pressing issue for the police because of the continuing diversity of urban populations. As the business model of customer satisfaction extends to the citizen—now characterized as a "citizen–customer" (see Pegnato 1997)—police are confronted with an ever increasing assortment of persons with which they must interact. This is especially true for community-policing officers, who engage in a far greater range of activities and with a more diverse range of persons, than is the case for their counterparts in more traditional or "beat" policing (Frank et al. 1997).

Communities are network configurations located within an even larger assemblage of human organizations called cities (see Hillery 1968). Although in cities we often refer to police departments as encompassing the entire city (e.g., the Los Angeles Police Department), in reality police departments are broken up into districts or precincts, each of which typically serves a potentially diverse and distinct set of inhabitants within these communities. This returns us once again to Klinger's (1997, 2004) notion that modern police must possess a special set of skills for engaging in "negotiated order" with a diverse citizenry as required within each unique setting. Part of this special skill set is embodied in, and presumably ensured, via the police role of contact person, emphasizing as it does especially proactivity, boundary spanning, and the ability to multitask in relation to both human and technological resources.

The evolution of this contact person role is evident when considering the four functional requisites of communities, as mentioned above. Drawing on the systems theory of Talcott Parsons (1960a), these four functions are *residence* (serving the function of adaptation within the community network structure); *work* (serving the function of goal attainment); *jurisdiction* (serving the integrative function); and *communication* (serving the latency or pattern-maintenance function).[5] Residence refers to the most basic level of human reality, that is, to the requirement that human beings must be located somewhere in space and time at any given moment. The consideration of pure location per se is not something that police as a rule are concerned with, so police are rarely if ever implicated in helping to fulfill this particular function for communities.

Work refers to the productive activities of the persons located, or taking residence in, communities. The "work" can vary immensely by location and nature of community, and it need not even be geared toward economic productivity as that term (work) is usually understood. Police may start being utilized to oversee or regulate certain aspects of the work activities of communities, but in the earliest stages of the service community there tended to be a "hands off" or laissez faire attitude concerning governmental intervention in such activity. And most certainly, even with police involvement in some aspects of work, there is no real need for police to play the more advanced role of contact person here. [6]

The third function, serving the integrative function for the community, is jurisdiction. Jurisdiction typically refers to political control of a particular territory, and makes sense only with the rise of the state and especially the service city (Monkkonen 1988). Within this more formalized system of human organization, laws are passed and formal agents of control (police) are assigned various duties whether law enforcement, order maintenance, or service. Also, with political oversight of a territory, human populations increase in density, hence also creating more diversity and a greater range of activities with which the police, as formal agents of control, may be called on to deal. Jurisdictional issues, especially with the move into later modernity corresponding with the second and especially third eras of policing, are those requiring police to gain more flexibility, acumen, and abilities in problem solving for the technological and human challenges they face in their daily work. Integration, which is the functional problem jurisdiction is set up to solve, becomes a more pressing issue with increasing population density and diversity, and this is one of the set of factors giving rise to the police contact person role.

Finally, communication serves the latent pattern-maintenance function for the community. Parsons (1960a, pp. 266–275) actually refers to this as the "communicative complex" because it involves more than the transfer of messages from one person to another. To wit, the communicative complex refers to the much broader notion of communicative performance within social roles. Hence, the communicative complex includes not only messages being sent and received between persons, but also goods and services being transmitted between physical locations. This serves the pattern-maintenance function for the community because everyone must be on the same page to communicate. For example, pertaining to language, persons communicating verbally must be able to understand each other, so the symbols used in the linguistic system must be understood and interpreted by all equally. Likewise, transportation systems link potentially disparate as well as distant members of a communal organization or network, and these throughways represent the lifeblood of social intercourse for virtually all activities taking place within the jurisdiction.

Law must "communicate" control across a jurisdiction, and the work of pattern maintenance, whether through communication, transportation, or analogous procedures, is carried out in various ways. For example, legal socialization—the effort to inculcate in citizens a sense of respect for the legal system and its officers and representatives—is carried out not only by the criminal justice and juvenile justice systems, but also by families, schools, and various community organizations (Fagan and Tyler 2005). Additionally, beyond gaining compliance of the citizenry through inculcating respect for the law and its agents, there is also the strategy of holding over the heads of citizens the threat of coercion if laws are not complied with. Law communicates "power" through the coercive potential of police officers, but pure coercion of the citizenry as a limiting strategy is tantamount to authoritarianism. Indeed, there exists a massive power asymmetry between police and the citizenry, and in their interactions police always have the potential to use this extraordinary power advantage in ways that are not approved by the citizenry (Skogan 2006b). A more effective use of the police, as has been discovered in the third era of community policing and beyond, is to downplay the coercive aspect of police power while emphasizing the special abilities of the "new police," presumably assured through increased educational and training requirements of officers, especially in the area of soft skills. Beginning in the community-policing era, the "ideal" police officer influences citizens into norm-conformity through sheer respect for the office, but also can resort to coercive force when needed.

Police are extremely concerned with the communicative complex, and are used in various and shifting configurations based upon local needs or exigencies. For example, patrol constitutes the bulk of work carried out in police departments, whether carried out by way of automobile, on foot, or by other methods. The "slower" or more person-focused patrol techniques, e.g., bike and foot, are more geared to making connections between police and citizens, and the contact person role for the police is deliberately configured here. On the technological side, patrol officers are having more things added to their patrol cars, and hence the multitasking requirements of the contact person are evident here as well (Anderson et al. 2005). Finally, police departments are more and more concerned with communicating a positive image to the communities they serve, and hence public relations and the co-opting of media gatekeepers, as described by Hirsch (972), become a paramount consideration for community policing.

CONCLUSION

The advent of the contact person role in policing coincided with changes in the organization of human populations over the last 170 years. Human society is not static but rather dynamic. For theorists and practitioners of policing alike, the concept of the contact person could be helpful in pointing toward strategies for how police organizations should manage and utilize their personnel and resources to coincide with shifts in society, culture, and local institutional environments over the foreseeable future. Some of this is going on right now with the emergence of post 9-11 policing (see, e.g., Brown 2007; Deflem 2004; Thacher 2005). Additionally, if indeed community policing is to remain a viable concept in the eyes of police practitioners and administrators, even in light of many of the changes discussed above, it is helpful to understand what community itself means, and which elements (structures and functions) of community are most pertinent to ongoing police operations. Given the direction of change within communities, police will be called on to perform as contact persons for many of the tasks assigned to them.

Additionally, from the perspective of the analyst, the role of contact person takes police even beyond community policing by interrogating the concept of "community" itself and, in so doing, shedding light on its functional aspects (as discussed above). The A- and G-functions, namely adaptation to the environment (jurisdiction) and goal attainment within the community context (work), respectively, provide no purchase for police activities or expertise embodied in the contact person role. With the I-function, namely jurisdiction, communities become more concerned with the integration and adjustment of and between members of the community, as well as establishing formal systems of control beyond those already in place through the work of members themselves. As a social control agency, modern municipal policing attempts to go beyond their original grounding in power emanating from the polity (G) by also adopting some of the elements of persuasion or influence part and parcel to the integrative functions originally carried out by members of the societal community writ large. In other words, glimpses of the contact person role for policing are seen here, at the level of jurisdiction. Finally, the full flowering of a new contact person role for policing in the community correlates with the L-function, namely communication, including face-to-face communication through transportation, the flow of ideas beyond the individual or small group level (for example, public opinion), and the use and cooptation of media technologies by the police in an effort to improve their image and facilitate collaboration with civilians and other stakeholders in the community (Sanders 1958, p. 345).

NOTES

[1] The term "contact man" was formulated by Paul Hirsch in the early 1970s before explicit attention was given to the use of language in describing categories of persons. In other words, for eons "generic he" was accepted as a standard way of referring to all persons. It is frankly awkward to change Hirsch's original "contact man" to "contact man or woman" or even "contact person" for purposes of comporting with modern literary sensibilities. To the extent possible, however, I have done this, but the major point to be made is that, wherever it is retained, "contact man" should be understood as equivalent to alternative uses such as "contact man or woman" or "contact person."

[2] For literature on these various programs, see Redmond and Baveja (2002), Walsh (2001), and Willis et al. (2007).

[3] For useful discussions concerning the conceptualization of boundary spanning in organizations, see Balogun et al. (2005), Dal Fiore (2007), Oliver and Montgomery (2005), and Yan and Louis (1999).

[4] Funding for community policing has waxed and waned over the last decade. According to the Law Enforcement Management and Administrative Statistics (LEMAS) survey, community-oriented police practices increased sharply between 1997 and 1999. However, between 2000 and 2003 the percent of local police departments using full-time community-policing officers declined, with the 2003 figure falling almost as far as the 1997 level. Since 2006, however, under the federal Community Oriented Policing Services (COPS) program, funding for community policing has increased once again (James 2008). It is unclear, however, whether this increase in funding has led to actual reimplementation of existing community-policing programs or the development of new ones.

[5] Although Parsons' AGIL schema was gone into in some detail in Chapter 5, I did not cover how these functions are understood at the micro-level or interactional level of social reality. The building blocks of the social system are unit acts, consisting of a person or persons (A) pursuing goals (G) in a social situation (I) guided by an overarching system of norms and values (L) constituting the cultural stocks of knowledge for that society (Parsons 1937, 1961). Conceptualizing police as contact persons forces attention to police occasions and police–citizen interaction, yet, all the while broader organizational and institutional contexts within which such interactions take place must also be kept in mind.

[6] Police may indeed get involved whenever work-related disturbances reach critical stages, such as in the case of strikes or other forms of labor unrest, and the police sometimes engage in strikes themselves. Additionally, a number of social critics argue that urban policing amounts to policing the poor, a group of citizens which, at least in the American inner city, tend to be racial and/or ethnic minorities. This of course opens a pathway for the study of racially-biased policing. Hence, in one important sense, the policing of work-related activities within the community has increased over time with the general growth of urbanization and industrialization (see, e.g., Crowther 2000; Reynolds and Judge 1968).

9

Security and Private Policing

Throughout the book emphasis has been placed on government or public polic-ing, particular policing taking place within a local metropolitan area. However, the amount of money spent on private security or policing has increased sharply over the last twenty years. For every dollar spent on traditional public policing, more than two dollars is spent on private policing and security (Joh 2004; Shear-ing and Stenning 1981). Private policing is pervasive and it takes many forms, including uniformed guards in shopping malls and gated communities, security services for business and industry, home security services, loss prevention pro-fessionals, especially those working for large retailers, and private investigative agencies. We will follow Joh (2004, p. 55) in defining private policing as

> ...lawful forms of organized, for-profit personnel services whose pri-mary objectives include the control of crime, the protection of property and life, and the maintenance of order.

We have discussed the rise of policing since the 1830s, including the traditional forms appearing in the northeastern United States as well as the zigzag and haphazard patterns evident across the American West between 1850 and 1890. We noted that these public forms of policing emerged as a supplement to the informal systems of control, including self-policing, which were already present in most localities. In other words, public, government-based policing evolved from informal systems of control, some of which were legal or consistent with local traditions or customs (e.g., frankpledge groups, watch and ward systems, hue and cry), while others were either illegal or ethically suspect (e.g., vigilant-ism, mob rule and riots, lynchings; see Goeres-Gardner 2005). In this sense, private policing is not new, but rather has reappeared or reemerged due to vari-ous challenges—economic, cultural, and political—facing modern public polic-ing (Johnston 1992).

Manning (1999) suggests that private, for-profit policing grew under conflict conditions, paralleling the efforts of local city or territorial governments to establish legal control systems to address citizen perceptions of conflict, unrest, or disorder. A takeoff point was the 1850s, coinciding with the invention of the alarm and massive commitments to new transportation technologies, especially trains and stagecoaches. Great banking and financial institutions appearing with the advent of early industrialization—Wells Fargo and Brink's to name two—needed to guard money and other valuables being transported from and into points west of the Mississippi River. Private detective agencies such as Pinkerton's emerged and worked independent of both the U.S. Army and territorial policing whether sheriffs, constables, or federal marshals to help secure valuables, retrieve stolen merchandise, and bring perpetrators to justice (Manning 1999, p. 58).[1]

Although municipal policing claimed a monopoly on the use of legitimate coercive violence, accented especially strongly during the second era of reform and early professionalization as police claimed specialized and proprietary knowledge of law enforcement and crime control, over time this monopoly has diminished, or at least has been challenged, by impulses toward privatization of policing and security (Daleiden 2006). Before understanding the more recent phenomenon of privatization, however, it is imperative first to provide grounding for the concept of privacy itself.

THE CONCEPT OF PRIVACY

Privacy emerges slowly over human history. In the original state of nature, human beings were available to each other first in their nakedness, before norms of propriety regarding the wearing of clothes emerged, then in their spatial arrangements, to the extent that natural or built structures such as caves, huts, or teepees were rudimentary and limited as barriers to perception. Even early dwelling units were fashioned in such a way that privacy as we now understand it was not an issue. In ancient Rome and Greece, houses were built such that members of a family lived in one large room together. Only later were smaller additional rooms built inside houses, yet doors between rooms were not yet thought to be crucial features, so even here direct observation of persons in their rooms was still possible. Charles Dickens (1855, p. 529) provides a perceptive look at life before doors in the following passage:

> The savage has no door to his dwelling. Even when he has ceased to burrow in the ground like a rabbit or a wild dog, and has advanced to the dignity of a hut, or kraal, a hunting-lodge, a canoe turned keel upwards, or any one of those edifices in resemblance between a wasp's-nest and a dirt-pie, in which it is the delight of the chief and warrior to dwell, to dance, to howl, to paint himself and to eat his foes, he never

rises to the possession of a door. The early Greeks and Romans had doorways, but no doors.

Open spaces with few places available to shield one's activities was the birthright of ancient civilization, but even within the most primitive assemblage of humanity there were distinctions made on the basis of sex and age. These are the most archaic forms of human stratification, and very early on human beings came to an understanding that certain spaces were set aside for women and others for men (Chriss 1994). This was the beginnings of the physical separation of women and men, which Daphne Spain (1992, 1993) has cleverly referred to as "gendered spaces." With the advent of the heterosexual nuclear family and men's appropriation (and domination) of productive work outside the home, women were more or less limited to the domestic sphere to attend to the "private" functions of childrearing and homemaking. By the fifteenth century privacy starts becoming a tacitly understood "good," embodied in the patriarchal sentiment "A man's home is his castle."

With the emergence of industrial capitalism and the increasing gap between the haves and the have-nots, wealthy families were able to build lavish estates which effectively separated them even further from common folk. The wealthy tend to be the benchmark by which those with less resources judge themselves, so persons with even modest financial circumstances did what they could to attain a privileged lifestyle, or at least the outward appearance of such, including the adoption and internalization of the values of privacy and exclusivity (Veblen 1899). By the eighteenth century those who could afford their own homes took care to also build fences, high shrubs, and other barriers to perception.

During this time urbanization increased rapidly and with it also the emergence of the modern urban metropolis. Many persons—but especially women—viewed the household and the privacy it promised as a defense against the profanations and threats of an unpredictable urban environment (on this point, see especially Spacks 2003). Douglas Yates (1978) has described the modern city as "ungovernable," yet since the middle of the nineteenth century city governments have handed the task of dealing with the oftentimes unmanageable aspects of city life to the police. Beginning in the nineteenth century, the Victorian Era of sexual prudishness made an especially powerful statement regarding modesty and sexual propriety, especially as it related to women's appearance in public (Foucault 1978; Marsh 1989; Walker 2002). It was during this era that a full-blown "cult of domesticity" emerged, which also fit in well with the rise of the early American suburb, because it allowed those who could afford to move out of the central city more safeguards against the prying eyes of strangers, thereby also further reinforcing the sanctity of the home as a safe haven against urban grit and grime, crime, and even nosy "do-gooders" and government officials, including of course the police (Monkkonen 1981). It was ironic that by the time the modern service city came into prominence in western society beginning in the early 1800s, whereby governments promised a greater array of services to citizens (especially in the form of fire and police services), individuals were growing increasingly wary of anonymous others, especially in urban settings, including the very government workers that promised to make their lives better and more fulfilling (Monkkonen 1988).

But perhaps it is not so ironic. With the growth of government and increasing population densities, there was a clamor for protection from unsavory characters—criminals and the poor to name two of the most prominent disvalued groups—and the relatively faceless police bureaucracy could be understood as playing a useful role in dealing with these undesirables. What this meant, then, was that persons could steal away to the comforts of their private domiciles relatively assured that the urban barbarians would be held at the gates by the police who, in these incipient stages, were custodians of physical space using brute force to deal with those who did not or could not live up to middle-class standards of propriety. All that was needed at this time was a physical force to thwart the unsavory teeming among the growing urban masses. There was nothing really cerebral about this. Exigencies of time and place push human beings into particular configurations of available resources to deal with things on the ground, as they are happening. This is the operation of what Parsons (1961) refers to as the function of adaptation and the lower level cognitive complex, whereby organisms adapt to their environment as best they can. The government already had the market cornered on assemblages of power, and this combined with the growing perception that urban places were dangerous and that increasing diversity—cultural, religious, socioeconomic, racial, and ethnic—was systematically eroding the coziness and predictability of small town living.

The establishment of constitutional democracies across Europe and America, as well as the growth of welfare provisions in these societies served to further define privacy as a legal right which demanded constitutional protections (Chriss 2004). Although this was not a major preoccupation for policing in its earliest phases (especially in the first era of policing running from the 1830s to the 1920s), by the 1960s police were spending more of their time in training and out in the field dealing with the due process rights of citizens with whom they came into contact. Indeed, by the late 1800s something new emerged in the law of torts, namely, the right to not have one's privacy invaded. As Friedman (2007, p. 214) explains,

> A famous article written by Samuel D. Warren and Louis D. Brandeis, published in 1890 in the *Harvard Law Review*, launched the tort. The two writers argued that the common law had the right and the duty to act to protect a person's privacy.

As social control was slowly and inexorably shifted away from the informal control of citizens and defined as a specialized task for government functionaries, including most importantly the police, there was also the establishment of the principle that government is ultimately responsible for social order, crime control, public health, and other areas previously the domain of citizen oversight and control (Chriss 2007b). From the beginning of professional policing, then, policing was always a government—that is, a public—function and responsibility. Yet, this put policing especially—although also to a lesser extent the courts and correctional system—in a precarious position of having to defend the privacy rights of citizens while also exerting force, where needed, to deprive citizens of their privacy rights whenever it was necessary to detain, question, or arrest them on the allegation of law violation.

BACK TO THE WILD WEST

We covered issues regarding law enforcement in the American western frontier in Chapter 3. In that chapter we saw that, unlike the early pattern of settlement in the northeastern United States, the situation west of the Mississippi from the 1840s through the 1890s was unstable as towns were attempting to be established amidst multiple conflicts and the difficulties inherent in any project of settling a frontier. It should be reiterated that self-policing, or informal control, is the most archaic form of social control and predates the rise of the state and its government apparatus. From the 1840s onward the American western frontier could be described as "stateless," to the extent that persons were left to their own devices in carrying out their life projects. As Elliott (1944) has argued, before and during the settling of the western frontier the lack of effective government encouraged a sense of individualism, and sometimes this eventuated in violent confrontations between persons in disputes over land, resources, or simply the perception of bellicose or threatening interpersonal behavior.

Although the United States placed various peace officers at key points across the western frontier, such as federal marshals who acted as sheriffs in some cities or territories, as well as U.S. Army presence more generally, especially as this involved the "Indian problem" and providing safe passage to settlers involved in legitimate enterprise, for the most part the state was absent as a formal system for assuring proper conduct among those assembled there. In other words, absent government regulation of local activities and behavior, enterprising individuals across the western frontier came together to fashion various forms of private self-help until such time that cities were settled and local charters were established certifying public police forces.

Private justice on the western frontier proliferated in various forms before the widespread adoption of professional policing in most major western cities by the 1880s. Discussed below are four key forms of private justice taking place in particular settings and times across the western frontier, namely, land clubs, wagon trains, mining camps, and vigilantism (Benson 1998).

Land Clubs

The United States Congress created the Office of Surveyor General within the Treasury Department in 1796, and later opened the General Land Office in 1812 (Atwood 2008, p. 3). Even before surveyors were empowered to survey federal lands across the West, numerous individuals—called "squatters" by the government—moved onto these lands without formal permission or acknowledgment. Government surveyors as well as U.S. Army personnel found these squatters to be a nuisance, especially insofar as they were willing to risk death or injury from the wilderness conditions as well as the constant threat of raid or attack by Native Americans. As a result, a number of disputes arose over rights to land, and with the U.S. government having the upper hand in defining squatters as law-breakers, many of them formed extra-legal organizations called Land Clubs. These Land Clubs attempted to create solidarity among early settlers in their battle against the federal government. The Land Clubs went so far as designing local charters, establishing procedures for registering land claims as well as laying out guidelines for the protection of these claims against outsiders (Benson 1998, p. 101). Land Clubs provided protection for fellow squatters who played by the rules set forth by the club. Those that did not were often ostracized and hence were provided no protection against aggression whether from legitimate sources (i.e., the government) or other sources (e.g., Native American tribes).

Wagon Trains

As discussed in previous chapters, after gold was discovered in California in 1848 large numbers of persons began making the trek westward, and many of them travelled in covered wagons or wagon trains. Along these trails on the open frontier, there were very few established cities or acknowledged outposts (whether trading or Army posts) between starting and finishing points whereby formal standards of conduct could be upheld. As Benson (1998, p. 102) explains, "Most trains waited until they were out of the jurisdiction of the state law, for example, and then selected officers with responsibilities for enforcing their own rules." Many of the extralegal rules established on these wagon trains, enforced by and among members themselves rather than by government agents whether Army or police personnel, closely resemble laws officially recognized in a legal jurisdiction, including:

- Rules for creating, enforcing, and amending contracts;
- Rules for the banishment of lawbreakers;
- Rules for organizing jury trials;
- Laws regarding gambling, prostitution, intoxication, and Sabbath-breaking;
- Penalties for not performing sanctioned tasks, such as the shirking of guard duty.

Within the wagon trains themselves acts of violence were rare. Most who were part of the entourage accepted the informal rules for membership and engaged in self-policing to ensure others abided by the rules as well. Ostracism from the group was very serious because banished persons were left to deal with the unpredictable nature of the unsettled areas of the frontier through which they were traveling, especially as this involved attacks or threats from Indians or outlaws.

Consistent with all this, Unruh (1978) has documented the extraordinary level of voluntary cooperation among most of the people emigrating overland across the plains between 1840 and 1860. Rather than the solitary trek across the barren plains depicted in much of the history of early migration into the western frontier, the reality is that the trails were often congested. Unruh (1978, p. 119) notes, for example, that so many people left St. Joseph, Missouri in 1852 for points west that "teams travelled twelve abreast." Yet for the most part, westbound overlanders went out of their way to cooperate and to assist those who had run into some misfortune along the way, whether tracking horse or cattle which had broken from the pack, helping an emigrant get his wagon out of a mud hole, and even assisting in the burial of the dead for those who did not complete the journey (Unruh 1978, p. 141).

Mining Camps

In Chapter 3 we saw that the first police force established in the United States was in San Francisco in 1857. The San Francisco police force emerged initially from citizen concerns that rapid population growth fueled by the discovery of gold in 1848 was leading to increased lawlessness among miners and untoward activities directed at them (such as stealing gold or jumping claims). It should be emphasized, however, that at least initially the conditions in the gold mines were not altogether chaotic or lawless. With the arrival of scores of new people to the area in 1848 and 1849, San Francisco government officials sought ways to raise revenue to deal with the strain on city services. When John W. Geary took over the office of *alcalde* in 1849, the public treasury of San Francisco was almost completely depleted. Geary and the newly elected town council passed new ordinances to raise funds, including:

- Increasing sales of town lots;
- Renewing emphasis on requiring businesses to pay license fees;
- Levying fines on those convicted of violating local laws;
- Increasing license fees charged to gamblers (Lewis 1980, p. 58).

The new funds generated from these and other activities were used to establish a municipal court, to organize a police force, and to purchase the brig *Euphamia* for use as a city jail. The municipal court and jail went into operation almost immediately after official sanctioning by the town council. Indeed, as long as persons are around with knowledge of the law, and as long as there are places where persons who are accused of crimes can be held awaiting trial, then at least two-thirds of the modern criminal justice system becomes operational even on a provisional basis.

The establishment of a fully functioning, paid and sworn police force typically takes more time and lags behind the establishment of courts and corrections systems. This is because the system of informal control and self-help already in place in a jurisdiction can be used in the transition to a formal policing system. A city may elect a local sheriff, or the federal government may assign a marshal to act as peace officer in a particular city or territory, yet that lone figurehead of justice cannot serve as a police force, at least as understood according to modern sensibilities. In other words, a municipal court can try cases, and suspects can be detained in jails on the authority of judges or at the direction of a constable, marshal, or sheriff. Yet the head peace officer cannot go out and physically run down suspects, arrest them, or bring them to justice by himself, at least not very effectively. Before the establishment of a complete criminal justice system at the local level, the police system is incomplete or impoverished as it is initially structured on the basis of a lead law enforcement officer and other individuals he designates to help him carry out the tasks bequeathed to him. This extra "help" is typically in the form of citizens of the jurisdiction who are recruited to assist the sheriff or constable, and by his authority they are temporarily "deputized" and given rights to pursue, detain, capture, or even kill suspects. Yet for the most part, these citizen patrols, whether organized informally or at the behest of the local peace officer, are not paid and their services are understood to be informal, sporadic, and on a case-by-case or needs basis.

What happened in San Francisco with regard to the establishment of local criminal justice systems is fairly typical of the history of most other local jurisdictions, whether located west of the Mississippi or elsewhere. The village of Cleaveland was incorporated in 1814, and after the spelling of the city's name was changed in 1831, Cleveland's population began growing as a result of the completion of the Ohio and Erie Canal in 1832 (Coates 1924). As the social disorganization theorists have documented (see, e.g., Elliott and Merrill 1950; Faris 1955), rapid population growth is often associated with an increase in various social problems including crime. Although the mayor had acted as the police judge since the establishment of the city, it was not until 1853 that construction on a new municipal police court was completed. A jail and a police department located on the second floor were also part of the building, yet an official police force would not be established until 1866, thirteen years after the establishment of officially functioning court and corrections systems (Van Tassel and Grabowski 1987).

With this standard evolution of the development of subsystems of the criminal justice system in mind, we may now return to the particular case of the establishment of an official police department in San Francisco partly in response to the social disorganization associated with the discovery of gold in the region. In the first few years of the discovery, miners who arrived in the area immediately set about establishing an informal system of rules for negotiating the myriad activities and issues arising in the mining camps. Indeed, between 1848 and 1850 the state of California had no specific mining laws that were applicable to the then-current situation (Benson 1998). There was, however, a federal mineral rights law, but applying it to the specific case of what was happening in California was haphazard and largely ineffective. In the absence of formal guidelines, miners negotiated working rules more or less informally.

These informal contractual arrangements among the miners worked as well as could be expected, and rates of crime in the area were not high, at least not through 1852. Indeed, in these first several years there were very few robberies, thefts, or murders in the mining camps (Benson 2006, p. 170; Canlis 1961). As the number of persons in the area continued to increase, however, it became apparent that many persons were arriving with no intentions of engaging in legitimate mining operations. Some mining camps hired "enforcement specialists" as a result of the perception that more and more unsavory elements were being attracted to the camps. This perception combined with continuing rapid growth and lawlessness in San Francisco more generally led to the eventual replacement of miners' informal contractual relations with formal government guidelines, including the ability to enforce new local or state laws by way of the San Francisco Police Department, established officially in 1857 (Benson 1998, p. 106; Monkkonen 1981).

Vigilantism

As covered briefly in Chapter 3, vigilantism is one of the most widespread forms of private law enforcement. It arises whenever and wherever citizens feel that official systems of law enforcement are absent, ineffective, or corrupt. Although vigilantism or private violence is generally considered in a negative light, Culberson (1990) argues that it can be positive or functional when public, official violence is ineffective or dysfunctional. In such cases, private violence may lead to new laws that correct the conflictual aspects underlying earlier forms of private violence, thereby stabilizing the legal and political systems. Indeed, the vigilance movement that arose several years after the discovery of gold in California (1848–1856) led in turn to the establishment of the police department in San Francisco shortly thereafter.

One of the earliest vigilante groups to appear in San Francisco, the Sydney Ducks, was composed primarily of former convicts who had been deported from English penal colonies to Australia. At the news of the discovery of gold, many of those who could travel did so, and sailed for the west coast and specifically San Francisco. Another group, the Hounds, aimed much of their hostilities at foreign colonies in San Francisco, particularly the Chileans who lived in Telegraph Hill (Lewis 1980, p. 59). They along with several other vigilante groups raided parts of town as they saw fit, most often engaging in theft, burglary, and assault, but occasionally also murder. The activities of these vigilante groups were directed more at the growing social disorganization arising from rapid population growth and those less able to defend themselves, rather than at occupants of miners' camps per se. The miners had already developed informal systems of control and defense against those who threatened them, however, after 1852 other vigilante groups would begin targeting them as well. It did not help matters that during this time as well numerous fires broke out in San Francisco, including a particularly devastating fire in 1851 which destroyed twelve square blocks and caused $3 million in damages. As a result of these fires, previously all volunteer fire companies started banding together in clubs, and as they became more formally structured and organized they came to wield considerable influence in city politics. Eventually San Francisco established an official, paid fire department in 1866.

After the Civil War and with the continuing movement of large numbers of persons into the western frontier, many Americans believed that a crime wave had descended upon them. A notice in the *Tribune* newspaper in Chicago in 1882 stated that "...in our own city...footpads and sluggers pursue their violent calling with almost perfect impunity," which coincided with the sentiment that violent criminals often went unpunished, law enforcement was ineffective, and juries were unwilling to convict (Hallwas 2008, p. 241). And although lynch law had been in effect across many parts of the West since at least the 1840s, especially in unsettled areas devoid of Army or police presence, by the early 1880s lynchings were on the increase. Angry mobs would form and target those accused of murder or lesser offenses such as cattle rustling or horse stealing. Additionally, although earlier lynchings were conducted without regard to the race or ethnicity of the perpetrator, beginning in the 1880s in the South as well as in the Midwest and points further west, lynchings of Blacks increased precipitously. Garland (2005) notes that between 1890 and 1940 most lynchings in the Deep South were targeted at African-Americans, and they were abnormally cruel and often involved publicity and crowds. Sometimes these "public torture lynchings" had almost a festive feel to them, as persons cheerily posed for pictures with the burned, hanged bodies, and postcards were sent to family and friends commemorating the occasion. Law enforcement was often absent and sometimes facilitated the grotesque activities of these lynch mobs.[2]

We see, then, that on the American western frontier between 1840 and 1890 there was a mix of private and public law enforcement operating, and the roles of outlaw and lawman were fluid and sometimes indistinguishable. Wayne Gard (1949, p. 253) captured well this transition from the lone peace officer battling rustlers, outlaws, and other unsavory characters to the institutionalization of western criminal justice systems:

> Not all of the stern men who carried guns in the interest of order and law on the frontier were in public employ. Some were shotgun messengers seated behind the stagecoach drivers or guards who worked for the pioneer railroads and the express companies. Others were range

detectives of the livestock associations who followed the trails of thieves across the plains and through the mountain passes. Occasionally one of these men cast his lot with the outlaws he was paid to exterminate. ...Yet nearly all of the pioneer enforcement officers, public or private, gave a good account of themselves. They risked their lives to make the West safe, and more than a few carried desperadoes' bullets to their graves. Only through their work could the emerging courts gain the confidence of law-abiding citizens and the respect of wrongdoers.

PRIVACY AND SECURITY

By the time of the widespread establishment of police departments in most American cities by the late 1800s, and in combination with the continuing emphasis placed on service provision within the modern city, the expectation was firmly established that the government had an obligation to oversee and regulate numerous areas of life. There were legitimate private places where police and other government functionaries were expected to steer clear of absent good reasons to do otherwise. Paramount among these private enclaves were (and still are) the home, the church, schools, and various private enterprises such as local bars and small businesses. Granted, the police patrolled these neighborhood areas and looked for suspicious persons, but for the most part maintained distance from the interior spaces of everyday life.[3] In other words, police operated in the public spaces and byways of the modern city, providing security through law enforcement, order maintenance, and a variety of services not directly connected with either of the first two.

In the modern metropolis teeming with large numbers of persons, the majority of whom are not familiar with each other, the guarantees of regularity, predictability, and order are imperiled. Yet, one of the requirements of living together in a community is that persons have a sense of security about the area. Sanders (1958, pp. 166–168) identifies four types of security important in community life. First, there must be *physical* security of one's person and possessions. Absent an abiding sense of physical security, human assemblages will have trouble maintaining the critical mass necessary to form a community. Second, there must be *psychological* security. Such security is attained to the extent that the unpredictable and unexpected are held to a minimum. As Sanders (1958, p. 166) explains,

> The individual who constantly worries about unemployment, the threat of a flood, or the possible necessity of getting to a distant hospital is a person whose efficiency is impaired. One of the reasons for living in a community is to reduce through group action the threat and the consequences of these unpredictable events.

Third, there must be *societal* security. This state is achieved to the extent that persons feel secure in most social situations. One important way this is achieved is through the institutionalization of patterned ways of doing things, largely by way of the stability of role-status systems and the normative expectations for performance in those roles or positions (Parsons 1951). Fourth, there must be *cultural* security, meaning that a person recognizes the local area as his or hers and identifies with it as an important aspect of who he or she is. Echoing Durkheim's (1984) notion of moral solidarity, cultural security is reflected in the extent to which persons in the community agree on important issues, instead of being merely a collection of isolated family units.

As we have discussed throughout the book, before the rise of public policing individuals provided security for each other as best as they could manage within the limits of available resources and the guidance of cultural horizons for action. Slowly and inexorably, however, public policing started taking on the responsibility of providing security in many of these areas. Providing physical security, for example, making sure that conditions existed within which persons were not at high risk of crime victimization, was clearly one of the first areas ceded to the new police. And with the rise of reassurance policing—nowadays also referred to as neighborhood policing (see Innes 2005)—under the auspices of community policing and beyond, police are also concerned with psychological security, especially as it relates to policy mandates regarding the reduction in citizens' fear of crime.

Ongoing research on fear of crime suggests that it is multifaceted, encompassing not only social, physical, and environmental variables, but also psychological and emotional ones. As police accept fear of crime as a legitimate area to which their energies and activities should be directed, they also expand their mandate to encompass all those aspects of society touching upon this diverse range of fear of crime factors. Specifically, fear of crime includes the following dimensions:

- Level of objective crime;
- Physical or social incivilities;
- Urban life in general;
- Key sociodemographic variables including gender and age;
- Psychosocial variables, including most importantly the perception of vulnerability (Carro et al. 2010, p. 304).

In essence, this transition reflects the rise and continuing domination of the state, whereby previously local and private social orders, overseen by persons within the contexts of their everyday lifeworlds, were now transferred into the hands of official, sworn police forces empowered to maintain a single, dominant public peace. As Shearing and Stenning (1986, p. 12) elaborate, once the notion of a stable and identifiable public sphere emerges,

...a "publicly" defined peace should properly be "publicly" mandated. Thus, the emergence of modern public police, as full-time salaried employees of the nation-state claiming a monopoly over order maintenance, is constituted as both proper and inevitable.

It should be noted that even with the police taking on the bulk of responsibilities of managing public spaces, because of their high levels of street discretion they have the opportunity to work "off the books" and elect to act or not act in their official capacity as they see fit. Police as contact persons sift through the myriad combinations of occasions and persons that they encounter on patrol, and have the power to define persons as assholes, know-nothings, or suspicious persons according to the situational exigencies of the occasion. Sometimes their utilization of do-nothing discretion upsets citizens of the community, further contributing to the heightening of tensions between the police and the communities they serve. In such cases, police as publicly accountable servants of the people are taken to task for allegedly shirking their duties, or playing favorites, or not caring about the real problems confronting real people in the community. Community policing was supposed to smooth over these discrepancies between the ideal and the real in police-community relations, and newer variants going beyond community policing—such as reassurance policing, pulling levers policing, and even post 9/11 policing—are further aimed at fulfilling the ideals of a fully professional, competent, and compassionate police force.

In many respects do-nothing discretion pushes police into acting like private security guards rather than public police. The official, public orientation toward troubles is typically backed with a legal code requiring government functionaries to exert force against citizens to compel them to comply with criminal law. This is the public face of policing, its principal operational logic being compliance and deterrence. Private policing, on the other hand, operates with the logic of administrative regulation, the aim of which is to maintain private order and prevent disruption (Reiss 1986). Even public police will forego the invocation of their formal powers of arrest if a situation can be managed in such a way that local, "private" troubles do not spill over into the public realm. Or, to restate, sometimes police forego compliance in favor of regulation, in which case they are acting more like administrators than law enforcement agents.

Let us consider the following example. One of the characteristics of the urban inner city is an underground economy which offers economic resources to the poor who otherwise are cut off from securing these valued goods through legitimate means. One of the characteristic social types operating among the urban poor is the hustler, with hustling described by Venkatesh (2006, pp. 17–18) as "the indefatigable and creative attempts by the down-and-out to find work, make a buck, and make ends meet." Hustling often involves illegal activity, including the selling of stolen or illegal merchandise (drugs for example), settling disputes, and enforcing underground contracts. Some hustlers brazenly operate in open daylight, whether selling pirated videos or CDs on a street corner, hanging out in parks or near schools offering stereo equipment or other items from the trunk of a car, or separating passersby from their money through panhandling or other creative forms of (illegal) entrepreneurship. Impoverished social conditions in socially disorganized communities may create a critical mass of hustlers who, through their activities, create an array of social problems which do not go unnoticed by local residents. In one community-policing meeting in an inner-city area of Chicago, a forty-something woman complained to the police that they were not doing enough to rid the neighborhood of these pests, explaining that residents felt unsafe. The police officer running the meeting responded sympathetically to the woman, but went on to explain that on some levels toleration of, and sometimes even cooperation with, local hustlers is necessary to maintain a fragile peace and security. The officer's justification for this is especially enlightening:

> Let's be real. The realistic way is the best way. Think about it. From our standpoint, you can have three kinds of people in those [public] places: you can have a mom and her kid, you can have a gangbanger sell dope, or you can have some of these people who don't have anywhere else to go. I mean do you want a gangbanger out there? No. And so these men, who don't have a job, who have a lot of problems—they're on drugs, they drink, they're going to be there every day. You can't get rid of them. So you use these men—and the women too—to get information. You find out what's happening by getting them to tell you what they see. And believe me, they see everything. And you make sure you take care of the little things before they blow up (Venkatesh 2006, p. 203).

It is interesting to ferret out the model of policing implied by this officer's statement. Under certain circumstances, the best options for the police are to act like security guards detaining suspects and soliciting information from them. In most jurisdictions this is all private security guards can do, since they do not have the power of arrest. When public police act in this way, they simply forego the arrest powers officially designated to them, in favor of assuring security in local situations through detention and information gathering. In this same vein, would it possible for local communities to simply employ private security guards to fan out across the area, detaining suspicious persons, and, if need be, calling for the real police if an arrest has to be made? Part of the story of private security, continuing in the next sections, reflects this new reality of mixing and matching private and public resources in policing and security.

ECONOMICS AND PRIVATIZATION

A reality that continues to confront those in government and the public sector is that the costs of services and programs provided to citizens, whether in the form of public education, public health, sanitation and water services, or safety services (fire, police, and EMS), continue to grow unabated. According to Charles Ellwood (1910), in 1900 the estimated cost of crime in America was $600 million annually. Four-hundred million of the cost were losses resulting from criminal activities, while $200 million reflected the cost of the operation of the criminal justice system. Through 2006, costs of the criminal justice system continued to soar (see Figure 9.1).[4] Compounding this reality, since 2008 an economic decline has left many U.S. states with growing deficits, and cities across the country are scrambling to find ways to cut costs.[5] Facing record budget deficits, Oakland, California has considered replacing sworn law enforcement officers with private guards. Sixty-five percent of Oakland's budget goes to police and fire services, hence, it made sense to target the police department for budget cuts. The city hired International Services, Inc., a private security agency, to patrol areas of the city. Instead of spending roughly $250,000 a year on each sworn police officer (this includes benefits as well as salary), Oakland can spend only about $200,000 a year to hire four private guards. Other cities have either proposed or have actually implemented measures to replace some full-time sworn officers with private security guards, including Chicago and New Orleans.[6]

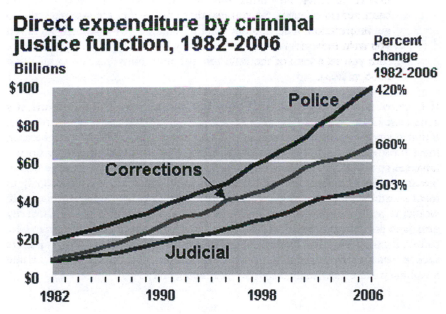

Figure 9.1. Criminal Justice System Costs

Accident Response Fees[7]

Here, government entities are acting like private, for-profit businesses, and much of it is due to economic expediency. In difficult financial times, government agencies are more concerned than normal with the bottom line, that is, with issues of profit and loss. Another way municipal governments are seeking to contain costs is through the imposition of controversial accident response fees (ARF). Under ARF programs, municipalities bill insurance companies for police, fire, and EMT responses to auto accidents and other service calls, no matter how minor or routine the events.

One company in particular, Cost Recovery Corporation (CRC) in Dayton, Ohio, has been the leading third-party vendor collecting fees on behalf of fire and police departments across participating municipalities. Here is how it works. A police department adopting the ARF strategy forwards their accident response reports to CRC, and then CRC calculates total costs based upon current market standards. CRC then writes up the claim and submits it to the insurance company of the at-fault driver. If the insurance company decides to pay either all or a portion of the bill, CRC keeps 10% of the total as their third-party fee, and sends the other 90% back to the police department. If the insurance company declines payment there is no service fee charged to the department. Accident response fees are not popular with the general public because people see this as inherently unfair in that a person involved in a wreck is receiving something akin to "double jeopardy": not only will the at-fault driver get additional points on his driving record and very likely higher rates from his or her insurance company, but will be burdened with an additional charge from the police department attempting to recoup the costs of the accident response. An average citizen's response to this is often incredulity, asking, "What do we pay the police for? That's their job!"

Another stakeholder opposed to accident response fees is the insurance industry. A recent issue brief from the National Association of Mutual Insurance Companies refers to the increase of municipal accident response fees as an "ominous trend." The authors of the report, Stanton and Thesing (2006), claim that the practice amounts to "double taxation," and that citizens rightly should be opposed to it. Insurance companies in Indiana have taken the position that the response fees are unconstitutional because they allow "a law enforcement officer to make an administrative adjudication, which usurps the role of the judicial process and which results in the taking of property (i.e., money), without due process of law" (Stanton and Thesing 2006, p. 2).

Those who defend the practice, primarily participating municipal safety departments and third-party providers such as Cost Recovery Corporation, argue that it makes sense to target those who are involved in automobile accidents, since they are the ones causing the majority of social harm on the roadways. And since it is especially difficult to collect the fees directly from at-fault drivers who are residents of the jurisdiction within which the accident occurred, it also makes sense to bill their insurance companies. And since police and fire departments are not set up to collect these fees from insurance providers, it seems natural for them to seek the services of companies like Cost Recovery Corporation who specialize in this sort of work. The insurance company response is that, if these fees were ever widely accepted as part of the calculation that goes into setting premiums of drivers, and if insurance companies actually started taking these bills seriously and started paying them, it would no longer affect only targeted drivers. That is, insurance companies would simply raise rates across the board to cover the extra cost of what is, from their perspective, a pernicious and possibly unconstitutional fee or double tax. Targeting insurance companies in this way only serves to raise rates for everyone, and the only entities receiving benefits are the third-party providers and the cities participating in the program.

Regina Moore, CEO of Cost Recovery Corporation, rejects many of these points.[8] For example, Moore argues that accident response fees are not a form of double taxation, because only dangerous, at-fault drivers are targeted, while the rest of the innocent taxpayers that reside in the jurisdiction are exempt. Moore also reports that, according to the most recent figures, 56% of insurance companies recognize the value of this program and are paying claims. As Ms. Moore states on the company website:

> Innocent taxpayers should not be forced to subsidize insurance companies' investigatory costs, thru-traffic or non-contributing individuals who require emergency response due to their own negligence.

It is also instructive to consider the logic or rationale behind the adoption of accident response fees from the perspective of participating police departments. The Longwood Police Department in Longwood, Florida is a client of Cost Recovery Corporation, and its chief, Thomas Jackson, has written a testimonial consistent with the position of Ms. Moore. Interestingly enough, Chief Jackson claims that traffic enforcement is a civil matter which takes police away from their "true" mandate as crime fighters. This harkens back to the position police departments were taking during the reform and early professionalization era, whereby claims of increasing professionalization were made on the basis of increasing task specialization, specifically, police as specialists in crime control while simultaneously divesting themselves of noncriminal matters. Community policing rejected this professionalization through specialization argument, and returned once again to the first era's generalist roles, including heavy emphasis on police as contact persons and service providers. Even broken windows policing, which suggests that police should direct their attention to noncriminal activities involving only lower-level problems of disorder or disruption (Wilson and Kelling 1982), would fall to the wayside as well, that is, if police divestment of civil entanglements is taken seriously.

Here is the opening paragraph of Chief Jackson's testimonial:

The primary responsibilities of the City's services, Police and Fire Departments, are investigating crimes, apprehending criminals and protection of the citizens, who in turn, provide funding for such through municipal tax assessment. However, an inordinate amount of safety services' time and resources are devoted to responding to vehicular crashes, which are basically civil issues. Services rendered at a vehicular crash are outside the scope of basic fire and police protection.[9]

This is an interesting wrinkle on the issue of privatization in policing and the criminal justice system more broadly, and in some ways the claims made by Chief Jackson could be construed as another strategy for "going beyond" community policing. Indeed, this move kills at least two birds with one stone. One, it fits in nicely with the increasing emphasis being placed on budget austerity in city governance. Safety services consume large portions of most city budgets, but rather than cutting back on police, fire, or EMS personnel, which is highly unpopular with the public and forces confrontations with powerful police and fire unions, why not simply recoup the cost of response operations by targeting negligent drivers and their insurance companies? Two, traffic patrol has always been unpopular among the police rank and file, because it often brings them into contact with irate and surly drivers, and also because it is dangerous. Indeed, more than 50% of police officers killed in the line of duty were involved in traffic-related incidents (White 2007, p. 142).[10]

Getting the human element "out of the loop" in traffic patrol and other areas of life is already well underway. The use of traffic cameras, automated ticketing, and closed-circuit television (CCTV) surveillance of public places has expanded tremendously over the last twenty years in Britain and the United States (Sharp 2000, Wells 2008). City leaders claim that the installation of red-light cameras in their cities serves to increase public safety by reducing speeding and red-light running, but critics argue it is simply a raw cash grab. The result is that police increasingly escape the everyday grind of routine traffic patrol, and when they are called out to an accident they can simply stick the at-fault driver's insurance company with a bill for services rendered.

Club Goods and Multilateralization

One of the more interesting social transformations contributing to the modern blurring of the line between private and public, and policing's role in monitoring and regulating activities taking place there, is the rise of "mass private property" (Shearing and Stenning 1981, 1983). Shearing (2006, p. 12) describes mass private property as privately owned property encompassing a relatively large area to which the general public has easy access. Examples include shopping malls, gated communities, and exercise clubs. Some of these clubs are fee- and/or membership-based, while others allow the general public entry and exit into the facility or compound just as long as they meet certain minimal requirements of entry, judgments of which are typically made and enforced by private security guards. For example, the general public is allowed in most shopping malls, and the assumption is made that people who enter the mall do so for "legitimate" reasons, namely to purchase the services or products being offered by merchants located there. These private security guards are concerned primarily with guarding against loss, but also with removing disruptive persons who threaten the social order of the establishment.

What this means is that increasingly security becomes a project of private governance, and in some ways the size and scope of the project equals if not surpasses the security work of public agencies and organizations. As we saw above in the case of accident response fees, the marketization of security does not affect only the police, but spills over into society more generally as security itself becomes a commodity to be bought and sold on an open market (Crawford 2006, pp. 112–113). Since it is funded by taxpayers, operated by governments, and legitimized through legislative enactment, policing has often been described as a "public good," to the extent that all citizens of the jurisdiction have access to its products and services and it is typically not operated on the basis of pay-as-you-go or user fees.

This is of course changing in some ways as discussed above. To put it more succinctly, since the rise of public policing there has been the conceit that policing and the work it does in assuring security, order, and safety are public goods, concerned more with fulfilling certain basic functions of government than with turning a profit. Yet, governments have never been configured as purely public entities. Even before explicit talk of the privatization of policing began, many local police departments routinely contracted out a variety of services to private firms, including police support services, the transportation of prisoners, collections, and so forth. Private security firms such as Wackenhut, for example, provide airport security to the city of Tampa Bay, as well as armed patrols of the Miami Metro Rail in Dade County, Florida (Benson 1998, pp. 17–18).

If indeed out in the real world the lines between public and private are becoming blurred, perhaps this means that we must also attempt to go beyond taken-for-granted notions of public and private in our scientific theories and concepts. Rather than thinking about public goods, perhaps it is more realistic to think about hybrid goods encompassing some aspects of public and private simultaneously. This leads us to the concept of club goods. *Club goods* are "'quasi-public' goods that are available to members of a club but restricted in some form or another to non-members" (Crawford 2006, p. 120). As discussed above, restrictions may be in the form of dues requirements, screening at entry points, or relative inaccessibility due to location within enclosures or some other purposeful architectural modification. For example, if some persons want to live in places away from certain "other" or "disvalued" persons, and if those "other" persons are more apt to ride buses because they cannot afford personal transportation, then why not build a bridge whose clearance is too low for buses to pass under? You could then build a gated community on the other side of the bridge, thereby keeping those "others" who are riding buses from making it to your side.

Clubs get to pick their members and make rules about exit, entry, behavior, characteristics or traits, occupational or employment status, and a host of other criteria. This ability to ensure selectivity and exclusivity means that, at least initially, members have to trust each other to abide by the rules, and if members step out of line they are dealt with by other members. The hope is that order is maintained through voluntary consensus of all the members. Indeed, as a club, the rules stipulate that anyone who does not abide by the rules can be kicked out of the club. Eventually with growth in membership or usage, clubs seek additional help with congestion and risk issues, and may hire outside help to further screen those attempting to enter and to enforce security both externally and internally. Most forms of mass private property can be thought of as clubs, whether industrial estates, business parks, sports stadiums, leisure venues, gated communities, swimming pools, and shopping centers (Crawford 2006, p. 125). Although public police patrol all these areas and can exert their authority where they see fit, for the most part they do not entangle themselves in doings within club enclosures. Yet they may "moonlight" there during off hours, working alongside private security guards.

Is this the new structure of policing that has emerged from the remnants of the presumably now archaic distinctions between public and private? In a provocative essay Bayley and Shearing (2001) believe it is. They begin by making a distinction between auspices of policing and providers of policing. *Auspices* of policing refers to those who authorize policing, while the *providers* of policing are those who actually do the work of policing. Since the beginning of the first era of policing, the state has been both auspice and provider of policing, and this is what is usually referred to whenever the claim is made that the state owns a monopoly on the use of coercive force through the work of a sworn police force. Since that time, however, the state is no longer the sole auspice of policing. Through the process of *multilateralization*—a more precise term than privatization, the latter of which is caught in the murkiness of the public–private conceptual divide—there are now at least five entities or groups that act as auspices of policing. These five auspices are economic interests, residential communities, cultural communities, individuals, and the state. Let us briefly look at each of these.

First, *economic interests* act as an auspice of policing, and shows up in both legitimate and illegitimate forms. On the legitimate side, businesses are keen on assuring the security of their operations as well as providing safe passage for customers. Businesses may pool their resources and form business improvement districts where money is used for trash pickup and removal, police patrols, and physical improvements to buildings, landscape, and other aspects of the environment (Bayley and Shearing 2001, p. 6). As we have seen, some of these businesses are in the form of mass private property, the shopping mall being the leading example. Economic interests may also spur illegitimate businesses such as criminal syndicates or juvenile street gangs, and they authorize the use of (illegal) force in protecting or regulating their own economic interests. The "code of the street," an informal set of rules for regulating violence on the streets of the inner city and enforced by local residents of the community, is an excellent example of this (Anderson 1999).

Second, *residential communities* may act as an auspice for policing. We have already discussed the obvious example of gated communities, but also in this category are realty groups, homeowners associations, and neighborhood watch groups. Residents of a neighborhood may collect dues for purposes of hiring private security guards, and residents themselves may form watch groups providing an extra set of eyes and ears to help the police under various community-policing programs. Of course, in earlier times, before the rise of sworn police forces, residents themselves provided policing services (so-called self-policing).

Third, rather than being based on place or location as in the case of residential communities, *cultural communities* can also act as police auspices. Cultural communities are assemblages of individuals who share some common beliefs or practices, such as the case of the Nation of Islam, an organization of Black Muslims whose members have formed a protective force known as the Fruit of Islam (Bayley and Shearing 2001, p. 8). In the same vein, tattoo enthusiasts often self-police activities taking place in tattoo parlors, ensuring, for example, that conditions are sanitary, that underage persons seeking tattoos are scrutinized, and that exotic requests, such as piercings of certain body parts, are kept to a minimum. In such cases, self-policing is engaged in to keep sworn police officers or the local health board from finding excuses to hassle the establishment.[11]

Fourth, *individuals* can act as auspices for policing. Anyone who engages in self-defense against some threat fits into this category. And the famous and the wealthy can hire body guards to keep fans, gawkers, and paparazzi at arm's distance.

The fifth category is the *state*, the entity which we have suggested all along is the major auspice, as well as the provider, of policing in society. Bayley and Shearing (2001, p. 9) argue that in many ways the state is a major force in the multilateralization of policing through the evolution of policy initiatives and programs—such as third-party policing, community policing, and problem-oriented policing to name a few variants—which seek to increase citizen involvement in policing and which thereby also contribute to the undermining of the state's monopoly on surveillance and use of coercive force. Governments have also occasionally passed laws which legitimate potential use of force by citizens, such as is the case for concealed carry permit provisions in a variety of U.S. jurisdictions.

CONCLUSION

Bayley and Shearing (2001) argue that multilateralization is occurring not only at the level of communities or cities within the United States, but it is expanding globally which is contributing to the internationalization of policing writ large. The earliest and most well-known international policing initiative was the International Criminal Police Commission (ICPC), founded in 1923 in Vienna, Austria, which was originally set up as a way for participating countries to share information about suspects, especially those that had crossed national borders in an attempt to evade capture, but also to help control the spread of radical groups (especially communists and anarchists) considered to be a threat to the political systems of sovereign nations (Deflem 2005). By 1940 some forty nations had joined ICPC.

The United States had initially resisted joining ICPC, which later came to be known as Interpol, because of concerns about the organization held by J. Edgar Hoover, head of the FBI. However, when Nazi Germany joined the organization in 1935, the United States starting taking interest in developments related to the organization (Deflem 2002). The United States joined ICPC in 1938 partly as a way of monitoring the infiltration of Nazi policing in the organization as well as securing America's national interests in light of the approach of World War II. With the creation of Interpol all participating nations operated under the assumption that policing was a government function which, because of the ability of suspects to cross national borders, sometimes required the cooperation and collaboration of police forces across national jurisdictions.

When some large multinational corporations started providing private police services for their own internal needs as well as to clients in business and governments wherever they were located, the privatization of police expanded globally as well. Many global or world bodies have established their own police forces, including the United Nations, the World Court, and the European Union (Bayley and Shearing 2001, p. 40). As national sovereignty and borders continue to erode, perhaps state-based public policing will do likewise. But rather than their complete disappearance, under this scenario it is more likely they will be replaced by national or international police forces as suggested by Bayley and Shearing (2001).

This prospect is fraught with difficulties. First, as the premier formal agents of control, police need to be accountable to the citizens of the communities they serve. Police operating under the auspices of some far-flung or remote controlling agency will be even less responsive to citizens' needs than they are now. Second, how will citizens be billed for local police services if the controlling agency is national or international? How will the cost structure of such an operation be worked out? It is highly likely that citizens who are forced to subsidize the work of police who may have no local ties to the area will grow resentful of a government increasingly operating behind the backs of citizens. Third, why would any sovereign nation be willing to cede the policing of its citizens to police forces which are international or based in other nations?

Community policing gained strength out of the impetus that police forces should more closely resemble the sociodemographic characteristics of the citizens of the local communities they serve.[12] The move to an international police force, whether public or private, providing services and security to any particular local community, would mark a significant regression from this ideal.

Fourth, countries have their own unique laws and systems of governance, and policing in each of these countries is presumably justified on the basis of enforcing those laws. International policing would have to presuppose international law, and the latter is by no means yet established. Perhaps one could have international policing without international law, but such a police force would be markedly different than traditional police forces which operate on the basis of a constabulary, namely, a legitimate coercive force empowered to enforce the laws of a jurisdiction. As Levi and Hagan (2006, pp. 234–235) note, international law relies on voluntary cooperation between member states, rather than the coercive work of a constabulary assigned to a particular sovereign jurisdiction. Hence, for now the prospects of an international police force are limited by the obdurate reality of this split between law and police.

Many intellectuals holding liberal ideological or political positions welcome the move to internationalization or globalization because it would represent the culmination of the slow and painful attempt to overcome divisive distinctions on the basis of place, nationality, and tradition. The founder of American sociology, Lester Ward, articulated such a position as far back as 1883. In the deep and dark past human beings were solitary and brutish, and they huddled together in their tribes or clans making war against anyone outside of their group. Slowly, however, human beings learned it was advantageous to set up communitarian and reciprocal relations with other groups, if for no other reason than to avoid an incessant war of all against all. Ward believed that the development of human society would at some unspecified point in the future take the form of the pantarchic, whereby human beings would be united in a world community as ideals such as altruism, reciprocity, and love of humanity would burst beyond the confines of the nation-state thereby rendering that concept obsolete (Chriss 2007c; Ward 1883, v. 1, pp. 464–468). Ward was prescient on this point, as he wrote these words well before the development of international organizations such as the World Court, the League of Nations, and the United Nations actually came to fruition.

The dream of secular humanism is that we are strengthened in our diversity, because as we hold fewer and fewer things in common the last remaining bond shared by all is our humanity (Durkheim 1984 [1893]). A one-world order would be based upon the most general and abstract good which is humanity, and human rights would be its major supporting plank. It is all feel-good and lovey-dovey, but why or how would something as profane and nitty-gritty as policing be folded into this? For some policing is a nagging reminder of the darker aspects of our humanity which gives the lie to lofty notions about the globalization of the human community. The nagging reminder is the truth of Bittner's Principle, namely that the core of the police role is the nonnegotiable distribution of coercive force. We believe that as enlightenment continues to expand, we will be able to leave behind, finally, all the undesirable aspects of our past which still linger in the present, including aggression, violence, coercion, lying, deceit, ill will, terrorism, and war. But that is just the point: the nastiness from the past still lingers, and that is why the police make sense and are still needed.

The police are packaged as a new and enlightened group of individuals who can be used in a constructive way (such as in the case of positive proactivity discussed in Chapter 7) to restore communities, to teach our children how to avoid the temptations of drugs and gangs, to help the elderly avoid becoming victims of crime, and to use the latest data-analysis techniques to understand the root causes of crime and disorder with an eye toward eliminating them. This is all well and good, but notice that while police stay busy doing this work most remain armed and uniformed, especially in a post 9-11 era where safety and security are the key public (and private) goods. Whatever lies beyond community policing and post 9-11 policing, it is very likely that Bittner's Principle will be retained as the key element.

NOTES

[1] Interestingly enough, the well-known Pinkerton detective agency has expanded over the years, and one part of their operation is the Pinkerton Global Intelligence Service. In this respect, Pinkerton's ongoing analysis and monitoring of international terrorism has been a major contributor to the Global Terrorism Database (GTD), a key resource utilized by law enforcement as well as criminologists in the study of terrorism (LaFree and Dugan 2009).

[2] Brown (1976) makes an analytical distinction between these two forms of vigilantism which is worth noting. The aim of the earlier type of vigilantism practiced primarily on the western frontier was aimed at crime control (punishing outlaws and rustlers), while the aim of the later wave of vigilantism was social control of particular groups (most notably Jews, African-Americans, and "radicals"). The latter form of vigilantism was fomented as well by the rise of organized hate groups such as the Ku Klux Klan, which formed in Tennessee in 1865.

[3] Undercover policing is, of course, an exception to this general rule. For an interesting analysis of how undercover policing mixes aspects of both public and private policing, see Marx (1986).

[4] This graph is available at http://bjs.ojp.usdoj.gov/content/glance/exptyp.cfm.

[5] This economic downturn has also gone global, and is affecting police operations and other vital functions of government in many areas of the world. We briefly covered Greek policing in Chapter 1, and it is interesting to note that among all European nations, Greece is operating with a crushing debt which pushed Eurozone leaders into agreeing to provide to Greece an emergency bail-

out, on the requirement that Greece climb out of its massive debt by 2012. Greece's debt problem has many observers concerned that other nations will require similar bailouts, which in turn would likely impact the United States which is struggling with its own massive deficits. And since the Greek debt problem has been publicized more widely, armed clashes between Greek police and citizens worried about how planned budget cuts will adversely affect their lives have resurfaced. See "Eurozone Leaders Back Greece Rescue Plan," published February 11, 2010 by the *Financial Times* and available at http://www.ft. com/cms/s/0/226231f0-16fd-11df-afcf-00144feab49a.html, and "Greek Police Clash with Protesters as National Strike Takes Hold," published February 24, 2010 by the *Guardian* and available at http://www.guardian.co.uk/world/2010/ feb/24/greek-police-clash-protesters-national-strike.

[6] Information on the situation in Oakland was taken from a *Wall Street Journal* article titled "Cash-Strapped Cities Try Private Guards over Police," which can be found at http://online.wsj.com/article/SB124027127337237011.html.

[7] I thank Regina Moore for providing feedback and clarifications on the topic of accident response fees.

[8] Some of the points made by Regina Moore discussed here arose during phone conversations I held with her in late January, 2010. Position statements from Ms. Moore can also be found on the company website at http://www. costrecovercorp.com.

[9] The testimonial of Chief Jackson was provided to me by Ms. Moore at Cost Recovery Corporation.

[10] White (2007) draws on a 2002 article by James J. Onder, a Highway Safety Specialist in the Traffic Law Enforcement Division of the National Highway Traffic Safety Administration. The article is titled "Traffic Safety" and is available at http://www.sussexcountysheriff.com/traffic_safety.htm.

[11] See the article "Self-Policing Tattoo Joints," originally published in the Colorado Springs *Gazette* on July 15, 2008, which can be found at http://findarticles. com/p/articles/mi_qn4191/is_20080715/ai_n27998307/?tag=content;col1.

[12] Whereas in earlier times the great majority of police officers were White and male, today the situation has changed rather dramatically. In 1970 Blacks made up about 6% of sworn officers, but today the figure is around 18%. And in 2005, for the first time in its history, the majority of graduating officers in the New York City Police Department were members of racial minorities (Sklansky 2006, pp. 1213–1214).

10

Police and Society:
A Summary of Principles

In this concluding chapter I summarize the major findings, or first principles, of this study. Any author studying the police makes certain decisions about what to cover, meaning that much that could potentially be covered pertinent to police and society issues is left out or merely glossed over. Keeping this caveat in mind, the first principles presented here reflect a condensation of key points made throughout the book, with additional comments and elaborations where appropriate.

Also, the concept of "first principles" is borrowed from Herbert Spencer (1864), but I use it in a somewhat different way than Spencer. From the mid to the late 1800s Spencer published a series of books, the total project of which he called "synthetic philosophy." Spencer presented a sweeping, cosmological vision of all current knowledge, and summarized key propositions or principles about all that was known in physics, chemistry, biology, psychology, sociology, ethics, and morals. The project was synthetic to the extent that Spencer did not limit himself to one topic or one field of study. He simply set out to document the first principles about everything known of his era which had a sound scientific foundation (rather than being grounded in speculative philosophy or religion), and this meant covering all phenomena whether inorganic, organic, or super-organic (that is, the social organization of living organisms). For example, from physics two of Spencer's first principles were the "conservation of energy" and the "persistence of force." Unlike later sociologists (such as Durkheim) who limited explanations of social phenomena to the frame of reference of human society or "social facts," cosmologists such as Comte, Spencer, and Ward believed that science must incorporate all philosophical truths into a total conceptual system, otherwise all you have are partial truths which do not speak to the continuities between all areas of knowledge (Haines 1992). For Spencer and other early cosmologists or grand synthetic philosophers,

fundamental laws of nature, of chemistry and biology, of zoology and astronomy, and even of psychology (earlier referred to as transcendental physiology or
biology), should all be incorporated into explanations of human social phenomena. Yet, for Spencer and these other cosmologists, the first principles of mass,
matter, motion, and energy were the foundation upon which all other secondary
principles or findings were built (Bitsakis 1991).

Of course, since Spencer's time the specialization of scientific knowledge has proceeded unabated, and the assumption now is that the growth of
knowledge is so vast that no field of study could hope to incorporate all that is
known from other fields. Even more to the point, by limiting the frame of reference to, say, the social, or cultural, or criminological, one is also saying that the
first principles lying outside the immediate field of study are simply irrelevant.
From the perspective of this conceptual strategy, one can simply take for granted
the first principles lying outside the immediate field of interest, as they are external to the conceptual system being developed connected with any particular
substantive agenda.

For the most part I follow the later trend of development and do not go
all the way back to the "simpler sciences" such as physics, chemistry, or biology
to derive what I am here calling the first principles of police and society. Actually, in many ways the utilization of the AGIL schema of Talcott Parsons does
allow some dipping into these areas, because with Parsons one may explain sociological or criminological phenomena with reference to organisms and the
environments to which they adapt (A); motivational complexes arising within
stable personality systems (G), the integration of the multitudes of human organisms seeking gratifications and other life plans within the patterns that have
come to be known as social structure, itself composed of the interlocking of unit
acts (I); and the guiding of these many and varied activities by an overarching
value system which helps to maintain patterns across time and from generation
to generation (L). The basis of the principles presented here is the wide-ranging
literature within sociology and criminology touching upon the particular topics
that I have chosen to cover in this particular book, and interpreted where appropriate by way of a conceptual frame of reference informed by Talcott Parsons,
Egon Bittner, and a few other key thinkers.

I now summarize the major principles of the study, listing them by
chapter and numbering them continuously 1 through 103.

CHAPTER 1

1. BITTNER'S PRINCIPLE: The core of the police role is the distribution of
nonnegotiably coercive force, applied in accordance with officers' intuitive
grasp of situational exigencies.

2. The great majority of persons who have had contact with the police in routine
situations (a call for police help, or police responses to a traffic accident) say

that the police acted properly, and there are no significant differences by respondents' race.

3. When persons are themselves targets of police actions, there are significant differences by race: Blacks are much less likely than Whites and Hispanics to say that the police acted properly.

4. Most encounters between citizens and the police are asymmetrical, to the extent that police hold far more power than citizens, and their version of events (as reflected in the police report) are more likely to be believed by key actors in the criminal justice system (prosecutors, judges, and juries to name a few).

5. The impact of a bad encounter with the police is four to fourteen times greater than the impact of a positive police encounter.

6. Police organizations are government agencies which pursue political goals, namely those of social control. Over time, however, the overtly political aspects of police operations have been deemphasized in favor of more social humanitarian goals such as community integration, building trust, and values identification and maintenance.

7. Police are oftentimes caught in the middle between two competing and sometimes contradictory goals of the criminal justice system, namely, to arrest the "bad guys" (crime control), while doing so in such a way that defendants' rights are ensured (due process).

8. Because professional status is typically linked with the quality of the clientele being served by that profession, and because the police are often involved with disreputable characters, police work may come to be viewed as a tainted profession.

9. Everyday troubles may eventuate in someone "calling the cops," and because reasons for doing so are enormously varied, by necessity the police mandate is diffuse, uncertain, and even unmanageable.

10. Although police are vested with the coercive power of the state, more often than not they *do not* employ physical force in their dealings with citizens.

CHAPTER 2

11. The oldest form of social control is self-help, whereby members of a group attempt to ensure the conformity of its members to tacitly understood and overtly enforced standards of conduct.

12. As society becomes more advanced work becomes more specialized, including the work of social control. With the rise of the state, formal agents of control specialize in enforcing laws of the state's political jurisdiction. These formal agents are the police.

13. The rise of municipal policing in Britain, the United States, and elsewhere was not viewed particularly favorably by citizens, but tolerated as a "necessary evil" given the worrisome changes afoot in these societies especially beginning in the early 1800s.

14. The first phase of policing, political spoils, ran from the 1830s through the 1920s, and was characterized by municipal policing being heavily controlled by the local political machine as well as powerful members of the community.

15. The second era of policing, reform and early professionalization, from the 1920s through the 1960s, was marked by attempts at professionalizing policing (largely through specialization in crime control), but also early reforms such as placing distance between the police and the untoward influences of both citizens and local politics.

16. Bureaucratic control of policing through quasi-military design came to prominence in this era thanks to the efforts of Ernest Vollmer and later O.W. Wilson.

17. The third era of policing, referred to as community policing, emerged beginning in the 1970s as a result of the turbulent 1960s and the fact that, as defenders of the status quo, the police were involved in a number of high-profile clashes with citizens engaged in various social movements of the era. As the legitimacy of the professional model of policing waned, calls went out for serious reform of the police beyond those initiated during the previous era. In essence, there was a move to ensure that police understood the needs and life circumstances of the members of the communities they served.

18. A form of policing closely allied to community policing is problem-oriented policing, which emphasizes citizen collaboration with the police to solve pressing problems in the community utilizing the methodology of SARA (scan, analyze, respond, and assess).

19. Generally, as population mobility increases in a community, implementation of community-policing programs increases as well.

20. The more formalized are the directives for community-policing implementation, the more likely such programs will actually be implemented in a community.

CHAPTER 3

21. The three eras of American policing pertain to the northeastern United States, which was settled first and which produced the earliest and largest urban metropolises—Boston, New York City, and Philadelphia—within which municipal policing developed. As a consequence, the three-era typology largely omits developments west of the Mississippi River between 1840 and 1890, in the so-called western frontier.

22. In the earliest stages the vast and unsettled American western frontier was primarily a problem of land management, assessment, and apportionment. The U.S. military along with government surveyors were initially assigned to controlling and surveying this territory.

23. The settling of towns on the western frontier was difficult because of endemic conflicts with Native American tribes, Mexicans to the south and the southwest, and an unpredictable and transient population of settlers, pioneers, cowboys, and outlaws.

24. The year of the establishment of a municipal police forced is based upon the year of uniform adoption. Upon this basis, the first western police force was that of San Francisco in 1857.

25. President Lincoln's Homestead Act of 1862 accelerated the populating and settling of the western plains, even while the Civil War and its aftermath introduced further challenges to the establishment of both cities and police forces in the region during this time.

26. The "code of the west" was an informal set of norms emphasizing masculinity and rugged individualism, and when threatened there was a duty to act to preserve physical security but also honor and dignity. Absent effective law enforcement, this system of informal control predominated across the western frontier until a critical mass of towns was established.

27. In the transition from the solitary peace officer to the institutionalization of policing and criminal justice on the western frontier, there was great fluidity between the roles of outlaw and lawman. Indeed, it was not uncommon for a person to occupy both roles at various points in his life.

28. The western frontier was unstable because of the extreme mobility of one of its most valuable personal assets: horses.

29. An importation model of settlement characterized the western frontier: persons coming to the region carried in their heads how social order looked and

felt, and they attempted to impose order where they could. This was made more difficult by the demographics of migration to the area, as there was an over-representation of single, unattached males, most importantly the cowboys.

30. Some western towns, such as Wichita, Kansas, moved from being incorpo-rated as a city to the establishment of a police department literally within a decade. This accelerated development in the west was unique in comparison to the slower and long-term pace which characterized the settling of towns and the establishment of police departments in the American northeast.

31. On the western frontier, as elsewhere, cities establish police departments for any number of reasons, including (1) concerns over crime real or perceived; (2) concerns over social disorder which fall short of criminal activities; (3) concerns over an influx of disreputable characters into the area, including immigrants, outlaws, rustlers, squatters and vagabonds, and other assorted groups; (4) com-petition between cities in close physical proximity which are seeking to attract new residents.

CHAPTER 4

32. Police are effective only to the extent that citizens view them as honest, fair, and impartial in the discharging of their duties.

33. Police are held to a higher standard of accountability because they are vested with the coercive power of the state.

34. Ensuring police integrity is one of the most demanding and difficult goals of police organizations, due in large part to the various dilemmas which holders of power confront on a daily basis (including entangled hands, many hands, and dirty hands).

35. Integrity tests are simulations which place officers in monitored situations where they have the opportunity to engage in illegal or unethical activities. The test is to see if the officer gives in to temptations presented.

36. Random testing is directed at an entire police department or specialized units within the department. Targeted testing is specially designed for particular offic-ers who are suspected of corruption.

37. Targeted integrity testing produces many more "hits"—that is, catching officers in corruption—than random testing.

38. Targeted integrity testing always has to contend with the problem of entrapment, that is, providing an officer with an inducement for some corrupt or criminal behavior which otherwise would not normally exist.

39. Police discretion is enormous, and of all the decisions facing police officers, the decision to arrest carries the greatest consequences for citizens.

40. The decision to arrest is complex, but among some of the key contributors to the decision are seriousness of offense, suspect's criminal record, victim willingness to file a complaint, availability of evidence at the scene, suspect's general demeanor, and level of suspect resistance.

41. Even when facing a situation in which an arrest could be made, most of the time police officers *do not* make an arrest.

42. Police officers are even less likely to fire their weapon in situations in which the legal elements are present which would allow them to do so.

43. The darker the uniform, the more positive impression citizens have of the police.

44. The most often cited reason for nonarrest is officer uncertainty over the illegality of the alleged act.

45. Officers often engage in adaptive arrest behavior. For example, if a police officer is seeking overtime he or she may seek arrests near the end of the shift. Likewise if an officer wants to finish a shift on time, he or she will avoid arrests in the latter half of the shift.

CHAPTER 5

46. In response to the terrorist attacks of September 11, 2001, a more tightly integrated network of U.S. law enforcement was generated. With the creation of the Department of Homeland Security, federal, state, and local law enforcement agencies work more closely together, sharing information and developing collaborative strategies with regard to counterterrorism and crisis response and preparedness.

47. As a result, some speak of a fourth era of policing, so-called post 9-11 policing. The emphasis of post 9-11 policing is on security, in ways a return to the second era where police specialized in crime control.

48. Like any organization, police organizations are embedded within broader institutional environments in which crucial services are provided (typically, law

enforcement, service, order maintenance, and security). Beyond functioning in a completely technical capacity (matching goals to available resources on the basis of the demand structure of the community) police also operate on the basis of rhetoric and other nontechnical aspects, seeking for example to justify their existence on the basis of comporting with prevailing cultural notions of propriety.

49. At the most general level of the institutional environment, government or polity serves the goal-attainment function for the broader social system, and utilizes power to pursue goals as well as ordering them in a goals hierarchy.

50. The administrative system serves the function of adaptation for the polity, as it utilizes the raw resources of the governmental institutional environment and adapts to changes therein.

51. Within the administrative subsystem, the criminal justice system serves the function of adaptation, as it utilizes power seated in the polity to deal with the raw material, namely people identified as potential lawbreakers, in the process adapting to and processing this material from the front end (contact with police) to the back end (conferring of a sanction via the correctional system).

52. Within the criminal justice system the police serve the function of goal attainment, as it attempts to link up with the demand structure of the wider community to provide essential services in the areas of crime control, order maintenance, service, and/or security.

53. Post 9-11 policing serves the functions of adaptation through readying for new operational realities of international terrorism.

54. Goal-attainment functions of post 9-11 policing include federally-led responses which local police departments must implement with regard to the unique demand structure of each local community.

55. The integrative function of post 9-11 policing comes by way of information sharing across levels of law enforcement (federal, state, and local), identifying "best practices" for counterterrorism and community preparedness.

56. The pattern-maintenance function of post 9-11 policing operates through the institutionalization of the USA Patriot Act, and these operational guidelines fan out across lower levels of law enforcement (state and local) which, when properly implemented according to legal and normative guidelines, also work to preserve public trust regarding new mission configurations.

57. With regard to police field operations in general, service serves the adaptation function, law enforcement the goal-attainment function, order maintenance

the integrative function, and the provision of security (a more general undertaking than law enforcement) the pattern-maintenance function. Of course, these various functions rise or decline in prominence according to the unique demand structures and institutional environments of the communities within which police departments operate.

CHAPTER 6

58. Discretion is the freedom of an official to act or not act in his or her official capacity in ways not specifically prescribed by the rules designating expected conduct in the position.

59. Among criminal justice personnel, field operations police officers have the most discretion. Court personnel have high discretion as well, but not as high as police. Corrections personnel have the lowest level of discretion relative to personnel in policing and the courts.

60. Both organizational and operational factors contribute to levels of discretion among police officers. However, the written rules of the organization do a poor job of following officers out into the field, so the operational rules, that is, the tacit understandings about the world informed by actually working the streets and meeting various social types, are more important in guiding actual police behavior.

61. Three other factors contribute to police officers' high levels of discretion: openness of work horizons, personnel density, and visibility. Because patrol officers wear uniforms, they are more visible than undercover or plainclothes officers, and hence the latter enjoy higher levels of discretion relative to the former.

62. In the community-policing era police are asked to do a variety of things beyond simply law enforcement and order maintenance, and these diverse role requirements also lead to heightened discretion so that police can multitask in and across these roles.

63. Police discretion does not occur at only one specific point in time and place, but operates across multiple decision points, and hence discretion is a complex and multifaceted phenomenon.

64. There are a number of "working rules" which police officers formulate out of their collective work experiences. Rather than bureaucratic directives codified in the standard operating procedures, these working rules form part of the background subculture of police work, and hence are vital resources officers draw upon for acting and making decisions out in the field.

65. Upon contact between police and citizens, a police occasion emerges, and eight basic types of police occasions can be noted. These police occasions are produced on the basis of four factors, namely structure, schedule, focus of attention, and contact rules. And each of these factors may exist in a high or low state, thereby producing the eight types of police occasions.

66. Although there is a popular movement to continue to work on ways to reduce police discretion, it is easier said than done. For example, evidence that is gained by way of an illegal search by the police cannot be admitted into the record at a criminal trial. But because police hold the power of the police report, they can claim that the evidence was in plain sight, thus sidestepping the question of the illegality of the search. Time and time again, for the police the power of operations (on-the-ground discretion) trumps the power of organization (bureaucratic rules and mandates).

67. Although these typically high levels of discretion provide police officers with ample opportunities to violate the fiduciary trust of their position, most police officers most of the time engage in lawful policing.

CHAPTER 7

68. Although historically policing has been reactive (responding to citizen calls for help), especially since the community-policing era police are acting more proactively.

69. Negative proactivity is acting to keep bad things from happening (for example, vice operations under standard policing or later broken windows policing), while positive proactivity is acting to promote a desired future state of affairs. Among policing, examples of positive proactivity include problem-solving policing and information-led policing.

70. Within sociology, the innovator of proactivity was the early American sociologist Lester F. Ward (in 1883), whose concept of indirect conation is equivalent to the later developed concept of proactivity.

71. The most important early forms of proactivity were new technologies which allowed persons to escape from direct conation (merely reacting to stimuli in direct fashion) to indirect conation (that is, using the new technology as a means to achieve new and improved ends).

72. The first scholarly article which mentioned proactivity with regard to policing was a 1966 paper by David Bordua and Albert J. Reiss published in *American Journal of Sociology*. In the article the authors noted that the traditional

command-and-control structure of policing was reactive, that is, sending officers to persons requesting help through the dispatch system. As education and training for officers increased, they were released from centralized control and allowed to use their expertise and discretion to adjudicate situations as they saw them out in the field, hence opening the way to greater proactivity.

73. The earliest form of proactive policing is vice work: since there is often no complainant in such victimless crimes, officers have to catch perpetrators in the act via sometimes elaborate sting operations and other forms of deception.

CHAPTER 8

74. Under conditions of community diversity and increasing decentralization of police operations under community policing and beyond, police do much of their work by way of negotiated order, relying less on the strict letter of the law and more on the specifics of places and persons within particular jurisdictions.

75. This emphasis on flexibility in dealing with diverse persons and places according to prevailing understandings of how best to maintain the peace within particular jurisdictions means that police play the part of contact men and women in the community.

76. Three basic social types police encounter in their daily work are know-nothings, suspicious persons, and assholes. Assholes are persons who are not initially seen as suspicious or threatening, but who within the unfolding police occasion act in ways which challenge police authority. Such persons, rightly or wrongly, may be singled out by police for extralegal actions falling under the rubric of "street justice."

77. Modern municipal police have returned to the role of generalists which they initially played in the first era of political spoils. However, unlike the first era where communities were homogeneous, modern communities are heterogeneous, fragmented, and diverse, and as a result police must be especially skilled at sorting through the mass of diverse humanity with which they come into contact in their daily rounds. These special skills are embodied in the contact person.

78. Demands for higher multitasking skills by the police are taking place on two fronts, namely the proliferation of technology with which police work ("hard skills"), as well as the proliferation of diverse places, persons, and situations police are likely to encounter on their beats ("soft skills"). Again, this special skill set points to police as contact men and women.

79. Municipal police officers are the primary boundary-spanning personnel for police departments, as they are the ones who are sent out into the field to deal with the empirical realities that await there.

80. Contact men in the arts industries (TV, film, and books) hit the streets and sign creative artists to the organizations they represent. They are given great discretion to weed through the mass of humanity for the purposes of connecting a mass audience to the creative products of the artists which they bring in to the organization. Police in the community-policing era and beyond act much in the same way.

81. Like contact men in the arts industries, modern police are boundary-spanning multitaskers who must connect with multiple stakeholders in the community. In the game of social order, police act as contact men, gatekeepers, and access brokers, having expertise in dealing with all manner of individuals in an attempt to maximize this public good. Besides the work of suppressing meat eaters and grass eaters—those that do not contribute to the production of social order—the police also cajole citizens into good works by using their special skills in human relations.

82. Conceptualizing police as contact persons takes the police organization beyond a reliance on power (traditional policing with emphasis on crime fighting) or influence (represented in later more "compassionate" and enlightened forms of policing such as community policing and problem-oriented policing), to a new reliance on communications (such as police as savvy users of media to portray themselves in the most flattering light possible).

83. This progression or evolution of policing makes sense if we keep in mind the functional aspects of communities, and how police organizations are situated within the broader institutional environments of the communities within which they are embedded. Police as proactive, boundary-spanning multitaskers are equipped to deal with the random arrivals of individuals across network configurations within communities (a Poisson distribution), and can sort through this sea of humanity to help promote community solidarity while still fulfilling traditional goals of crime control and order maintenance utilizing power from the polity and influence from the societal community.

84. Police are differentially concerned with or pertinent to different functional aspects of communities. In the modern condition, police as contact persons are not particularly involved with helping to fulfill either the adaptation function (residence) or the goal-attainment function (work). By the time of the rise of the service city in the late 1700s, police were in a position to help fulfill the jurisdiction or integrative function of communities beginning in the 1830s (the first era of political spoils). Beginning in the community-policing era and now moving beyond it, police as contact persons have elevated to primacy the overseeing and

supervision of the communicative or latent pattern-maintenance function for communities.

CHAPTER 9

85. In the United States, more than twice as much money is spent on private policing and security as on public policing and security.

86. Public or government-based policing arose with the emergence of the state, and coexists alongside the much more ancient forms of social control carried out by persons within their own groups, tribes, and communities. The primordial form of social control was self-help. Later developments in public policing more or less evolved from and supplemented informal systems of self-help.

87. The urban environment is in many respects chaotic and unpredictable due to high population densities and emphasis on mobility via transportation systems. Even if the urban metropolis is described as "ungovernable," it was nevertheless the case that by the middle-1800s city governments handed the task of public order to the police. This is because persons could no longer effectively hold others in check through informal systems of oversight and surveillance.

88. Four prominent forms of self-help (or private justice) which existed before the institutionalization of criminal justice systems on the American western frontier were land clubs, the movement of wagon trains, the rise of mining camps with the discovery of gold in the southwest, and the rise of vigilantism.

89. The story of the settling of the western frontier was as much as anything the story of the slow and difficult transition from the solitary peace officer battling an assortment of disreputable characters, to the establishment and institutionalization of criminal justice systems.

90. The sense of security of an area includes physical security (A) of one's person and possessions; psychological security (G) in the form of assurances that the unpredictable will be held to a minimum; societal security (I), namely familiarity with the patterns and habits of forms of life prevalent in the area; and cultural security (L), whereby persons recognize the local area, identify with it, and are in solidarity with a critical mass of persons residing there. These can also be thought of as functional elements of security in general according to AGIL designations as noted.

91. Before the rise of public policing citizens attempted to provide for all these forms of security. Police first assured the A-function or physical side of security, then later started defining the remaining areas of security (such as psychological security or fear of crime) as their responsibility as well. This continuing

expansion of more and more aspects of society being defined as pertinent to policing contributes in large part to the "impossible mandate" of policing.

92. Public or government police are concerned primarily with compliance and deterrence, while private police operate more with the logic of administrative regulation.

93. In 2006 the cost of operating the American criminal justice system was immense, with $100 billion spent on policing, about $70 billion on corrections, and about $45 billion on the courts.

94. In order to cut costs, many cities are experimenting with the use of various types of private security, as well as designating more civilian and nonsworn positions in local law enforcement.

95. Some cities are collecting extra fees whenever safety forces (fire, police, and EMS) respond to accident scenes. These so-called accident response fees are controversial, not least because the city attempts to charge the cost of the accident response to the insurance company of the at-fault driver.

96. One implication of imposing accident response fees on drivers and insurance companies is making the argument that police should divest themselves of civil matters such as traffic accidents. This implies that police should attend narrowly to criminal matters, returning them once again to the second era of reform and early professionalization and the argument of professionalization through specialization in law enforcement and crime control.

97. The blurring between public and private, both in society in general and policing in particular, has been prodded along with the cultural formation known as mass private property, namely, large areas privately owned but which serve the general public (examples being shopping malls, gated communities, and exercise clubs).

98. It is typically private security guards employed by the owners of these mass private properties who determine the entrance and exit of members of the general public, as well as supervising use of the facilities while inside.

99. Although police hold a monopoly on the use of coercive force in society, they do not hold a monopoly on the provision of public security and safety. Indeed, in modern society there is a multitude of both public and private providers of such services.

100. It is also useful to make a distinction between auspices or authorizers of policing on the one hand, and providers of policing services on the other. With the rise of the state, government was both the auspice and provider of policing.

But today, through the process of multilateralization, the auspices of policing are numerous and can be determined by economic interests, by members of residential communities, by cultural communities in the abstract, by individuals (such as in the case of self-defense), and of course by the state.

101. With the growth of large multinational corporations, the multilateralization of policing has spread to the global level. However, the internationalization of policing, representing a chaotic mix of national police forces as well as private police forces connected with business and international entities (such as the United Nations), does not provide clear guidelines regarding how laws of particular sovereign nations could be enforced by international law enforcement forces.

102. Globalization or internalization in the abstract is a dream of many political liberals, for it would represent an important step in moving beyond invidious distinctions of place, tradition, and nationality. If national borders are soon to become obsolete, merely a dim relic of the past now cast off in a new era of global enlightenment, what becomes of the concept of police? Does it survive at the national level? Does it make sense at the international level? Before asking such questions, we must first grapple with an even more fundamental question: what do we want the police to do?

103. Whatever configuration it may take, it is hard to imagine policing in terms other than that implied in Bittner's Principle, namely, that the core of the police role is the distribution of coercive force in society. Until we reach the utopian goal of eradicating war, terrorism, crime, ill will, lying, stealing, cheating, or the coveting of that which is not ours, policing will be needed.

Bibliography

Adams, Ramon F. 1963. "Cowboys and Horses of the American West." Pp. 323–376 in *The Book of the American West*, edited by J. Monaghan and C.P. Hornung. New York: Julian Messner Inc.

Alpert, Geoffrey P. and Jeffrey J. Noble, Esq. 2009. "Lies, True Lies, and Conscious Deception: Police Officers and the Truth." *Police Quarterly* 12 (2):237–254.

Anderson, Elijah. 1999. *Code of the Street: Decency, Violence, and the Moral Life of the Inner City*. New York: Norton.

Anderson, G.S., A. Courtney, D. Plecas, and C. Chamberlin. 2005. "Multitasking Behaviors of General Duty Police Officers." *Police Practice and Research* 6 (1):39–48.

Ankony, Robert C. and Thomas M. Kelley. 1999. "The Impact of Perceived Alienation on Police Officers' Sense of Mastery and Subsequent Motivation for Proactive Enforcement." *Policing* 22 (2):120–132.

Arcuri, Alan F. 1977. "Criminal Justice: A Police Perspective." *Criminal Justice Review* 2 (1):15–21.

Atwood, Kay. 2008. *Chaining Oregon: Surveying the Public Lands of the Pacific Northwest, 1851–1855*. Blacksburg, VA: McDonald and Woodward Publishing.

Bailey, John and Lucía Dammert. 2006. "Public Security and Police Reform in the Americas." Pp. 1–23 in *Public Security and Police Reform in the Americas*, edited by J. Bailey and L. Dammert. Pittsburgh, PA: University of Pittsburgh Press.

Bales, Robert F. 1950. *Interaction Process Analysis: A Method for the Study of Small Groups*. Reading, MA: Addison-Wesley.

———. 1953. "The Equilibrium Problem in Small Groups." Pp. 111–161 in *Working Papers in the Theory of Action*, edited by T. Parsons, R.F. Bales, and E.A. Shils. New York: Free Press.

Ball, Durwood. 2001. *Army Regulars on the Western Frontier, 1848–1861*. Norman: University of Oklahoma Press.

Balogun, Julia, Pauline Gleadle, Veronica Hope Hailey, and Hugh Willmott. 2005. "Managing Change across Boundaries: Boundary-Shaking Practices." *British Journal of Management* 16:261–278.

Bannister, Robert C. 1987. *Sociology and Scientism*. Chapel Hill: University of North Carolina Press.

Barth, Alan. 1961. *Law Enforcement versus the Law*. New York: Collier Books.

Bartlett, Richard A. 1962. *Great Surveys of the American West*. Norman: University of Oklahoma Press.

Bayley, David H. and Clifford D. Shearing. 2001. "The New Structure of Policing: Description, Conceptualization, and Research Agenda." *NIJ Research Report*. Washington, DC: National Institute of Justice.

Bayley, David H. and David Weisburd. 2009. "Cops and Spooks: The Role of the Police in Counterterrorism." Pp. 81–99 in *To Protect and to Serve: Policing in an Age of Terrorism*, edited by D. Weisburd, T.E. Feucht, I. Hakimi, L.F. Mock, and S. Perry. Dordrecht: Springer.

Belvedere, Kimberly, John L. Worrall, and Stephen G. Tibbetts. 2005. "Explaining Suspect Resistance in Police-Citizen Encounters." *Criminal Justice Review* 30 (1):30–44.

Benedict, William Reed, Douglas J. Bower, Ben Brown, and Roger Cunningham. 1999. "Small Town Surveys: Bridging the Gap between Police and the Community." *Journal of Contemporary Criminal Justice Review* 15 (2):144–154.

Bendix, Reinhard. 1947. "Bureaucracy: The Problem and Its Setting." *American Sociological Review* 12 (5):493–507.

Bennett, Trevor. 1995. "Identifying, Explaining, and Targeting Burglary 'Hot Spots.'" *European Journal on Criminal Policy and Research* 3 (3):113–123.

Benson, Bruce L. 1998. *To Serve and Protect: Privatization and Community in Criminal Justice*. New York: New York University Press.

———. "Contractual Nullification of Economically-Detrimental State-Made Laws." *Review of Austrian Economics* 19:149–187.

Bernard, Thomas J., Eugene A. Paoline, III, and Paul-Philippe Pare. 2005. "General Systems Theory and Criminal Justice." *Journal of Criminal Justice* 33:203–211.

Bitsakis, Eftichios. 1991. "Mass, Matter, and Energy: A Relativistic Approach." *Foundations of Physics* 21 (1):63–81.

Bittner, Egon. 1967. "The Police on Skid-Row: A Study of Police Keeping." *American Sociological Review* 32 (5):699–715.

———. 1970. *The Functions of the Police in Modern Society*. Chevy Chase, MD: National Institute of Mental Health.

———. 1990. *Aspects of Police Work*. Boston: Northeastern University Press.

Black, Donald J. 1970. "Production of Crime Rates." *American Sociological Review* 35 (4):733–748.

———. 1971. "The Social Organization of Arrest." *Stanford Law Review* 23: 1087–1111.

———. 1976. *The Behavior of Law*. San Diego: Academic Press.

———. 1980. *The Manners and Customs of the Police*. New York: Academic Press.

Black, Donald J. and Albert J. Reiss, Jr. 1970. "Police Control of Juveniles." *American Sociological Review* 35 (1):63–77.

Bohannan, Paul. 1973. "The Differing Realms of the Law." Pp. 306–317 in *The Social Organization of Law*, edited by D. Black and M. Mileski. New York: Seminar Press.

Booth, Charles. 1970 [1902–1904]. *Life and Labour of the People in London*, final volume. New York: AMS Press.

Bordua, David J. and Albert J. Reiss, Jr. 1966. "Command, Control, and Charisma: Reflections on Police Bureaucracy." *American Journal of Sociology* 72 (1):68–76.

Brodeur, Jean-Paul. 1983. "High Policing and Low Policing: Some Remarks about the Policing of Political Activities." *Social Problems* 30:507–521.

———. 2007a. "High and Low Policing in Post 9/11 Times." *Policing* 1:25–37.

———. 2007b. "An Encounter with Egon Bittner." *Crime, Law and Social Change* 48:105–132.

Brodeur, Jean-Paul and Stéphane Leman-Langlois. 2006. "Surveillance Fiction or Higher Policing?" Pp. 171–198 in *The New Politics of Surveillance and Visibility*, edited by K.D. Haggerty and R.V. Ericson. Toronto: University of Toronto Press.

Brown, Ben. 2007. "Community Policing in Post-September 11 America: A Comment on the Concept of Community-Oriented Counterterrorism." *Police Practice and Research* 8 (3):239–251.

Brown, Mary M. and Jeffrey L. Brudney. 2003. "Learning Organizations in the Public Sector? A Study of Police Agencies Employing Information and Technology to Advance Knowledge." *Public Administration Review* 63 (1):30–43.

Brown, Richard M. 1976. "The History of Vigilantism in America." Pp. 79–109 in *Vigilante Politics*, edited by H.J. Rosenbaum and P.C. Sedeberg. Philadelphia: University of Pennsylvania Press.

Brunson, Rod K. 2007. "'Police Don't Like Black People': African-American Young Men's Accumulated Police Experiences." *Criminology and Public Policy* 6 (1):71–101.

Buerger, Michael E. 1994. "The Limits of Community." Pp. 270–273 in *The Challenge of Community Policing*, edited by D.P. Rosenbaum. Thousand Oaks, CA: Sage.

Burgess, Ernest W. and Harvey J. Locke. 1945. *The Family, from Institution to Companionship*. New York: American Book Co.

Burris, Scott. 2006. "From Security to Health." Pp. 196–216 in *Democracy, Society and the Governance of Security*, edited by J. Wood and B. Dupont. Cambridge: Cambridge University Press.

Butler, Anne M. 1997. *Gendered Justice in the American West*. Urbana: University of Illinois Press.

Canlis, Michael N. 1961. "The Evolution of Law Enforcement in California." *Far Westerner* 2:1–13.

Carlson, Joseph R. 1995. "The Future Terrorists in America." *American Journal of Police* 14 (3-4):71–91.

Carro, D., S. Valera, and T. Vidal. 2010. "Perceived Insecurity in the Public Space: Personal, Social, and Environmental Variables." *Quality and Quantity* 44:303–314.

Chan, Janet B.L. 2001. "The Technological Game: How Information Technology Is Transforming Police Practice." *Criminal Justice* 1 (2):139–159.

———. 2007. "Making Sense of Police Reforms." *Theoretical Criminology* 11 (3):323–345.

Chappell, Allison T., John M. MacDonald, and Patrick W. Manz. 2006. "The Organizational Determinants of Police Arrest Decisions." *Crime and Delinquency* 52 (2):287–306.

Chriss, James J. 1994. "Spain on Status and Space: A Comment." *Sociological Theory* 12 (1):106–109.

———. 1999a. *Alvin W. Gouldner: Sociologist and Outlaw Marxist*. Aldershot, UK: Ashgate.

———. 1999b. "Introduction." Pp. 1–29 in *Counseling and the Therapeutic State*, edited by J.J. Chriss. New York: Aldine de Gruyter.

———. 2001. "Alvin W. Gouldner and Industrial Sociology at Columbia University." *Journal of the History of the Behavioral Sciences* 37 (3):241–259.

———. 2004. "The Perils of Risk Assessment." *Society* 41 (4):52–56.

———. 2005. "Mead, George Herbert." Pp. 486–491 in *Encyclopedia of Social Theory*, edited by G. Ritzer. Thousand Oaks, CA: Sage.

———. 2006. "The Place of Lester Ward among the Sociological Classics." *Journal of Classical Sociology* 6 (1):5–21.

———. 2007a. "The Functions of the Social Bond." *Sociological Quarterly* 48:689–712.

———. 2007b. *Social Control: An Introduction*. Cambridge, UK: Polity Press.

———. 2007c. "Norm of Reciprocity." Pp. 3227–3229 in *Blackwell Encyclopedia of Sociology*, Vol. 7, edited by G. Ritzer. Malden, MA: Blackwell.

———. 2008. "Addams, Ward, et al.: American Sociology Past to Present." *Journal of Classical Sociology* 8 (4):491–502.

Clarke, Ronald V. and Graeme R. Newman. 2007. "Police and the Prevention of Terrorism." *Policing* 1 (1):9–20.

Clutterbuck, Lindsay. 2006. "Countering Irish Republican Terrorism in Britain: Its Origin as a Police Function." *Terrorism and Political Violence* 18 (1):95–118.

Coates, William R. 1924. *A History of Cuyahoga County and the City of Cleveland*. Chicago: American Historical Society.

Cohen, Lawrence E. and Kenneth C. Land. 1987. "Age Structure and Crime: Symmetry versus Asymmetry and the Projection of Crime Rates through the 1990s." *American Sociological Review* 52 (2):170–183.

Comstock, Donald E. 1971. "Boundary Spanning Processes in Complex Organizations." Master's thesis, University of Denver.

Cooley, Charles H. 1930. *Sociological Theory and Social Research.* New York: H. Holt and Co.

Corra, Mamadi and David Willer. 2002. "The Gatekeeper." *Sociological Theory* 20 (2):180–207.

Crank, John P. 1989. "Civilianization in Small and Medium Police Departments in Illinois, 1973–1986." *Journal of Criminal Justice* 17 (3):167–177.

Crank, John P. 2003. "Institutional Theory of Police: A Review of the State of the Art." *Policing* 26:186–207.

Crank, John P. and Robert H. Langworthy. 1996. "Fragmented Centralization and the Organization of the Police." *Policing and Society* 6 (2):213–229.

Crant, J. Michael. 2000. "Proactive Behavior in Organizations." *Journal of Management* 26 (3):435–462.

Crawford, Adam. 2006. "Policing and Security as 'Club Goods': The New Enclosures?" Pp. 111–138 in *Democracy, Society and the Governance of Security*, edited by J. Wood and B. Dupont. Cambridge, UK: Cambridge University Press.

Crowther, Chris. 2000. "Thinking about the 'Underclass': Towards a Political Economy of Policing." *Theoretical Criminology* 4 (2):149–167.

Culberson, William C. 1990. *Vigilantism: Political History of Private Power in America.* New York: Praeger.

Dal Fiore, Filippo. 2007. "Communities versus Networks: The Implications on Innovation and Social Change." *American Behavioral Scientist* 50 (7):857–866.

Daleiden, J. Robert. 2006. "A Clumsy Dance: The Political Economy of American Police and Policing." *Policing* 29 (4):602–624.

Davis, James A. 1961. "Compositional Effects, Role Systems, and the Survival of Small Discussion Groups." *Public Opinion Quarterly* 25 (4):574–584.

Davis, Rebecca. 1997. "What Fourth Amendment? HR 666 and the Satanic Expansion of the Good Faith Exception." *Policing* 20 (1):101–112.

De Lint, Willem. 2003. "Keeping Open Windows: Police as Access Brokers." *British Journal of Criminology* 43:379–397.

Deflem, Mathieu. 2002. "The Logic of Nazification: The Case of the International Criminal Police Commission ('Interpol')." *International Journal of Comparative Sociology* 43 (1):21–44.

———. 2004. "Social Control and the Policing of Terrorism: Foundations for a Sociology of Counterterrorism." *American Sociologist* 35 (2):75–92.

———. 2005. "'Wild Beasts without Nationality': The Uncertain Origins of Interpol, 1898–1910." Pp. 275–285 in *Handbook of Transnational Crime and Justice*, edited by P. Reichel. Thousand Oaks, CA: Sage.

Denhardt, Robert M. 1947. *The Horse of the Americas*. Norman: University of Oklahoma Press.

Dewey, John. 1896. "The Reflex Arc Concept in Psychology." *Psychological Review* 3:357–370.

Di Paola, Pietro. 2007. "The Spies Who Came in from the Heat: The International Surveillance of the Anarchists in London." *European History Quarterly* 37 (2):189–215.

Dickens, Charles. 1855. *Household Words: A Weekly Journal*, Vol. 10. London: Lenox Library.

DiMaggio, Paul J. and Walter W. Powell. 1983. "The Iron Cage Revisited: Institutional Isomorphism and Collective Rationality in Organizational Fields." *American Sociological Review* 48:147–160.

———. 1991. "Introduction." Pp. 1–38 in *The New Institutionalism in Organizational Analysis*, edited by W.W. Powell and P.J. DiMaggio. Chicago: University of Chicago Press.

Drabek, Thomas E. 1965. "Laboratory Simulation of a Police Communication System under Stress." Ph.D. diss., Ohio State University.

Durkheim, Emile. 1984 [1893]. *Division of Labor in Society*, translated by W.D. Halls. New York: Free Press.

Durose, Matthew R., Erica L. Smith, and Patrick A. Langan. 2007. "Contact between Police and the Public, 2005." Bureau of Justice Statistics. Washington, DC: U.S. Department of Justice.

Dykstra, Robert R. 1968. *The Cattle Towns*. New York: Alfred A. Knopf.

Eck, John E. 2006. "Science, Values, and Problem-Oriented Policing: Why Problem-Oriented Policing?" Pp. 117–132 in *Police Innovation: Contrasting Perspectives*, edited by D. Weisburd and A.A. Braga. Cambridge, UK: Cambridge University Press.

Eckberg, Douglas Lee and Lester Hill, Jr. 1979. "The Paradigm Concept and Sociology: A Critical Review." *American Sociological Review* 44:925–937.

Elazar, Daniel J. 1996. "The Frontier as a Chain Reaction." Pp. 173–190 in *Frontiers in Regional Development*, edited by Y. Gradus and H. Lithwick. Lanham, MD: Rowman and Littefield.

Elliott, Mabel A. 1944. "Crime on the Frontier Mores." *American Sociological Review* 9:185–192.

Elliott, Mabel A. and Francis E. Merrill. 1950. *Social Disorganization*. New York: Harper.

Ellwood, Charles A. 1910. *Sociology and Modern Social Problems*. American Book Company.

Ericson, Richard V. 2007. "Rules in Policing: Five Perspectives." *Theoretical Criminology* 11 (3):367–401.

Fagan, Jeffrey and Tom R. Tyler. 2005. "Legal Socialization of Children and Adolescents." *Social Justice Research* 18 (3):217–241.

Fararo, Thomas J. and Kent A. McClelland. 2006. "Introduction: Control Systems Thinking in Sociological Theory." Pp. 1–27 in *Purpose, Meaning, and Action: Control Systems Theories in Sociology*, edited by K.A. McClelland and T.J. Fararo. New York: Palgrave.

Faris, Robert E.L. 1955. *Social Disorganization*. New York: Ronald Press Company.

Farr, James. 2004. "Social Capital: A Conceptual History." *Political Theory* 32 (1):6–33.

Feldman, Leonard C. 2002. "Redistribution, Recognition, and the State: The Irreducibly Political Dimension of Injustice." *Political Theory* 30 (3):410–440.

Felson, Richard B., Steven F. Messner, Anthony W. Hoskin, and Glenn Deane. 2002. "Reasons for Reporting and Not Reporting Domestic Violence to the Police." *Criminology* 40 (3):617–648.

Feucht, Thomas E., David Weisburd, Simon Perry, Lois Felson Mock, and Idit Hakimi. 2009. "Policing, Terrorism, and Beyond." Pp. 203–224 in *To Protect and to Serve: Policing in an Age of Terrorism*, edited by D. Weisburd, T.E. Feucht, I. Hakimi, L.F. Mock, and S. Perry. Dordrecht: Springer.

Fletcher, Joseph. 1850. "Statistical Account of the Police of the Metropolis." *Journal of the Statistical Society of London* 13 (3):221–267.

Foucault, Michel. 1978. *History of Sexuality*, Vol. 1, translated by R. Hurley. New York: Vantage.

Frank, James, Steven G. Brandl, and R. Cory Watkins. 1997. "The Content of Community Policing: A Comparison of the Daily Activities of Community and 'Beat' Officers." *Policing* 20 (4):716–728.

Frantzen, Durant and Claudia San Miguel. 2009. "Mandatory Arrest? Police Response to Domestic Violence Victims." *Policing* 32 (2):319–337.

Frazer, Robert W. 1965. *Forts of the West: Military Forts and Presidios and Posts Commonly Called Forts West of the Mississippi River to 1898*. Norman: University of Oklahoma Press.

Friedman, Lawrence M. 2007. *Guarding Life's Dark Secrets: Legal and Social Control over Reputation, Propriety, and Privacy*. Stanford, CA: Stanford University Press.

Gabbay, Edmond. 1973. *Discretion in Criminal Justice*. London: White Eagle Press.

Gard, Wayne. 1949. *Frontier Justice*. Norman: University of Oklahoma Press.

———. 1963. "The Law of the American West." Pp. 261–322 in *The Book of the American West*, edited by J. Monaghan and C.P. Hornung. New York: Julian Messner Inc.

Garland, David. 2005. "Penal Excess and Surplus Meaning: Public Torture Lynchings in Twentieth-Century America." *Law and Society Review* 39 (4):793–833.

Garner, Joel H., Thomas Schade, John Hepburn, and John Buchanan. 1995.
    "Measuring the Continuum of Force Used by and against the Police."
    Criminal Justice Review 20 (2):146–168.
Gelsthorpe, Loraine and Nicola Padfield. 2003. "Introduction." Pp. 1–28 in *Ex-
    ercising Discretion: Decision-Making in the Criminal Justice System
    and Beyond*. Devon, UK: Willan Publishing.
Gerstein, Lawrence H. 2006. "Counseling Psychology's Commitment to
    Strengths: Rhetoric or Reality?" *Counseling Psychologist* 34 (2):276–
    292.
Giddens, Anthony. 1984. *The Constitution of Society: Outline of the Theory of
    Structuration*. Cambridge, UK: Polity Press.
Giddings, Franklin H. 1896. *Principles of Sociology*. New York: Macmillan.
———. 1922. "The Measurement of Social Forces." *Journal of Social Forces* 1
    (1):1–6.
Girodo, Michel. 1998. "Undercover Probes of Police Corruption: Risk Factors in
    Proactive Internal Affairs Investigations." *Behavioral Sciences and the
    Law* 16:479–496.
Goeres-Gardner, Diane L. 2005. *Necktie Parties: Legal Executions in Oregon,
    1851–1905*. Caldwell, ID: Caxton Press.
Goffman, Erving. 1963. *Behavior in Public Places*. New York: Free Press.
Gouldner, Alvin W. 1954. *Patterns of Industrial Bureaucracy*. Glencoe, IL: Free
    Press.
Gouldner, Alvin W. 1960. "The Norm of Reciprocity: A Preliminary State-
    ment." *American Sociological Review* 25 (2):161–178.
———. 1970. *The Coming Crisis of Western Sociology*. New York: Avon.
Gowri, Aditi. 2003. "Community Policing is an Epicycle." *Policing* 26 (4):591–
    611.
Graybill, Andrew R. 2007. *Policing the Great Plains: Rangers, Mounties, and
    the North American Frontier, 1875–1910*. Lincoln: University of
    Nebraska Press.
Groeneveld, Richard F. 2005. *Arrest Discretion of Police Officers: The Impact
    of Varying Organizational Structures*. El Paso, TX: LFB Scholarly
    Publishing.
Guetzloe, Eleanor. 1992. "Violent, Aggressive, and Antisocial Students: What
    Are We Going To Do With Them?" *Preventing School Failure* 36
    (3):4–9.
Hadden, Sally E. 2001. *Slave Patrols*. Cambridge, MA: Harvard University
    Press.
Haggerty, Kevin D. 2006. "Visible War: Surveillance, Speed, and Information
    War." Pp. 250–268 in *The New Politics of Surveillance and Visibility*,
    edited by R.V. Ericson and K.D. Haggerty. Toronto: University of
    Toronto Press.
Haines, Valerie A. 1992. "Spencer's Philosophy of Science." *British Journal of
    Sociology* 43 (2):155–172.

———. 2005. "Spencer, Herbert." Pp. 781–787 in *Encyclopedia of Social Theory*, Vol. 2, edited by G. Ritzer. Thousand Oaks, CA: Sage.

Hallwas, John E. 2008. *Dime Novel Desperadoes: The Notorious Maxwell Brothers*. Urbana: University of Illinois Press.

Hamilton, Peter. 1996. "Systems Theory." Pp. 143–170 in *Blackwell Companion to Social Theory*, edited by B.S. Turner. Oxford, UK: Blackwell.

Haupt, Edward J. 2001. "Laboratories for Experimental Psychology: Göttingen's Ascendancy over Leipzig in the 1890s." Pp. 205–250 in *Wilhelm Wundt in History*, edited by R.W. Rieber and D.K. Robinson. New York: Plenum.

Hawkins, Keith. 2003. "Order, Rationality, and Silence: Some Reflections on Criminal Justice Decision-Making." Pp. 186–219 in *Exercising Discretion: Decision-Making in the Criminal Justice System and Beyond*. Devon, UK: Willan Publishing.

Haywood, C. Robert. 1991. *Victorian West: Class and Culture in Kansas Cattle Towns*. Lawrence: University Press of Kansas.

Hays, Sharon. 1994. "Structure and Agency and the Sticky Problem of Culture." *Sociological Theory* 12 (1):57–72.

Henry, Vincent E. and Douglas H. King. 2004. "Improving Emergency Preparedness and Public-Safety Responses to Terrorism and Weapons of Mass Destruction." *Brief Treatment and Crisis Intervention* 4 (1):11–35.

Herbert, Steve. 2006a. *Citizens, Cops, and Power: Recognizing the Limits of Community*. Chicago: University of Chicago Press.

———. 2006b. "Police Subculture Reconsidered." *Criminology* 36 (2):343–370.

Hillery, George A., Jr. 1968. *Communal Organizations: A Study of Local Societies*. Chicago: University of Chicago Press.

Hirsch, Paul M. 1972. "Processing Fads and Fashions: An Organization-Set Analysis of Cultural Industry Systems." *American Journal of Sociology* 77 (4):639–659.

Hirsch, Paul and Michael Lounsbury. 1997. "Ending the Family Quarrel: Towards a Reconciliation of 'Old' and 'New' Institutionalism." *American Behavioral Scientist* 40 (4):406–418.

Hoffmann, Gabi and Paul Mazerolle. 2005. "Police Pursuits in Queensland: Research, Review, and Reform." *Policing* 28 (3):530–545.

Hogenboom, Ari. 1959. "The Pendleton Act and the Civil Service." *American Historical Review* 64 (2):301–318.

Huberts, Leo W.J.C., Terry Lamboo, and Maurice Punch. 2003. "Police Integrity in the Netherlands and the United States: Awareness and Alertness." *Police Practice and Research* 4 (3):217–232.

Hutcheon, Pat Duffy. 1972. "Value Theory: Towards Conceptual Clarification." *British Journal of Sociology* 23 (2):172–187.

Innes, Martin. 2005. "Why 'Soft' Policing is Hard: On the Curious Development of Reassurance Policing, How it Became Neighbourhood Policing and what this Signifies about the Politics of Police Reform." *Journal of Community and Applied Social Psychology* 15 (3):156–169.

———. "Policing Uncertainty: Countering Terror through Community Intelligence and Democratic Policing." *Annals of the American Academy of Political and Social Science* 605:222–241.

International Association of Chiefs of Police. 2005. "Post 9-11 Policing: The Crime Control–Homeland Security Paradigm." Washington, DC: US Department of Justice, Bureau of Justice Assistance, Office of Justice Programs.

Jackson, Arrick L. and John E. Wade. 2005. "Police Perceptions of Social Capital and Sense of Responsibility: An Explanation of Proactive Policing." *Policing* 28 (1):49–68.

James, Nathan. 2008. "Community Oriented Policing Services (COPS): Background, Legislation, and Issues." Congressional Report RL33308. Washington, DC: Congressional Research Service.

Joh, Elizabeth. 2004. "The Paradox of Private Policing." *Journal of Criminal Law and Criminology* 95 (1):49–131.

Johnson, David R. 1981. *American Law Enforcement: A History*. St. Louis, MO: Forum Press.

Johnson, Herbert A., Nancy Travis Wolfe, and Mark Jones. 2008. *History of Criminal Justice*, 4th ed. Newark, NJ: LexisNexis.

Johnston, Les. 1992. *The Rebirth of Private Policing*. London: Routledge.

Jones, Robert Huhn. 1961. *The Civil War in the Northwest: Nebraska, Wisconsin, Iowa, Minnesota, and the Dakotas*. Norman: University of Oklahoma Press.

Kaptein, Muel and Piet van Reenen. 2001. "Integrity Management of Police Organizations." *Policing* 24 (3):281–300.

Kelling, George L. 1999. *"Broken Windows" and Police Discretion*. Washington, DC: National Institute of Justice.

Kelling, George L. and Mark H. Moore. 1988. "The Evolving Strategy of Policing." In *Perspectives on Policing*, No. 4. Washington, DC: National Institute of Justice.

Kennedy, David M. 2006. "Old Wine in New Bottles: Policing and the Lessons of Pulling Levers." Pp. 155–170 in *Police Innovation: Contrasting Perspectives*, edited by D. Weisburd and A.A. Braga. Cambridge, UK: Cambridge University Press.

King, W.R. 1998. *Innovations in American Municipal Police Organizations*. Ph.D. diss., University of Cincinnati.

Kinkaid, Harold. 2007. "Functional Explanation and Evolutionary Social Science." Pp. 213–247 in *Philosophy of Anthropology and Sociology*, edited by S.P. Turner and M.W. Risjord. Amsterdam: North-Holland.

Klinger, David A. 1997. "Negotiating Order in Patrol Work: An Ecological Theory of Police Response to Deviance." *Criminology* 35 (2):277–306.

———. 2004. "Environment and Organization: Reviving a Perspective on the Police." *Annals of the American Academy of Political and Social Science* 593:119–136.

———. 2005. "Social Theory and the Street Cop: The Case of Deadly Force." *Ideas in American Policing* 7:1–15.

Klockars, Carl B. 1980. "The Dirty Harry Problem." *Annals of the American Academy of Political and Social Science* 452:33–47.

———. 2006. "Street Justice: Some Micro-Moral Reservations." Pp. 150–153 in *Police and Society: Touchstone Readings*, edited by V.E. Kappeler. Long Grove, IL: Waveland Press.

Klockars, Carl B., Sanja K. Ivkovic, and M.R. Haberfeld. 2006. *Enhancing Police Integrity*. Dordrecht: Springer.

Knapp Commission. 1973. *The Knapp Commission Report on Police Corruption*. New York: George Braziller.

Kowalski, Brian R. and Richard J. Lundman. 2007. "Vehicle Stops by Police for Driving while Black: Common Problems and Some Tentative Solutions." *Journal of Criminal Justice* 35 (2):165–181.

KPMG. 1996. *Report to the New York City Commission to Combat Police Corruption*. New York: NYC Commission to Combat Police Corruption.

Krader, Lawrence. 1968. *Formation of the State*. Englewood Cliffs, NJ: Prentice-Hall.

Kuhn, Thomas S. 1962. The *Structure of Scientific Revolutions*. Chicago: University of Chicago Press.

Lab, Steven P. 2007. *Crime Prevention: Approaches, Practices and Evaluations*, 6th ed. Albany, NY: LexisNexis.

LaFree, Gary and Laura Dugan. 2009. "Tracking Global Terrorism Trends, 1970–2004." Pp. 43–80 in *To Protect and to Serve: Policing in an Age of Terrorism*, edited by D. Weisburd, T.E. Feucht, I. Hakimi, L.F. Mock, and S. Perry. Dordrecht: Springer.

Lane, Roger. 1992. "Urban Police and Crime in Nineteenth-Century America." Pp. 1–50 in *Modern Policing*, edited by M. Tonry and N. Morris. Vol. 15 of *Crime and Justice*, edited by M. Tonry. Chicago: University of Chicago Press.

Leichtman, Ellen C. 2008. "Complex Harmony: The Military and Professional Models of Policing." *Critical Criminology* 16 (1):53–73.

Levi, Ron and John Hagan. 2006. "International Police." Pp. 207–247 in *The New Police Science: The Police Power in Domestic and International Governance*, edited by M.D. Dubber and M. Valverde. Stanford: Stanford University Press.

Lewis, Oscar. 1980. *San Francisco: Mission to Metropolis*, 2nd ed. San Diego, CA: Howell-North Books.

Librett, Mitch. 2008. "Wild Pigs and Outlaws: The Kindred Worlds of Policing and Outlaw Bikers." *Crime, Media, Culture* 4 (2):257–269.

Lidz, Victor. 2001. "Language and the 'Family' of Generalized Symbolic Me-
    dia." 141–176 in *Talcott Parsons Today*, edited by A.J. Trevino.
    Lanham, MD: Rowman and Littlefield.
Liebling, Alison. 2000. "Prison Officers, Policing, and the Use of Discretion."
    Theoretical Criminology 4 (3):333–357.
Liebling, Alison and David Price. 2003. "Prison Officers and the Use of Discre-
    tion." Pp. 74–96 in *Exercising Discretion: Decision-Making in the
    Criminal Justice System and Beyond*. Devon, UK: Willan Publishing.
Linn, Edith. 2009. *Arrest Decisions: What Works for the Officer?* New York:
    Peter Lang.
Llewellyn, Karl N. 2008. *Jurisprudence: Realism in Theory and Practice*. New
    Brunswick: Transaction Publishers.
Loader, Ian. 2006. "Policing, Recognition, and Belonging." *Annals of the Amer-
    ican Academy of Political and Social Science* 605:202–221.
Loader, Ian and Neil Walker. 2006. "Necessary Virtues: The Legitimate Place of
    the State in the Production of Security." Pp. 165–195 in *Democracy,
    Society and the Governance of Security*, edited by J. Wood and B. Du-
    pont. Cambridge, UK: Cambridge University Press.
Maguire, E.R. 2003. *Organizational Structure in American Police Agencies:
    Context, Complexity, and Control*. Albany, NY: SUNY Press.
Maguire, E.R. and S.D. Mastrofski. 2000. "Patterns of Community Policing in
    the United States." *Police Quarterly* 3:4–45.
Manning, Peter K. 1978. "The Police: Mandate, Strategies, and Appearances."
    Pp. 7–32 in *Policing: A View from the Street*, edited by P.K. Manning
    and J. Van Maanen. Santa Monica, CA: Goodyear.
———. 1997. *Police Work: The Social Organization of Policing*, 2nd ed.
    Prospect Heights, IL: Waveland Press.
———. 1999. "A Dramaturgical Perspective." Pp. 49–125 in *Privatization
    of Policing: Two Views*, B. Forst and P.K. Manning. Washington, DC:
    Georgetown University Press.
———. 2006. "Two Case Studies of American Anti-Terrorism." Pp. 52–85 in
    Democracy, Society and the Governance of Security, edited by J. Wood
    and B. Dupont. Cambridge: Cambridge University Press.
Marks, D.E. and I.Y. Sun. 2007. "The Impact of 9/11 on Organizational Devel-
    opment among State and Local Enforcement Agencies." *Journal of
    Contemporary Criminal Justice* 23:159–173.
Marsh, Margaret. 1989. "From Separation to Togetherness: The Social Con-
    struction of Domestic Space in American Suburbs, 1840–1915."
    Journal of American History 76 (2):506–527.
Marx, Gary T. 1986. "The Interweaving of Public and Private Police in Under-
    cover Work." Pp. 172–193 in *Private Policing*, edited by C.D. Shearing
    and P.C. Stenning. Newbury Park, CA: Sage.
———. 1992. "When the Guards Guard Themselves: Undercover Tactics
    Turned Inward." *Policing and Society* 2 (3):151–172.

Maslow, Abraham H. 1934. "The Effect of Varying Time Intervals between Acts with a Note on Proactive Inhibition." *Experimental Psychology* 17 (1):141–144.

Mastrofski, Stephen. 1998. "Community Policing and Police Organization Structure." Pp. 161–189 in *How to Recognize Good Policing*, edited by J. Brodeur. Thousand Oaks, CA: Sage.

———. 2004. "Controlling Street-Level Police Discretion." *Annals of the American Academy of Political and Social Science* 593:100–118.

———. 2006. "Community Policing: A Skeptical View." Pp. 44–73 in *Police Innovation: Contrasting Perspectives*, edited by D. Weisburd and A.A. Braga. Cambridge, UK: Cambridge University Press.

Mazerolle, Lorraine and Janet Ransley. 2006. "The Case for Third-Party Policing." Pp. 191–206 in *Police Innovation: Contrasting Perspectives*, edited by D. Weisburd and A.A. Braga. Cambridge, UK: Cambridge University Press.

McCallum, Henry D. and Frances T. McCallum. 1965. *The Wire that Fenced the West*. Norman: University of Oklahoma Press.

McConville, Mike and Chester Mirsky. 1995. "Guilty Plea Courts: A Social Disciplinary Model of Criminal Justice." *Social Problems* 42 (2):216–234.

McGrath, Roger D. 1984. *Gunfighters, Highwaymen, and Vigilantes: Violence on the Frontier*. Berkeley: University of California Press.

McKelvey, Blake. 1969. *The City in American History*. London: Allen and Unwin.

McMahon, Pamela M. 2000. "The Public Health Approach to the Prevention of Sexual Violence." *Sexual Abuse* 12 (1):27–36.

Mead, George H. 1934. *Mind, Self, and Society from the Standpoint of a Social Behaviorist*, edited by C.W. Morris. Chicago: University of Chicago Press.

Melbin, Murray. 1987. *Night as Frontier: Colonizing the World after Dark*. New York: Free Press.

Meliala, Adrianus. 2001. "The Notion of Sensitivity in Policing." *International Journal of the Sociology of Law* 29:99–111.

Merton, Robert K. 1957. "The Role-Set: Problems in Sociological Theory." *British Journal of Sociology* 8 (2):106–120.

———. 1968. *Social Theory and Social Structure*. New York: Free Press.

Meyer, J. and B. Rowan. 1977. "Institutional Organizations: Formal Structures as Myth and Ceremony." *American Journal of Sociology* 83:340–363.

Miller, Nyle H. and Joseph W. Snell. 1963. *Great Gunfighters of the Kansas Cowtowns, 1867–1886*. Lincoln: University of Nebraska Press.

Miolanti, John M. 1996. "Police Suicide: An Overview." *Police Studies* 19 (2):77–89.

Monkkonen, Eric H. 1981. *Police in Urban America, 1860–1920*. Cambridge, UK: Cambridge University Press.

————. 1988. *America becomes Urban: The Development of U.S.Cities and Towns, 1780–1980*. Berkeley: University of California Press.

Morgan, Dale. 1963. "Opening of the West: Explorers and Mountain Men." Pp. 9–82 in *The Book of the American West*, edited by J. Monaghan and C.P. Hornung. New York: Julian Messner Inc.

Mosher, Clayton J., Terance D. Miethe, and Dretha M. Phillips. 2002. *The Mismeasure of Crime*. Thousand Oaks, CA: Sage.

Moskos, Peter. 2008. *Cop in the Hood: My Year Policing Baltimore's Eastern District*. Princeton, NJ: Princeton University Press.

Muir, William Ker, Jr. 1977. *Police: Streetcorner Politicians*. Chicago: University of Chicago Press.

Mumford, Lewis. 1961. *The City in History*. New York: Harcourt, Brace, and World.

Murray, Henry A. 1951. "Toward a Classification of Interactions." Pp. 434–464 in *Toward a General Theory of Action*, edited by T. Parsons and E.A. Shils. Cambridge, MA: Harvard University Press.

Nacy, Michele J. 2000. *Members of the Regiment: Army Officers' Wives on the Western Frontier, 1865–1890*. Westport, CT: Greenwood Press.

National Commission on Terrorist Attacks upon the United States. 2004. "Law Enforcement, Counterterrorism, and Intelligence Collection in the United States Prior to 9/11." Staff Statement No. 9. Washington, DC.

Newham, Gareth. 2003. "Preventing Police Corruption: Lessons from the New York City Police Department." Johannesburg, RSA: Centre for the Study of Violence and Reconciliation.

Nickels, Ernest L. 2007. "A Note on the Status of Discretion in Police Research." *Journal of Criminal Justice* 35:570–578.

————. 2008. "Good Guys Wear Black: Uniform Color and Citizen Impressions of Police." *Policing* 31 (1):77–92.

Nobles, Gregory H. 1993. "The Frontier." Pp. 1183–1196 in *Encyclopedia of American Social History*, Vol. 2, edited by M.K. Cayton, E.J. Gorn, and P.W. Williams. New York: Charles Scribner's Sons.

Nolan, James J., Norman Conti, and Jack McDevitt. 2005. "Situational Policing." *FBI Law Enforcement Bulletin* 74 (11):1–9.

Novak, Kenneth J., Brad W. Smith, and James Frank. 2003. "Strange Bedfellows: Civil Liability and Aggressive Policing." *Policing* 26 (2): 352–368.

Nunn, Samuel. 2001a. "Cities, Space, and the New World of Urban Law Enforcement Technologies." *Journal of Urban Affairs* 23 (3-4):259–278.

————. 2001b. "Police Information Technology: Assessing the Effects of Computerization on Urban Police Functions." *Public Administration Review* 61 (2):221–234.

————. 2001c. "Police Technology in Cities: Changes and Challenges." *Technology and Society* 23:11–27.

———. 2003. "Seeking Tools for the War on Terror: A Critical Assessment of Emerging Technologies in Law Enforcement." *Policing* 26 (3):454–472.

Nye, F. Ivan. 1955. "What Patterns of Family Life?" *Coordinator* 4 (2):12–17.

Oaks, Dallin H. 1970. "Studying the Exclusionary Rule in Search and Seizure." *University of Chicago Law Review* 37:665–757.

Oates, Stephen B. 1984. *Abraham Lincoln, the Man behind the Myths*. New York: Harper and Row.

Odum, Howard W. 1922. "Editorial Notes." *Journal of Social Forces* 1 (1):56–61.

Ogburn, William F. 1922. *Social Change: With Respect to Culture and Original Nature*. New York: B.W. Huebsch.

———. 1929. "The Changing Family." *Publications of the American Sociological Society* 23:124–133.

———. 1933a. "The Influence of Invention and Discovery." Pp. 122–166 in *Recent Social Trends in the United States: Report of the President's Research Committee on Social Trends*. New York: McGraw-Hill.

———. 1933b. "The Family and Its Functions." Pp. 661–708 in *Recent Social Trends in the United States: Report of the President's Research Committee on Social Trends*. New York: McGraw-Hill.

———. 1937. "Culture and Sociology." *Social Forces* 16 (2):161–169.

Oliver, Amalya L. and Kathleen Montgomery. 2005. "Toward the Construction of a Profession's Boundaries: Creating a Networking Agenda." *Human Relations* 58 (9):1167–1184.

Oliver, Willard M. 2000. "The Third Generation of Community Policing: Moving through Innovation, Diffusion, and Institutionalization." *Police Quarterly* 3 (4):367–388.

———. 2006. "The Fourth Era of Policing: Homeland Security." *International Review of Law, Computers, and Technology* 20 (1-2):49–62.

Olson, James C. 1966. *History of Nebraska*. Lincoln: University of Nebraska Press.

O'Reilly, Conor and Graham Ellison. 2006. "'Eye Spy Private High': Reconceptualizing High Policing Theory." *British Journal of Criminology* 46:641–660.

Otterstrom, Samuel M. and Carville Earle. 2002. "The Settlement of the United States from 1790 to 1990: Divergent Rates of Growth and the End of the Frontier." *Journal of Interdisciplinary History* 33 (1):59–85.

Packer, Herbert. 1968. *The Limits of the Criminal Sanction*. Stanford, CA: Stanford University Press.

Palmiotto, Michael J. 2000. *Community Policing: A Policing Strategy for the 21st Century*. Gaithersburg, MD: Aspen Publishers.

Parsons, Talcott. 1937. *The Structure of Social Action*. New York: Free Press.

———. 1946. "The Science Legislation and the Role of the Social Sciences." *American Sociological Review* 11 (6):653–666.

———. 1951. *The Social System*. New York: Free Press.

————. 1960a. *Structure and Process in Modern Societies*. Glencoe, IL: Free Press.

————. 1960b. "Pattern Variables Revisited: A Response to Robert Dubin." *American Sociological Review* 25 (4):467–483.

————. 1961. "An Outline of the Social System." Pp. 30–79 in *Theories of Society*, edited by T. Parsons, E. Shills, K. Naegele, and J. Pitts. New York: Free Press.

————. 1966. "The Political Aspect of Social Structure and Process." Pp. 71–112 in *Varieties of Political Theory*, edited by D. Easton. Englewood Cliffs, NJ: Prentice Hall.

————. 1967a. "On the Concept of Political Power." Pp. 297–354 in *Sociological Theory and Modern Society*. New York: Free Press.

————. 1967b. "Some Reflections on the Place of Force in Social Process." Pp. 264–296 in *Sociological Theory and Modern Society*. New York: Free Press.

————. 1968. "An Overview." Pp. 319–335 in *American Sociology: Perspectives, Problems, Methods*, edited by T. Parsons. New York: Basic Books.

————. 1975. "Social Structure and the Symbolic Media of Interchange." Pp. 94–120 in *Approaches to the Study of Social Structure*, edited by P.M. Blau. New York: Free Press.

————. 1977. *The Evolution of Societies*. Englewood Cliffs, NJ: Prentice Hall.

————. 1991. "The Integration of Economic and Sociological Theory: The Marshall Lectures." *Sociological Inquiry* 61 (1):10–59.

————. 2007. *American Society: A Theory of the Societal Community*, edited by G. Sciortino. Boulder, CO: Paradigm Publishers.

Parsons, Talcott and Gerald M. Platt. 1973. *The American University*. Cambridge, MA: Harvard University Press.

Pearse, John and Gisli Gudjonsson. 1999. "Measuring Influential Police Interviewing Tactics: A Factor Analytic Approach." *Legal and Criminological Psychology* 4 (2):221–238.

Pegnato, Joseph A. 1997. "Is a Citizen a Customer?" *Public Productivity and Management Review* 20 (4):397–404.

Pelfrey, William V., Jr. 2005. "Parallels between Community Oriented Policing and the War on Terrorism: Lessons Learned." *Criminal Justice Studies* 18 (4):335–346.

Prassel, Frank Richard. 1972. *The Western Peace Officer: A Legacy of Law and Order*. Norman: University of Oklahoma Press.

Prenzler, Tim. 2006. "Senior Police Managers' Views on Integrity Testing, and Drug and Alcohol Testing." *Policing* 29 (3):394–407.

————. 2009. *Police Corruption: Preventing Misconduct and Maintaining Integrity*. Boca Raton, FL: CRC Press.

Prenzler, Tim and Carol Ronken. 2001. "Police Integrity Testing in Australia." *Criminal Justice* 1 (3):319–342.

Prothrow-Stith, Deborah. 1993. *Deadly Consequences*. New York: Harper Perennial.

Psathas, George. 1960. "Phase Movement and Equilibrium Tendencies in Interaction Process in Psychotherapy Groups." *Sociometry* 23 (2):177–194.

Rausch, Sharla and Gary LaFree. 2007. "The Growing Importance of Criminology in the Study of Terrorism." *The Criminologist* 32 (6):1, 3–5.

Reckless, Walter C. 1941. "The Implications of Prediction in Sociology." *American Sociological Review* 6 (4):471–477.

Redmond, Michael and Alok Baveja. 2002. "A Date-driven Software Tool for Enabling Cooperative Information Sharing among Police Departments." *European Journal of Operational Research* 141:660–678.

Reed, Wilson E. 1999. *The Politics of Community Policing: The Case of Seattle*. New York: Garland Publishing.

Reiss, Albert J., Jr. 1986. "The Legitimacy of Intrusion into Private Space." Pp. 19–44 in *Private Policing*, edited by C.D. Shearing and P.C. Stenning. Newbury Park, CA: Sage.

Renauer, Brian C. 2007. "Reducing Fear of Crime: Citizen, Police, or Government Responsibility?" *Police Quarterly* 10 (1):41–62.

Reynolds, Gerald William and Anthony Judge. 1968. *The Night the Police Went on Strike*. London: Weidenfeld and Nicolson.

Richardson, Heather Cox. 2007. *West from Appomattox: The Reconstruction of America after the Civil War*. New Haven, CT: Yale University Press.

Riechers, L.M. and R.R. Roberg. 1990. "Community Policing: A Critical Review of Underlying Assumptions." *Journal of Police Science and Administration* 17:105–114.

Rigakos, George S. and Georgios Papanicolaou. 2003. "The Political Economy of Greek Policing: Between Neo-Liberalism and the Sovereign State." *Policing and Society* 13 (3):271–304.

Riley, K. Jack, Gregory F. Treverton, Jeremy M. Wilson, and Lois M. Davis. 2005. *State and Local Intelligence in the War on Terrorism*. Santa Monica, CA: Rand Corporation.

Ritzer, George. 1975. *Sociology: A Multiple Paradigm Science*. Boston: Allyn and Bacon.

Roberg, Roy R. 1994. "Can Today's Police Organizations Effectively Implement Community Policing?" Pp. 249–257 in *The Challenge of Community Policing*, edited by D.P. Rosenbaum. Thousand Oaks, CA: Sage.

Rosa, Joseph G. 1993. *The Taming of the West: Age of the Gunfighter: Men and Weapons on the Frontier, 1840–1900*. New York: Smithmark.

———. 1996. *Wild Bill Hickok: The Man and His Myth*. Lawrence: University Press of Kansas.

Rosenbaum, Dennis P. 2006. "The Limits of Hot Spots Policing." Pp. 245–263 in *Police Innovation: Contrasting Perspectives*, edited by D. Weisburd and A.A. Braga. Cambridge, UK: Cambridge University Press.

Rosenfeld, Richard. 2009. "Homicide and Serious Assaults." Pp. 25–50 in *Oxford Handbook of Crime and Public Policy*, edited by M. Tonry. Oxford, UK: Oxford University Press.

Rosenfeld, Richard and Scott H. Decker. 1993. "Where Public Health and Law Enforcement Meet: Monitoring and Preventing Youth Violence." *American Journal of Police* 12:11–57.

Roth, Wendy D. and Jal D. Mehta. 2002. "The *Rashomon* Effect: Combining Positivist and Interpretivist Approaches in the Analysis of Contested Events." *Sociological Methods and Research* 31 (2):131–173.

Russell, Don. 1963. "Indians and Soldiers of the American West." Pp. 193–260 in *The Book of the American West*, edited by J. Monaghan and C.P. Hornung. New York: Julian Messner Inc.

Russell, James W. 1994. *After the Fifth Sun: Class and Race in North America*. Englewood Cliffs, NJ: Prentice Hall.

Sanders, Irwin T. 1958. *The Community: An Introduction to a Social System*. New York: Ronald Press.

Sanders, William B. 1979. "Police Occasions: A Study of Interaction Contexts." *Criminal Justice Review* 4 (1):1–13.

Schafer, Joseph A. and Thomas J. Martinelli. 2008. "First-line Supervisor's Perceptions of Police Integrity: The Measurement of Police Integrity Revisited." *Policing* 31 (2):306–323.

Schwab, William A. 1992. *The Sociology of Cities*. Englewood Cliffs, NJ: Prentice Hall.

Selznick, Philip. 1949. *TVA and the Grass Roots*. Berkeley: University of California Press.

———. 1957. *Leadership in Administration*. New York: Harper & Row.

Sennett, Richard. 1990. *The Conscience of the Eye: The Design and Social Life of Cities*. New York: Knopf.

Seron, Carroll, Joseph Pereira, and Jean Kovath. 2004. "Judging Police Misconduct: 'Street Level' versus Professional Policing." *Law and Society Review* 38 (4):665–710.

Sharp, Arthur. 2000. "Smile You're on CCTV." *Law and Order* 48 (3):53–58.

Shearing, Clifford D. 2006. "Reflections on the Refusal to Acknowledge Private Governments." Pp. 11–32 in *Democracy, Society and the Governance of Security*, edited by J. Wood and B. Dupont. Cambridge: Cambridge University Press.

Shearing, Clifford D. and Philip C. Stenning. 1981. "Modern Private Security: Its Growth and Implications." *Crime and Justice* 3:193–245.

———. 1983. "Private Security: Its Implications for Social Control." *Social Problems* 30:125–138.

———. 1986. "Reframing Policing." Pp. 9–18 in *Private Policing*, edited by C.D. Shearing and P.C. Stenning. Newbury Park, CA: Sage.

Sherman, Lawrence W. and David Weisburd. 1995. "General Deterrent Effects of Police Patrol in Crime 'Hot Spots': A Randomized Controlled Trial." *Justice Quarterly* 12:626–648.

Short, James F. 1984. "The Social Fabric At Risk: Toward the Social Transformation of Risk Analysis." *American Sociological Review* 49 (6):711–725.

Sklansky, David A. 2006. "Not Your Father's Police Department: Making Sense of the New Demographics of Law Enforcement." *Journal of Criminal Law and Criminology* 96 (3):1209–1243.

Skogan, Wesley G. 1994. "The Impact of Community Policing on Neighborhood Residents: A Cross-Site Analysis." Pp. 167–181 in *The Challenge of Community Policing*, edited by D.P. Rosenbaum. Thousand Oaks, CA: Sage.

———. 2006a. *Police and Community in Chicago: A Tale of Three Cities*. Oxford, UK: Oxford University Press.

———. 2006b. "Asymmetry in the Impact of Encounters with the Police." *Policing and Society* 16 (2):99–126.

———. 2006c. "The Promise of Community Policing." Pp. 27–43 in *Police Innovation: Contrasting Perspectives*, edited by D. Weisburd and A.A. Braga. Cambridge: Cambridge University Press.

Skogan, Wesley G. and Tracey L. Meares. 2004. "Lawful Policing." *Annals of the American Academy of Political and Social Science* 593:66–83.

Skolnick, Jerome H. 1966. *Justice without Trial: Law Enforcement in Democratic Society*. New York: Wiley.

Skolnick, Jerome H. and James F. Fyfe. 1993. *Above the Law: Police and the Excessive Use of Force*. New York: Free Press.

Small, Albion W. 1895. "Static and Dynamic Sociology." *American Journal of Sociology* 1 (2):195–209.

Smith, Brad W., Kenneth J. Novak, James Frank, and Christopher Lowenkamp. 2005. Explaining Police Officer Discretionary Activity." *Criminal Justice Review* 30 (3):325–346.

Smith, Michael R., Matthew Petrocelli, and Charlie Scheer. 2007. "Excessive Force, Civil Liability, and the Taser in the Nation's Courts: Implications for Law Enforcement Policy and Practice." *Policing* 30 (3):398–422.

Spacks, Patricia Meyer. 2003. *Privacy: Concealing the Eighteenth-Century Self*. Chicago: University of Chicago Press.

Spain, Daphne. 1992. *Gendered Spaces*. Chapel Hill: University of North Carolina Press.

———. 1993. "Gendered Spaces and Women's Status." *Sociological Theory* 11 (2):137–151.

Spencer, Herbert. 1864. *First Principles*. New York: Appleton.

———. 1872 [1850]. *Social Statics*. New York: Appleton and Co.

Sprey, Jetse. 1966. "Family Disorganization: Toward a Conceptual Clarification." *Journal of Marriage and the Family* 28 (4):398–406.

Stanton, Tami and Joe Thesing. 2006. "Ominous Trend: Growth of Municipal Accident Response Fees." *NAMIC Issue Brief*. Washington, DC: National Association of Mutual Insurance Companies.

Stinchcombe, Arthur L. 2001. *When Formality Works*. Chicago: University of Chicago Press.

Stroshine, Meghan, Geoffrey Alpert, and Roger Dunham. 2008. "The Influence of 'Working Rules' on Police Supervision and Discretionary Decision Making." *Police Quarterly* 11 (3):315–337.

Sumner, William G. 1906. *Folkways*. Boston: Ginn & Company.

———. 1909. "The Family and Social Change." *American Journal of Sociology* 14 (5):577–591.

Sun, Ivan Y. 2003. "Officer Proactivity: A Comparison between Police Field Training Officers and Non-field Training Officers." *Journal of Criminal Justice* 31:265–277.

Taylor, Charles. 1994. "The Politics of Recognition." Pp. 25–73 in *Multiculturalism*, edited by A. Gutmann. Princeton, NJ: Princeton University Press.

Teasley, C.E. 1978. "Police Role Perceptions: Their Operationalization and Some Preliminary Findings." *Criminal Justice Review* 3 (1):17–29.

Terrill, William and Eugene A. Paoline, III. 2007. "Nonarrest Decision Making in Police–Citizen Encounters." *Police Quarterly* 10 (3):308–331.

Thacher, David. 2005. The Local Role in Homeland Security." *Law and Society Review* 39 (3):635–676.

Thacher, David and Martin Rein. 2004. "Managing Value Conflict in Public Policy." *Governance* 17 (4):457–486.

Thale, Christopher. 2004. Assigned to Patrol: Neighborhoods, Police, and Changing Deployment Practices in New York City before 1930. *Journal of Social History* 37 (4):1037–1064.

Theriault, Sean M. 2003. "Patronage, the Pendleton Act, and the Power of the People." *Journal of Politics* 65 (1):50–68.

Thompson, James D. 1967. *Organizations in Action*. New York: McGraw-Hill.

Tilley, Charles. 1976. "Major Forms of Collective Action in Western Europe 1500–1975." *Theory and Society* 3 (3):365–375.

Toffalo, Douglas A. Della. 2000. "An Investigation of Treatment and Outcomes in Wraparound Services." *Journal of Child and Family Studies* 9 (3):351–361.

Turner, Frederick Jackson. 1996 [1920]. *The Frontier in American History*. New York: Dover.

Unruh, John D., Jr. 1978. *The Plains across: The Overland Immigrants and the Trans-Mississippi West, 1840–1860*. Urbana: University of Illinois Press.

Van Maanen, John. 1974. "Working the Street: A Developmental View of Police Behavior." Pp. 83–130 in *The Potential for Reform of Criminal Justice*, edited by H. Jacob. Beverly Hills, CA: Sage.

———. 1978. "The Asshole." Pp. 221–238 in *Policing: A View from the Street*, edited by P.K. Manning and J. Van Maanen. Santa Monica, CA: Goodyear.

Van Maanen, J. and B.T. Pentland. 1994. "Cops and Auditors: The Rhetoric of Records." Pp. 53–90 in *The Legalistic Organization*, edited by S.B. Sitkin and R.J. Bies. Beverly Hills: Sage.

Van Tassel, David D. and John J. Grabowski. 1987. *Encyclopedia of Cleveland History*. Bloomington: Indiana University Press.

Veblen, Thorstein. 1899. *The Theory of the Leisure Class*. New York: Macmillan.

Venkatesh, Sudhir Alladi. 2006. *Off the Books: The Underground Economy of the Urban Poor*. Cambridge, MA: Harvard University Press.

Virilio, Paul. 1986. *Speed and Politics*, translated by M. Polizotti. New York: Semiotext(e).

Vollmer, August. 1974 [1924]. *Law Enforcement in Los Angeles*. New York: Arno Press.

Wagner, Helmut. 1963. "Types of Sociological Theory: Toward a System of Classification." *American Sociological Review* 28 (5):735–742.

Walby, Sylvia. 2001. "From Community to Coalition: The Politics of Recognition as the Handmaiden of the Politics of Equality in an Era of Globalization." *Theory, Culture and Society* 18 (2-3):113–135.

Walker, Lynn. 2002. "Home Making: An Architectural Perspective." *Signs* 27 (3):823–835.

Walker, Samuel. 1993. *Taming the System: The Control of Discretion in Criminal Justice, 1950–1990*. New York: Oxford University Press.

Walsh, William F. 2001. "Compstat: An Analysis of an Emerging Police Managerial Paradigm." *Policing* 24 (3):347–362.

Ward, Lester F. 1883. *Dynamic Sociology; or, Applied Social Science as Based upon Statical Sociology and the Less Complex Sciences*, 2 vols. New York: D. Appleton and Co.

———. 1893. *Psychic Factors of Civilization*. Boston: Ginn & Company.

———. 1895. "Static and Dynamic Sociology." *Political Science Quarterly* 10 (2):203–220.

———. 1903. *Pure Sociology: A Treatise on the Origin and Spontaneous Development of Society*. New York: Macmillan.

———. 1906. *Applied Sociology: A Treatise on the Conscious Improvement of Society by Society*. Boston: Ginn & Company.

Webb, Vincent J. and Charles M. Katz. 1997. "Citizen Ratings of Community Policing Activities." *Policing* 20 (1):7–23.

Weber, Max. 1978. *Economy and Society*, vol. 2, edited by G. Roth and C. Wittich. Berkeley: University of California Press.

Weisburd, David and Anthony A. Braga. 2006. "Hot Spots Policing as a Model for Police Innovation." Pp. 225–244 in *Police Innovation: Contrasting Perspectives*, edited by D. Weisburd and A.A. Braga. Cambridge, UK: Cambridge University Press.

Weisburd, David, Cody W. Telep, Joshua C. Hinkle, and John E. Eck. 2010. "Is Problem-Oriented Policing Effective in Reducing Crime and Disorder? Findings from a Campbell Systematic Review." *Criminology and Public Policy* 9 (1):139–172.

Weisheit, Ralph A. and John M. Klofas. 1998. "The Public Health Approach to Illicit Drugs." *Criminal Justice Review* 23 (2):197–207.

Weitzer, Ronald. 2000. "White, Black, or Blue Cops? Race and Citizen Assessments of Police Officers." *Journal of Criminal Justice* 28 (4):313–324.

Weitzer, Ronald and Rod K. Brunson. 2009. "Strategic Responses to the Police among Inner-City Youth." *Sociological Quarterly* 50 (2):235–256.

Wells, Helen. 2008. "The Techno-Fix versus the Fair Cop: Procedural (In)Justice and Automated Speed Limit Enforcement." *British Journal of Criminology* 48:798–817.

Wender, Jonathan M. 2008. *Policing and the Poetics of Everyday Life*. Urbana, IL: University of Illinois Press.

Westley, William A. 1970. *Violence and the Police: A Sociological Study of Law, Custom, and Morality*. Cambridge, MA: MIT Press.

Wharton, Amy S. 1991. "Structure and Agency in Socialist-Feminist Theory." *Gender and Society* 5 (3):373–389.

White, Michael D. 2007. *Current Issues and Controversies in Policing*. Boston: Allyn and Bacon.

White, Michael D. and Justin Ready. 2007. "The Taser as a Less Lethal Force Alternative: Findings on Use and Effectiveness in a Large Metropolitan Police Agency." *Police Quarterly* 10 (2):170–191.

———. 2010. "The Impact of the Taser on Suspect Resistance: Identifying Predictors of Effectiveness." *Crime and Delinquency* 56 (1):70–102.

White, Welsh S. 2001. *Miranda's Waning Protections: Police Interrogation Practices after Dickerson*. Ann Arbor: University of Michigan Press.

Willer, David and Henry A. Walker. 2007. *Building Experiments: Testing Social Theory*. Stanford, CA: Stanford University Press.

Williams, Hubert and Patrick V. Murphy. 2006. "The Evolving Strategy of Police: A Minority View." Pp. 27–50 in *The Police and Society*, 3rd ed., edited by V.E. Kappeler. Long Grove, IL: Waveland.

Williamson, Roger E. 2001. *Wichita Police Department, 1871–2000*. Wichita, KS: Wichita Police Benefit Fund Association.

Willis, James J., Stephen D. Mastrofski, and David Weisburd. 2007. "Making Sense of COMPSTAT: A Theory-Based Analysis of Organizational Change in Three Police Departments." *Law and Society Review* 41 (1):147–188.

Wilson, James Q. 1968. *Varieties of Police Behavior*. New York: Atheneum.

———. and George L. Kelling. 1982. "Broken Windows: Police and Neighborhood Safety." *Atlantic Monthly* 249 (3):29–38.

Wilson, Jeremy W. 2006. *Community Policing in America*. London: Routledge.

Wilson, O.W. 1958. *Police Planning*, 2nd ed. Springfield, IL: Charles C. Thomas.

Wingerd, Mary Lethert. 2001. *Claiming the City: Politics, Faith, and the Power of Place in St. Paul.* Ithaca, NY: Cornell University Press.

Winther, Oscar O. 1963. "Transportation in the American West." Pp. 83–136 in *The Book of the American West*, edited by J. Monaghan and C.P. Hornung. New York: Julian Messner Inc.

Wolf, Ross, Charlie Mesloh, Mark Henych, and L. Frank Thompson. 2009. "Police Use of Force and the Cumulative Force Factor." *Policing* 32 (4):739–757.

Wortley, Richard K. 2003. "Measuring Police Attitudes toward Discretion." *Criminal Justice and Behavior* 30 (5):538–558.

Wright, Will. 2001. *The Wild West: The Mythical Cowboy and Social Theory.* Thousand Oaks, CA: Sage.

Yan, Aimin and Meryl Reis Louis. 1999. "The Migration of Organizational Functions to the Work Unit Level: Buffering, Spanning, and Bridging up Boundaries." *Human Relations* 52 (1):25–47.

Yates, Douglas. 1978. *The Ungovernable City: The Politics of Urban Problems and Policy Making.* Cambridge, MA: MIT Press.

Yip, Kam-shing. 2006. "A Strengths Perspective in Working with an Adolescent with Self-cutting Behaviors." *Child and Adolescent Social Work Journal* 23 (2):134–146.

Zhao, Jihong "Solomon" and Kimberly D. Hassell. 2005. "Policing Styles and Organizational Priorities: Retesting Wilson's Theory of Local Political Culture." *Police Quarterly* 8 (4):411–430.

Index